ARCHITECTURE AND RURAL LIFE IN CENTRAL DELAWARE, 1700–1900

Architecture and Rural Life in Central Delaware, 1700–1900

Bernard L. Herman

THE UNIVERSITY OF TENNESSEE PRESS

Publication of this book has been aided by a grant
from the University of Delaware.

The paper in this book meets the minimum requirements of
the American National Standard for Permanence of Paper for
Printed Library Materials. ∞ The binding materials have
been chosen for strength and durability.

Library of Congress Cataloging-in-Publication Data

Herman, Bernard L., 1951–
    Architecture and rural life in central Delaware,
1700–1900.

    Bibliography: p.
    Includes index.
    1. Vernacular architecture—Delaware—New Castle
County.   2. Architecture and society—Delaware—New
Castle County.   3. Farm buildings—Delaware—New
Castle County.   4. Country homes—Delaware—New Castle
County.   5. Architecture—Delaware—New Castle
County—Details.   I. Title.
NA730.D32N474   1987   720′.9751′1   86-14608
ISBN 0-87049-519-4 (alk. paper)

For David G. Orr

Acknowledgments

T HE EXTENSIVE FIELDWORK AND documentary research for this study of vernacular architecture and agriculture in southern New Castle County, Delaware, requires an extended note of thanks. Without the energy of students in the American Studies Program and College of Urban Affairs and Public Policy at the University of Delaware and the cooperation of property owners I could never have brought this project to completion. I am indebted to Trish Bensinger, Bert Jicha, Mr. and Mrs. William Cross, Mr. and Mrs. William Brady, Hallie Bond, William Butler, Robert and Linda Beck, Anne Witty, Julie Riesenweber, Beth Twiss-Garrity, Louise Hite, and Valerie Cesna. Singular thanks are extended to Marcia Jarrell. For their work with the orphans court records, tax lists, and agricultural census returns, I am grateful to Rebecca Sheppard Siders, Laura Tuthill, and Karie Diethorn. Delaware historians John Munroe, Carol Hoffecker, Elizabeth Homsey and Richard Carter gave freely of their time and knowledge.

Jack Michel, David Allmendinger, and David Ames provided invaluable advice, enabling me to grasp analytical methods and historical analysis new to my way of considering the past. For innumerable insights into thinking about the data I happily thank fellow Vernacular Architecture Forum members: Robert Blair St. George, Jerry Pocius, Alice Schooler, Cary Carson, Abbott Lowell Cummings, Richard Candee, Tom Carter, Dell Upton, Edward A. Chappell, Catherine Bishir, Paul Touart, Dru Haley York, J. T. Smith, Richard Harris, R. Machin, Camille Wells, and William Tishler. My teachers at the University of Pennsylvania, in particular Henry Glassie, Don Yoder, Kenneth Goldstein, David Orr, and Drew Faust, provided ongoing lessons and inspiration. Kate Hutchins, Tracy

Kidder, Bruce Bigatel, and the editorial office of the University of Tennessee Press enabled me to make extensive revisions in the original text.

Financial support for research and writing came through matching grants from the Office of Archaeology and Historic Preservation, Delaware Division of Historical and Cultural Affairs. Without the enthusiastic support and non-stop encouragement from Dean Nelson, Steve Del Sordo, Joan Larrivee, Lawrence Henry, and Daniel Griffith, I would have reconsidered undertaking this study. Additional support from the University of Delaware Research Foundation enabled me to compile measured drawings of agricultural buildings. The dedication of fieldworkers and draftsmen Melinda Fike, Brian Fletcher, Charles Bergengren, and William Macintire insured the success of the recording project. A generous grant from the University of Delaware subsidized the production of this book.

For access to primary source materials I wish to acknowledge the kindnesses of Joanne Mattern and Russell McCabe (Delaware State Archives); Barbara Benson and Constance Cooper (Historical Society of Delaware); Stuart Dick (Special Collections, Morris Library, University of Delaware); Marti and Elizabeth Schiek, Ruth Tindall, and William Brady.

Without the love and perception provided by Rebecca Herman and the distractions offered by our daughter, Lania, there would be no humanity in this book.

Bernard L. Herman
May 1986

Contents

Illustrations

1. Introduction

IN 1778 THREE NEIGHBORS APPOINTED BY the orphans court of New Castle County visited the farm of Samuel Carpenter to appraise the contents and condition of the property and buildings. The observations they made concerning the farm describe a now-vanished architectural landscape and yield a glimpse into the textures of a rural world that was to undergo a dramatic and a nearly total architectural renewal in the next century:

> . . . one log dwelling house two stories high wants some repairs such as two hearths layed and twelve sash lights in the windows, one logg kitchen in good repair, one draw well, a pailed garden in middling order, one meat house in good repair, one smith's shop in repair, one logg stable and hen house in middling repair, one corn crib, one large barn wants some repairs on the south end struck with thunder.[1]

The types of buildings and means of construction listed in the appraisers' account were so common in the eighteenth and early nineteenth centuries as to account for the majority of vernacular architecture throughout southern New Castle County from the fall line cutting across Pencader, White Clay Creek, and New Castle hundreds down to and beyond the Kent County line. With the advent of agricultural reforms, an increasingly urban/industrial-oriented rural economy, and the emergence of a new agrarian world view in the early 1800s, the world from which Samuel Carpenter had departed was on the brink of profound changes destined to transform all aspects of traditional life and, specifically, the manner and style in which Carpenter's successors were to order their lives architecturally.

In fact, as we pass through southern New Castle County today, we see only a few remnants of the architectural landscape that existed prior to the mid-nineteenth century. What survive on the land are a multitude of farms and country estates that speak eloquently of generations of gradual change occurring from the first period of durable architecture in the early 1800s on through radical transformations in architecture and agriculture during the middle decades of the nineteenth century. Residents of southern New Castle County subsidizing local histories written in the late 1800s described their recent past in words like "improvement," "renewal," and "rebuilding."

The present study documents the character and significance of an agricultural countryside in the process of fitful transformations. On one level it is an attempt to reconstruct the physical environment shaped in the eighteenth century by Samuel Carpenter and his neighbors and improved, renewed, and rebuilt by their successors through the mid-nineteenth. On another level we will undertake an interpretation of the values and paradoxes of desired and perceived change as expressed in buildings. Architecture, as we shall see, is not a simple reaction to material circumstance and world view. It is one of many media used to create and maintain order, to project images of self and community, and to control meaning in social discourse.

New Castle County, Delaware, is bordered to the north by southeastern Pennsylvania, to the west by northeastern Maryland, to the east by the Delaware River, beyond which sits southwestern New Jersey, and to the south by lower Delaware (Fig. 1:1). The county is subdivided into nine smaller political units equivalent to townships or parishes and known as "hundreds" (Fig. 1:2). The lower reaches of the county contain all or parts of several hundreds, including Pencader, Red Lion, New Castle, St. Georges, Appoquinimink and Blackbird (partitioned from Appoquinimink in 1875). Two non-political topographic divisions, however, have contributed more to the overall historical development of the area. The first of these is the fall line separating the Piedmont Plateau of the northern third of the county from the coastal plain making up the lower two-thirds of the county. The second division, somewhat south of the fall line, is man made—an east-west canal designed to carry ocean-going traffic which links the Delaware River to the Chesapeake Bay and which, since its completion in the late 1820s, has cut the county in half.[2]

These two nearly coterminous boundaries across the county

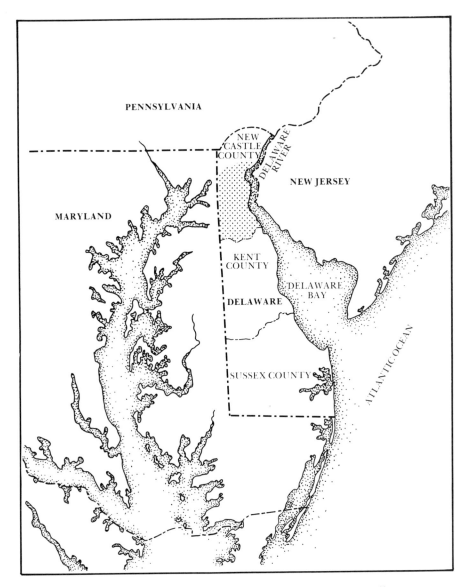

Figure 1:1. Southern New Castle County in the lower Delaware Valley. Map: Center for Historic Architecture and Engineering (CHAE), Teresa Miller and William Macintire.

have provided a pair of cultural borders: one corresponding to general historic settlement patterns and the other providing a cognitive frontier for a regional identity. "South of the canal" is a label for a separation in the folk topography of the county between two landscapes—one representing the southern edge of the rolling foothills

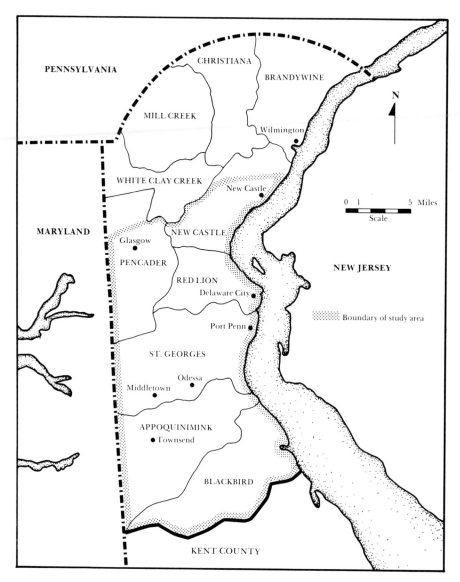

Figure 1:2. New Castle County hundreds. The study area (within the shaded margins) includes parts of Pencader and New Castle hundreds and all of St. Georges, Red Lion, Appoquinimink, and Blackbird hundreds. Map: CHAE, Teresa Miller and William Macintire.

and industrialized valleys of the Pennsylvania Piedmont and the other the beginning of the Eastern Shore (or Delmarva Peninsula), with its generally flat terrain cut by slow-flowing streams and tidal creeks and marshes.

Southern New Castle County is very much a part of the Eastern

Shore, as defined by an economy historically rooted in agriculture, in working the river, bays, and marshes, and in trade. Settlement from the seventeenth to the mid-twentieth century has been non-centralized, with towns serving as points for local politics, commerce, and transportation. Until well into the nineteenth century, even churches were more likely to be found in the back country than in a village setting.

The general history of the lower hundreds from the seventeenth to the twentieth centuries has been well documented.[3] Studies of the seventeenth-century development of the county focus on the early settlement efforts of first the Swedes and then the Dutch, the later presence of the British, and the separation of the three lower counties of New Castle, Kent, and Sussex from Pennsylvania by charter in 1701. The architectural legacy left by the earliest European settlers is in dispute, and writers traveling through the region in the first half of the eighteenth century remarked on the prevalence of British characteristics in local buildings. The most famous of these individuals, Peter Kalm, repeatedly sought out vestiges of Scandinavian building practices. Typically, he describes log construction and hearth placement as being in the English or Irish manner. Those Scandinavian features he did identify were seen by Kalm as either debased or unusual survivals. The prevailing architectural styles and practices were English or Scotch-Irish. In a similar vein New Englander Joshua Hempstead noted the log houses he saw in the 1740s as being built "crib fashion" by locals of Scotch-Irish descent. The architectural landscapes described by Kalm and Hempstead were the product of the intensive British settlement sponsored under William Penn, beginning in the 1680s.[4]

William Penn and his agents aggressively promoted immigration into the lower Delaware Valley in the late seventeenth century. As a result large numbers of Welsh and English settlers entered what is now New Castle County. Their numbers and consequent political power led to the rapid acculturation of the existing European population. Dutch and Scandinavian family and place names survived, and, initially, so did material aspects of their colonial culture, but by the mid-eighteenth century, the latter existed only as relics or curiosities. Thus, architecturally and demographically the ethnic character of early eighteenth-century southern New Castle County was Anglo-American.

Events particular to our study of the lower hundreds unfold in the late 1700s. As the northern reaches of the county became the scene for early developments in the Industrial Revolution, including experimentation and technological innovations in flour milling, paper making, iron casting, and gunpowder manufacture, the southern areas remained almost wholly agrarian.[5]

The land itself is the starting point for the study of the building traditions that created the architectural landscapes of southern New Castle County. The terrain is flat with subtly rolling hills, is near the coast, and rises only to a hundred feet at the highest elevation (Fig. 1:3). Resting on sediments of sand, clay, and gravel, the area is covered primarily with fertile well-drained soils; however, the soils in the south and northwest reaches have tended historically to be neither as productive in terms of crop yields nor as well drained. The climate is temperate and humid with an average growing season extending from mid-April through October. Although rainfall is fairly evenly distributed throughout the year, destructive summer droughts can and do occur. The generally favorable combination of soil and climate have, historically, made lower New Castle County the wealthiest agricultural district in Delaware.[6]

In 1798 James Tilton, a progressive agriculturalist in adjacent Kent County, Delaware, wrote an article for a national magazine in which he outlined statewide conditions of soil and climate and devoted considerable space to a discussion of livestock and farming.[7] Sheep (for wool) and cattle (for meat and dairy products) were, along with grain, the mainstays of the farm economy. Grains included wheat, buckwheat, barley, and Indian corn. Wheat, the principal crop, was "distinguished in various ways, sometimes by the chaff, according to the colour, either red or white; sometimes by the ear, as it is either bearded or otherwise: and in selling by the grain, the millers prefer the white grain to the red, and all smooth wheat to the bearded."[8] In Tilton's day, farmers rotated crops and pasture in a three- to six-field system, fertilized with manures and ashes, sowed and harvested by hand, and hand-threshed with flails or used horses to tread out the grain. The other crops noted by Tilton were oats, potatoes, cabbage, timothy, clover, and Indian corn—all used as animal feeds.

Tilton's observations are central to this study. Just as the 1778 valuation of Samuel Carpenter's farm portrays an architectural landscape on the eve of transformation, Tilton's remarks on agriculture describe a rural economy on the brink of industrialization.

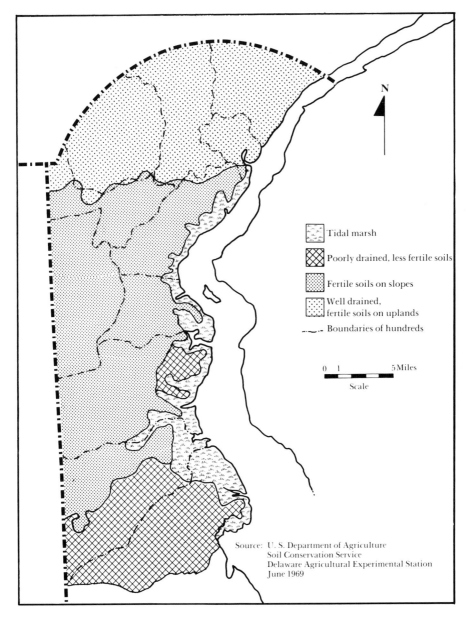

Figure 1:3. Simplified soils map for New Castle County. Map: CHAE, Teresa Miller and William Macintire.

The notion that wheat could be grown to the satisfaction of millers is one aspect of the incipient changes to be wrought in this society, but the fact of Tilton himself is an even better index to the coming of new ways to farming and domestic life. His was an early voice arguing for agricultural reform. A spokesman for agricultural societies, he advocated soil improvement, improved tillage, and mechanization. His contemporary, John Spurrier, a New Castle County farmer to the north, offered a guide to achieving these ends in a book, *The Practical Farmer*, published in 1793.[9] Spurrier emphasized the conjunction between practical knowledge and theoretically based experimentation. He encouraged "book farming" and the keeping of written accounts. The kind of change Spurrier promoted was equated with "improvement" and manifested itself in the adoption of a "regular system" of farming. This desire for a system was a call for order, an order that was to be theoretically and experimentally grounded. This new order would transform traditional relationships into commercial concerns, and, as we shall see, become the theme for architectural innovation and social history.

The rural history of southern New Castle County in the nineteenth century was marked by several transportation-related events: 1829—the opening of the Chesapeake and Delaware Canal; 1831—the opening of the New Castle and Frenchtown Railroad, adding another east-west transportation route across the upper peninsula; and 1856—the opening of the Delaware Railroad from Wilmington south to Dover, the state capital. There were other, more gradual forces at work in nineteenth-century rural New Castle County, but these are less easy to isolate[10] or to date precisely. One exception—the second founding of the New Castle County agricultural society in 1819—was a central influence. But the development of an orchard industry from the mid-1800s until around 1880, the widespread incorporation of service wings into the main block of the house beginning in the 1820s, or the emergence of a local sense of history—all these are gradual but important changes, aspects of a quieter and in some ways more revealing history.

What often defines history are the dates, circumstances, people, and places fixed into a chronology and charting a progression that seems to be characterized by a prevailing desire on the historian's part to illustrate forward movement. Similarly, architectural studies of Delaware have typically examined buildings in a chronology of style periods that are tied to movements in national fashion or bound to the life and work of significant men and women. Houses are studied as bearers of style and often judged inferior when compared to more academically accomplished parallels and antecedents located elsewhere in the mid-Atlantic region or in the British Isles. Just as history has been measured out by a chronology of national and local events, architectural history has been mapped out by great houses. What is lost in such narratives is the significant influence on both history and architecture of the mainstream of community thought and action.[11]

One level of meaning that can be discovered in the past compilations of historic chronologies and the recognition of locally important landmark architecture is the rationale that guided their selection of items for inclusion. General state and local histories typically sought to place local experience and knowledge in wider contexts, so that the sense of self and place was articulated in the framework of a larger identity. Thus one historical chronology for Delaware advances the dates for occurrences of purely sub-regional interest, such as violent storms and lynchings, between dates of national consequence. The process of imbedding one history within another has the advantage of lending to local lives and anecdotes the unity of a greater narrative: there is coincidence between what is ordinary and what is exceptional.

The dwellings, farm buildings, mills, and other structures discussed here were selected on the basis of a comprehensive architectural inventory undertaken by the Delaware Division of Historical and Cultural Affairs for all of southern New Castle County. Between 1970 to 1977, a historic structures survey had been conducted throughout the area that emphasized studying the earliest or most stylish of eighteenth- and nineteenth-century building. In 1977 the survey activity undertaken in the lower hundreds adopted a more comprehensive methodology that yielded the raw data for the present undertaking.[12]

In the second half of the nineteenth century, four atlases were published for New Castle County (1849, 1868, 1881, and 1893).[13] Each of these maps, whether bound into a folio volume or produced as a single large sheet, showed not only basic topographical features and political boundaries, but also plotted individual farms and townscapes, designating the locations of dwellings and the names of their owners. Because these atlases were often compiled by a subscription process through which an individual could pay an additional fee to have the name of his farm included on the final copy, there is the chance that some houses were not plotted. Furthermore, the atlases excluded most lesser structures, such as tenant houses or barns. Still, when compared to the actual location of sites in the field, even today these maps prove to be accurate and indispensable for completing fieldwork-based research.

The folio atlases of 1868 and 1893 contained maps of individual hundreds and the towns included within their borders. For the present study, reproductions of these early maps were made, then compared and correlated to a modern road map, and all three gridded with equal-sized squares, depending on the scale of the map being used. All three maps were used in planning out fieldwork, in order to ensure a systematic survey of all the structures standing in each block of the grid. Once the full extent and volume of the architectural resources had been identified and roughly counted, a more detailed survey was begun. Students working in Blackbird, Appoquinimink, and St. Georges hundreds, together with the county historic preservation planner surveying Red Lion, Pencader, and New Castle hundreds, systematically visited individual sites one by one. Except in a small number of cases, exterior photographs and written architectural descriptions were made of each site. In many instances interior data (including measured floor plans, photographs of decorative techniques, and sections of roofing systems) were also recorded. All of this information was organized within the guidelines provided by the Delaware Bureau of Archaeology and Historic Preservation and entered into the state archives, where microfiche copies were produced and the originals stored for research and planning use.[14]

The utility of this data base rests in its comprehensiveness, uniformity, and coherent methodology. The new social history is predicated upon the study of traditional life from the bottom up.[15] Using mass-oriented source materials like censuses, tax lists, land, and probate records, historians have been able to plumb the deeper attitudes and assess key movements in society and culture. It is quite significant that social shifts tend to occur independently of the actions of great figures and great events—that the prolonged effect of falling grain prices is of far greater regional impact than are political manifestos issued by nearby city leaders. Enumerating houses, like counting heads of households or assessing property values, provides both a sample and an index to the actions and circumstances shaped and directed by individuals functioning within community systems. Whether quantitative methods start from collective biography, systemic analysis, or networks of communication, they all seek to understand the deep, often reified social, cultural, and economic forces binding individuals together.[16] What the new social historians, folklorists, archaeologists, and others using quantitative methods seek is to set up vigorous methodologies which enable them to focus on the social relationships that simultaneously order and are ordered by the participants in a society.

This study of the architecture and history of southern New Castle County begins by counting houses. Other sources, however, play a vital role in providing comparative information for testing the reliability of traditional buildings as a primary and central source. Documents—including tax records, probate inventories, agricultural censuses, and orphans court property valuations—are instrumental to evaluating the development of a cultural landscape. Each record group contains its own biases in terms of content and context: only the houses of the better sort tend to survive, tax lists are generated to produce public revenues, and orphans court assessments are maintained to protect the property rights of minors. Still, these records yield data which can be counted. Those counts in turn suggest patterns of ownership, household structure, family size, agricultural and industrial practice, and other aspects of rural life and work. To determine history through quantitative methodologies designed to seek out the ordering principles of a given society often entails a dramatic departure from the traditional reliance on narrative chronologies that present the flow of settlement as a rational, sequential progression.[17]

The real meaning in numbers rides on the individual lives they describe. To maintain the fundamental humanity of the cultural expression described here, individual builders and buildings are advanced as representatives of a broad-based historical moment. Those singled out for discussion compose a cross-section of all involved in the architectural shaping of the land. In some instances builders left considerable documentary information to go with their houses and farms; for others only buildings remain; and still other structures and individuals are remembered only in an isolated documentary reference. The selected buildings and individual references are intended as examples, incorporating the patterned behavior and expressed values found in the whole of the area's building traditions. What emerges is a history written through the actions of individuals—a history where meaning is found not in great events but in the continuum of architectural thought realized upon the land.

The cycles of building in southern New Castle County can be read almost as archaeological layers of prolonged human settlement. The layers from the first extended cycle reveal patterns of impermanent housing, a shift to durable buildings, the introduction of stair-passage-plan dwellings, and movement toward incorporating service functions into the house. Each of these factors can be read as a separate, yet overlapping, architectural development, important in individual terms. However, the method used in this book reveals that in terms of numbers and degree of intensity, all four are distinguishing characteristics of a larger single building cycle running from circa 1700 to circa 1820. The beginning date is derived from the period of the first intensive occupation of the land and the closing date from the last period of radical formal change and the advent of a locally founded agricultural reform movement.

The second building period of lower New Castle County ran from approximately 1820 to 1870. A time of architectural renewal and rebuilding, this fifty-year period saw three types of domestic architectural activity. Roughly concurrent, they comprised the extensive remodeling of existing structures, the replacement of old buildings with completely new ones, and the substantial remodeling of new buildings within a few years of their initial construction. The layers of architectural activity apparent in the nineteenth-century rebuilding represent a uniform codification and consolidation of spatial concepts and social organization that had been formally worked out in the first building cycle. There were few new substantive ideas in the rebuilding period, but there was a general push towards a prevailing architectural sameness by class-oriented individuals who could afford to build.

From the 1870s into the twentieth century, few building projects were undertaken except those needed to house the gradually swelling village populations. The houses built in this third period represent a continuation of house-types worked out in the mid 1800s but now condensed into the compact parameters of bungalows or modestly priced pattern-book houses. A few people continued to build in the old way—commissioning two-story, center-passage-plan farmhouses with service wings. More importantly, during the 1880s people of substance and ambition gave considerable attention to building a past by sponsoring the publication of local histories. The architectural present was with them and its future secured, so those who had commissioned houses subscribed to campaigns to produce a written history, and, as patrons, bought their place in the final codification of values initiated a century before.

As an architectural landscape, southern New Castle County presents us with the buildings of a social minority. By the 1810s the majority of all available land was owned by slightly less than a third of the taxable population. Landholders also composed the segment of society that commissioned the bulk of architectural projects, varying from mansion houses to tenant dwellings and agricultural structures. Within this economic and social reality—one common to many American historic landscapes—how are we to define vernacular architecture? The answer lies in the social purpose of building. Vernacular architecture is the architecture of common usage and communication. The surface issues are to determine what a building or group of buildings are in terms of their constructural, stylistic, or spatial character. At a deeper level, though, one must address how those various elements are brought together in individual buildings and manipulated as media for expressions of thought, everyday interaction, and the signification of social and cultural relationships and meanings. It is important that a social majority of a society lacked opportunity to design and erect their own dwellings, but it is equally important to recognize that the majority who did not build were deeply affected by the minority who did. Not everyone has an equal hand in the expressive culture of a society, but everyone who participates in or observes that society is affected to varying degrees by the decisions implemented by a demographic minority and perceived and experienced by many. An agricultural and architectural writer whose works were read in mid-nineteenth-century Delaware remarked on the instructive and historical values incorporated in rural architecture:

> A house is always a teacher; it may become an agent of civilization. While builders minister to deceit and vanity, those vices will prevail; when their works embody fitness truth and dignified simplicity, these republican virtues will be firmly rooted in the nation. Few are aware how strong an influence is exerted by the dwelling on its inhabitants.[18]

2. House Types, 1700–1820

THE DEFINITION OF BUILDING TYPES is a major theme in studies of American folk architecture. It is in the recognition of house forms or plans that we find the basis for workable typologies, and these typologies, in turn, allow us to formulate interpretations about continuity and change.[1] Simply speaking, by identifying all the building types in a given area and then plotting the frequency of their occurrence historically, we are able to see when and where change takes place in the organization of household and domestic space.

In southern New Castle County, we will see that a core of house types built during the early decades of the eighteenth century continued in use well into the nineteenth century. But, by the 1740s those first forms had been supplemented by a house type in which an unheated entryway and stair passage were incorporated into the overall plan of the house. With the introduction of the new style, the preference for one style over the other paralleled growing economic and social divisions within the community. The shift in architectural choices took place gradually through the eighteenth century, but by the middle of the nineteenth century (the building period with which the second half of this study is concerned) the transformation of the architectural landscape was complete. To comprehend the extent and significance of those later changes we must examine first the formative traditions of house types found in the colonial and early national periods.

Form is the one aspect of traditional architecture least susceptible to casual change, and it also has the least number of options and therefore becomes the easiest for historians to describe.[2] Between 1700 and 1820 southern New Castle County was punctuated with a variety of functional buildings—dwellings, barns, granaries, sheds, stables, churches, and public buildings. Among these, dwellings represent the category most likely to yield insight into how the occupants of the area saw fit to order their lives.[3]

The house forms common throughout southern New Castle County's first building period (1700 to 1820) are of two historical types: those with traditional options built from the moment of initial settlement onward, and those based on academically inspired ideals of symmetry and balance that were introduced in the mid-eighteenth century. Based on extant buildings and fragmentary documentary evidence, these first period houses had one-, two-, three-, or four-room plans, within which considerable variation occurred.

In the waning years of the eighteenth century, the majority of houses in the Chesapeake Bay country and on the Delmarva Peninsula consisted of one-room plans in one- or sometimes two-story dwellings.[4] These small houses averaged sixteen to twenty feet square (400 square feet or less)[5] such as Benjamin Abraham's "one old log house twenty by 18 feet and one story." Such a structure we identify as a hall-plan house. Typically, it contained a chimney pile constructed against one gable, with a boxed-in winder stair and sometimes a storage closet placed between one chimney jamb and the corner of the room. In one-story dwellings, a ladder might provide the only access to the loft. The single room was entered directly from the outside. In some instances the interior of the house was illuminated with a window on either side of a central doorway, but the norm appears to have been one window located in the gable end, away from the hearth, and possibly a window between the doorway on each side of the building and the hearth wall. What defined this room was that it contained the sum of domestic life; it was the space where children were born and visitors entertained, and where adults died amid the ebb and flow of household activities.

Despite an architecturally undifferentiated space and limited size, the one-room-plan house could range in quality from an insubstantial structure without proper floors or chimney to a decoratively elaborated two-story brick plantation house. Not surprisingly, those substantial homes built by wealthier families have survived in more than an archaeological state. The dwelling that comes closest to illustrating a normative hall-plan house is the original block of the Christopher Vandergrift House situated west of Port Penn (Fig. 7:3). Built of sawn logs, this one-story structure with a loft was approximately 18 by 20 feet. First erected in the 1700s, the dwelling has had numerous additions and alterations since, but as late as 1818—after the house had been substantially enlarged with a two-story frame wing—the older section was still described as a common room and loft.[6] As originally built, Vandergrift's dwelling exhibited several features common in hall-plan residences. The hearth located inside the west gable consisted of two brick jambs carrying a hewn timber lintel that supported the masonry flue. The ceiling beams, or joists, were exposed and finished with chamfered edges. Stairs, adjacent to the chimney jamb, led to a storage loft, which in 1818 contained only a barrel churn and "miscellaneous sundries." Windows were located between the door frames and hearth wall. The fine log construction and full brick cellar indicate the Vandergrift House was above the average. A hall-plan dwelling of the meanest sort, as in the case of a tenant's house, contained only minimal furnishings; Walter Fellow's "Red House" had two rush-bottom chairs, a feather bed, a tub, a flax wheel, and a chest—all described as "old."[7]

Although the hall-plan house containing a single common room was the dominant architectural idea in the first half of the eighteenth century, there were also one-room-plan, two-story dwellings known as chambered halls, in which the two rooms had more particular functions. Two such houses, the Dilworth House and the Trap, survive in St. Georges Hundred and are of brick construction, a full two stories in elevation, and originally had support buildings including kitchens and smokehouses. In their form, both structures are clearly a part of the one-room-plan house tradition. Built about 1714, the Dilworth House contained a single room on each floor, with a gable-end hearth and a stair closet (Fig. 2:1). The Trap, later known as the McDonough House, erected circa 1730–40, was identical to the Dilworth House in form, although it differed in details of construction and decorative elements. Both structures had paneled hearth walls (Fig. 2:2), which are still in place in the second-floor rooms of the Trap, and molded fireplace surrounds, mantel cornices, chimney closets, vertical, beaded-board walling, and raised paneling.

A 1723 probate inventory of John Hales, taken in St. Georges Hundred, lists the rooms and contents of a house similar in form and elevation to the Dilworth House.[8] Within the house proper there were three basic spatial divisions: "the House below," "cham-

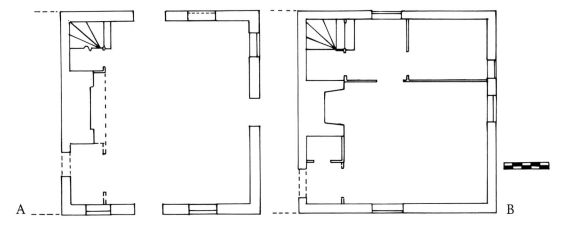

Figure 2:1. Chambered-hall plan: Dilworth House, Port Penn vicinity, St. Georges Hundred (ca. 1714). The Dilworth House was enlarged into a two-room (hall-parlor) plan dwelling before 1720. Shown here is the original block of the house. Dotted lines indicate the position of known original architectural features. The doorways in the first-floor (A) gable end, opposite the fireplace, and the subdivision of the second floor (B) are later alterations.

ber," and "garrett." The ground-floor room, or "the House below," was furnished with an oval table, several old chairs, an old chest, a bedstead, and a cradle; while the second-story room, or "chamber," held similar pieces—a chest of drawers, a bedstead, two chests, seven chairs, and a table. The two rooms differed most in the amount of their smaller contents. The ground-floor room contained a couple of small boxes, baskets, a parcel of leather, and "furniture" (ornaments) on the mantlepiece. In the room above, the small items included additional boxes, a bottle case with two bottles, stoneware jugs, flask bottles, a Bible, wool yarn, linen yarn, homespun cloth, and a looking glass. Both rooms served as combination sitting rooms and sleeping chambers. The only material distinction between the two spaces is made by the furniture on the mantelpiece; the miscellaneous small items listed for both rooms may well have been stored in a chimney closet or a chest. What is curious here is what is *not* in either room.

That the single room functioned as the theatre of domestic activity is not apparent from the items in the 1723 inventory nor is it evident in Dilworth House or the soon-to-be-built Trap. Missing from the main rooms are spaces for general storage, for spinning and weaving, and for cooking. Some objects were stored in the loft or attic, and, in the 1723 inventory, the loft contained a variety of

Figure 2:2. The Trap (McDonough House), McDonough vicinity, St. Georges Hundred (1730–40). Shown in the photograph is a section of the original paneling in the second-floor chamber. Of particular note is the cupboard built into the chimney breast and finished with glass-paneled doors and "butterfly" display shelves. Photograph: Delaware State Archives (DSA), Dean Nelson.

textiles, pewter, knives, forks, a tankard, and some loose bedding; but the bulk of storage needs as well as all the food preparation and spinning and weaving were housed apart from the main dwelling in a kitchen.

The presence and importance of separate kitchens in southern New Castle County is known almost exclusively through written references in various records, including inventories, tax assessments and estate valuations; no such eighteenth-century structures have survived. Yet they were important and distinct. They are mentioned repeatedly in property valuations made between 1770 and 1820. Over 80 percent of all farms in the southern hundreds are listed as having separate or adjoining kitchens, usually of log or frame construction. In 1775 one such kitchen was in particularly bad condition. The court ordered the guardian to take it down and rebuild it, but allowed him to use the same materials (logs) wherever possible."[9]

Whatever the details of their construction, throughout the eighteenth century the kitchens on a great many farms were intended as household work spaces. The 1723 inventory of the John Hales residence describes the contents of the kitchen: tools for cooking, tools for textile production, and tools for farming and working wood. The kitchen loft held a jumble of pewter, livery, more farm tools, and corn meal; and the cellar housed a cheese press, milk pans, and various barrels and casks. The Hales inventory is unusually detailed, and it describes a pattern of living that is reflected in other room-by-room household inventories taken throughout the eighteenth century.

The relation of kitchens to one-room houses is that their presence or absence defines categories for hall-plan dwellings. Where a separate kitchen is present, the hall assumes the character of a common sitting room, bedchamber, and, possibly dining room, while household work is carried on in a kitchen. One-room-plan houses without separate kitchens remain the spatially undifferentiated scenes of domestic activities. Thus, as early as the first quarter of the eighteenth century, within the single formal option of a one-room-plan house, the organization of space had begun to break down along lines of social and functional differentiation.

The range of formal options exercised in the first building period also included multi-room houses. The most typical of these was the hall-parlor-plan house, containing two rooms side by side, with the ridge of the roof running parallel to the long wall of the structure (Fig. 2:3). One or two stories in elevation, with gable chimney piles, the hall-parlor plan had been in use on the lower Delmarva Peninsula since at least the mid-seventeenth century, and in one general regional variation had become so closely identified with the Chesapeake Bay settlements that it was called a "Virginia House."[10] These structures, some of which survive in Delaware, appear more Anglo-American than English in origin and, in construction and detailing, are more characteristic of local rather than

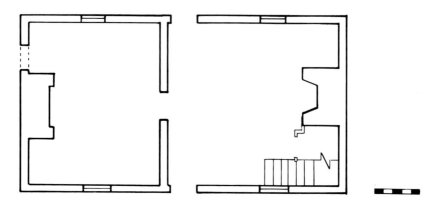

Figure 2:3. Hall-parlor plan: Liston House, Taylors Bridge vicinity, Blackbird Hundred (1739). The first-floor plan illustrates a typical hall-parlor arrangement, with access through opposed entries into the hall and then from the hall into the inner room or parlor. The fireplaces in both rooms have been closed down from their original configuration (a common alteration in the nineteenth and twentieth centuries), and a later door has been cut into the gable end wall of the parlor.

broad regional traditions. The earliest hall-parlor houses still standing in southern New Castle County (and perhaps the earliest in all of Delaware) have a hall that is directly entered from the outside, and an adjacent parlor or inner room. The parlor is entered from the hall, and only rarely does it have a second doorway to the outside. The second story and the garret commonly echoed the arrangement of the first floor and were reached through a stair located in the hall against the partition wall between the two rooms or in the corner between the hearth jamb and the wall. When the stair was placed against the partition, the parlor contained the actual stair structure. There are also a few examples in which there are separate stairs in both rooms.

The hall-parlor house of the lower Delaware Valley typically had three openings across the facade—a doorway and a single window on either side illuminating each of the rooms. In the earliest houses of this type additional small gable-end windows, usually no more than eighteen inches high and twelve inches wide, provided light for stairs and chimney closets. The first hall-parlor houses were partitioned with non-load-bearing scantling walls of vertical plank nailed to the sides of the ceiling joists and toed to a nailing strip tacked to the floor. The hall functioned as a day room in much the same way as it did in one-room-plan houses. The hall—with its larger fireplace, access to the upper stories, entry from the outside, and a greater amount of floor space—formed the social and working center of the house. The parlor, set off to the side, was most often fitted out as a downstairs chamber and later on in the colonial period as the finer sort of sitting room that came to be associated with the term "parlor" in the nineteenth century.

The 1818 inventory of David Ross, New Castle Hundred, details the room use of his hall-parlor house.[11] The hall, furnished only with a mahogany dining table, card tables, chairs, curtains and a set of mantel ornaments, had been set aside as a room designated for more public activities. The parlor, containing a sofa, sideboard, oval table, French clock, stands, numerous chairs, and a clutter of smaller items including four prints of "Naval Actions" hung together with two prints of the "Benediction," had become the room to which the householder and specially invited guests could withdraw. The two chambers on the second floor were furnished with bedsteads, bureaus, tables, washstands, and textiles. In Ross's household (as with others of this era) the degree to which the upper-story rooms were used as storage spaces had diminished; furthermore there was a marked absence of tools, grain, and other rough materials in the principal rooms of the house. As with other house types, the utilitarian functions of interior space were still defined by the presence or absence of outbuildings. David Ross, like John Hales a century before, relegated the bulk of household labor to a separate kitchen building, outfitted with cooking utensils, an open stove, food storage, and a "copper bathing tub." Farm implements and other tools were stored for the most part in a separate "Cool Room" that also contained wine casks and barrels of honey.

Hall-parlor-plan dwellings averaged between sixteen to twenty feet in width and twenty-four to forty feet in length. While width was limited by the ability of unsupported timbers to span a room, the length of the house was more responsive to the builder's own preference. Houses such as "one logg dwelling house a partition through the same, plank floors above and below, two brick chimneys" are repeatedly mentioned in the estate valuations of the orphans court and periodically appear in eighteenth-century inventories.[12] Dimensions, however, are seldom specified except in unusual instances: for example, a late seventeenth-century inventory listed a house twenty by thirty-five feet to be built of frame and weatherboarded.[13] Throughout the first half of the eighteenth century hall-parlor houses were the plantation and mansion houses of the region;

in the latter half of the century, following the rapid and widespread acceptance of stair-passage plans, they endured as the predominant plan-type selected by middle income farmers for themselves.

Although hall and hall-parlor plans were used for the majority of houses in the first three generations of building on the coastal plain of New Castle County, other spatial options, or floor plans, were available and were used to a limited extent. The two major alternatives were houses two rooms deep rather than two rooms long, and dwellings with a three-room plan consisting of a large hall with two adjoining equal-sized rooms that could serve as parlors, storage rooms, or downstairs sleeping chambers. While no identified examples of these forms survive in the region from before 1750, their presence is well documented, and some such houses can still be found in the northern half of the county. These houses reflected the architectural influence of the Pennsylvania Piedmont.

Houses one room wide and two rooms deep have been called "double-cell" houses elsewhere on the Delmarva Peninsula and "Quaker plan" houses in the rural districts west of Philadelphia (Fig. 2:4).[14] While these structures provide no measurably larger amount of household space than the more common hall-parlor plans, they do present themselves as a separate house-type. On the ground floor the front and the back rooms are entered directly from the outside. The front room appears to have been cast in the image of the old parlor and contained a hearth smaller than that in the hall, which was usually set diagonally into the corner of the room farthest from the doorway. The rear room was fitted out either with a second corner-hearth backed up to the one in the front room or with a large open fireplace capped with a beam lintel typical of the early hall. In either case, the parlor was either a bit smaller than or equal in size to the hall, and the stairs to the upper stories were placed against the wall away from the chimney pile, where they could be entered from the front parlor or through doorways from both rooms.

In the lower Delaware Valley the origins of the double-cell house have been ascribed to the architectural environment of early eighteenth-century Philadelphia, where row houses with one-room-wide facades crowded the city's streetscapes. The earliest surviving rural examples in Chester, Delaware, and northern New Castle Counties, however, suggest that they were contemporaneous with their superficially similar urban cousins. By the mid-eighteenth century in southern New Castle County the double-cell houses had been largely supplanted by the hall-parlor type.

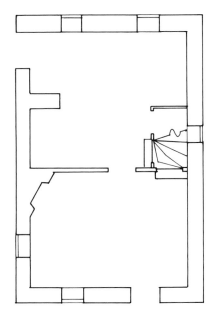

Figure 2:4. Double-cell-plan farmhouse in southeastern Pennsylvania: West Chester vicinity, Chester County (late eighteenth century).

In the villages of Port Penn and Odessa a variant of the double-cell plan continued to be erected as free-standing structures into the early 1800s (Fig. 2:5). The double-cell, village housing, which is concentrated in the period from 1790 to 1820, is characteristically of frame construction, with a free-standing masonry chimney rising through the center of the house and thereby allowing back-to-back fireplaces on each floor. By 1807, one householder had placed a bed and desk in the front first-floor room and a dining table, card table, chairs, and items related to food service in the back room; the owner kept mostly chamber furnishings on the second floor and filled the garret with textiles and spinning equipment.[15] Although there was precedent in rural housing at this time for two-room-deep structures, the surviving village double-cell houses clearly owe a greater formal debt to prevailing ideas of urban housing.

Three-room-plan dwellings were occasionally built in southern New Castle County throughout the colonial era (Fig. 2:6). Reference to a house plan containing a partition wall near the middle and another, at right angles to the first, further subdividing half the dwelling into two smaller rooms was first published in 1684 as part of William Penn's colonization literature.[16] This so-called beginner's house was provided with a chimney only at the gable end of the hall, thus leaving the two opposing chambers or storage rooms unheated. Three-room plans were built in the mid-Atlantic region as

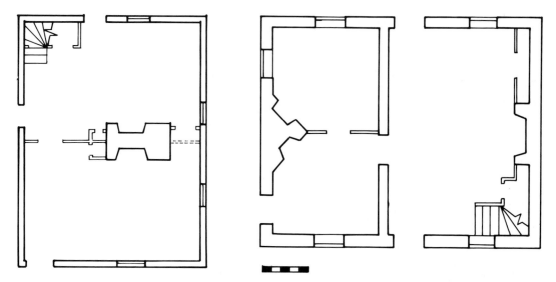

Figure 2:5. (Left) Double-cell village house: Merchant Street, Port Penn (ca. 1800).

Figure 2:6. (Right) Three-room plan: Townsend House, Townsend vicinity, Appoquinimink Hundred (ca. 1780). Built as a miller's house, the house contains three rooms on the first floor, with exterior access into a large, paneled hall and interior entry into two smaller inner rooms. The three-room arrangement was repeated on the second floor.

late as the mid-nineteenth century and as far south as central North Carolina (in the latter region they are still popularly known as Quaker plans). But by the mid-1750s the three-room-plan houses of New Castle County had been conceptually enlarged by the addition of a second chimney pile at the gable end, opposite the hall. As a result the two small ground-floor rooms achieved the comfort of downstairs parlors or chambers. At the same time, the three-room-plan house became increasingly square in its overall dimensions and demanded additional intermediate support, requiring the use of summer beams to enable the joists to span the breadth of the hall.

Finally, a few houses laid out in a four-room plan were built in New Castle County's lower hundreds and in neighboring communities to the north and east (Fig. 2:7). These houses were typically large, nearly square in their proportions, and contained two front and two back rooms. As with the hall-parlor plan, entry into the house was made directly into a common room containing both a fireplace and the stair leading to the upper stories. The common room could be richly paneled or relatively plain, but it does not

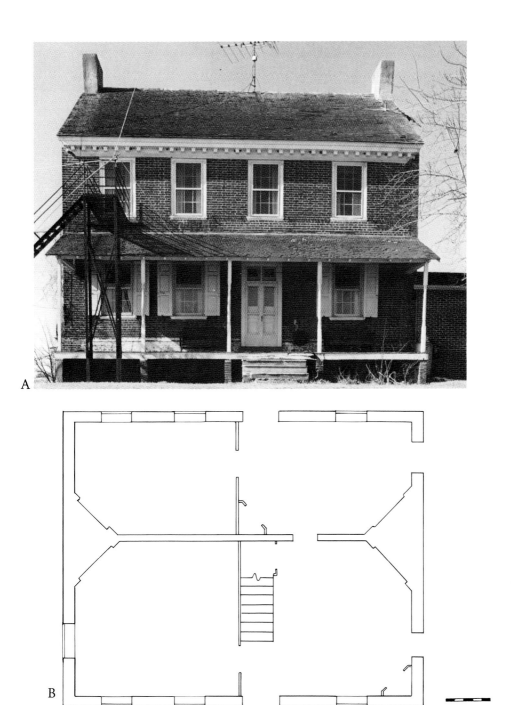

Figure 2:7. Four-room plan: Mount Jones, Odessa vicinity, St. Georges Hundred (ca. 1770). Behind the balanced, four-bay elevation (A) is a four-room plan (B) containing exterior entry into a heated hall and back room and segregated entries into the front and back inner rooms.

appear to have been used as a kitchen in any surviving examples. To the side of the room, away from the hearth, was an inner room or parlor finished with more elaborate decorative detailing. Behind the front rooms were two back rooms of equal length but shallower in depth. In most instances these were clearly secondary rooms that may have served any number of functions, including dining and sleeping. At Mount Jones, north of Odessa, the back rooms were fitted out with paneled overmantels and, in the room behind the hall, with a glass-paneled corner cupboard, indicating display and possibly public usage. Other examples of the four-room arrangement outside the area of this study subdivide the back rooms into even smaller spaces, resulting in an occasional unheated fifth or sixth space. Still, these more extensively divided forms are subtypes of the four-room-plan arrangement and typically retain the four-room plan on the second floor.

What is most significant about these larger houses is the formal position they occupy in the architectural community. They are the largest houses not making use of a stair-passage plan, an observation made more interesting by the fact that the largest of the four-room-plan types were erected well after the concept of a separate stair passage had been introduced into dwelling design. While the often elaborate interiors do not betray an ignorance of stylistic concerns, the division of interior space in these dwellings does not embrace the academic, formal separations achieved with the Georgian plan types.

The hall, hall-parlor, double-cell, three- and four-room-plan dwellings composed a first wave of formal options that continued to be popular in southern New Castle County through the early nineteenth century. But, beginning in the 1740s, the conceptual pool of possibilities was dramatically altered by the gradual acceptance of a family of plans oriented around an entry way—an unheated passage opening into the principal rooms of the house and containing a stair (Fig. 2:8). The general impression created by this form was of a new domestic order. The stylistic antecedent was classical architecture, which had gained popular currency in northern Europe in the sixteenth and seventeenth centuries.[17] The hallmark of the style that has come to be identified as Georgian architecture was increased attention to geometric balance in design, coupled with the creation of a space specifically intended to function as a corridor leading to all the rooms of the house, as if they were satellites orbiting a central axis.

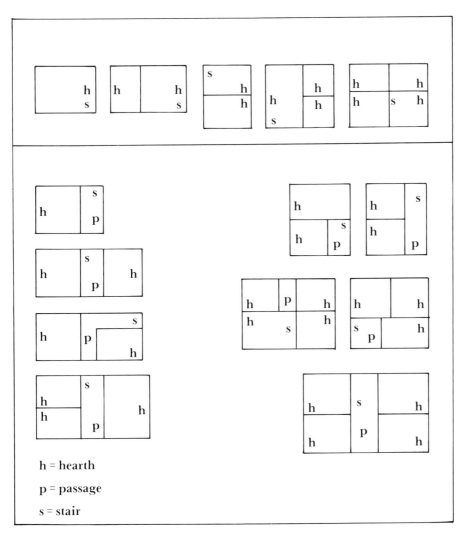

Figure 2:8. The increase in plan options for dwellings built in southern New Castle County prior to 1820 is illustrated in this schematic of basic types. Above the line are customary or traditional plans (hall, hall-parlor, double-cell, cross-passage, and four-room); below the line are common variations incorporating unheated stair entries. Not shown here are plans introduced in the later eighteenth century that incorporated original service wings.

While narrow passages are known to have been present in houses erected prior to the new "Georgian" look, they were typically quite narrow and functioned as lobbies or baffle-like entries providing some additional measure of separation between the hall and the outside world.[18] The introduction of broader entry spaces, often furnished with chairs, benches, and even cupboards, and with open rather than boxed-in stairs, has been interpreted in a number of ways. The consensus of these interpretations is that the presence of a substantial interior passageway physically distanced rooms and functioned as a transportation axis directing and isolating movement through the house. Rooms were no longer just separated by walls, but now also by space. Consequently, space was at once socially disruptive and desirable: disruptive because the passage removed entry into the heated, lived-in portions of the house by at least one more distance, desirable because those who opted for the new convention were the same individuals most concerned with expressing their social separation from the community at large.

In lower New Castle County the first dwellings to incorporate the open entry passage were one room deep, with either a single room to one side or with rooms flanking the passage (Fig. 2:9). The second-floor plan remained identical except for the partitioning off of a small unheated chamber over the principal entrance on the ground floor. The rooms off the passage were equipped with interior gable chimney piles and fitted with cupboards between the chimney jambs and the corners.

The Huguenot House and its first addition located in Appoquinimink Hundred contain several of the features common to the

Figure 2:9. Center-passage, single-pile plan: Naudain House, Middletown vicinity, Appoquinimink Hundred (1730–40).

new image in the mid-eighteenth century (Fig. 2:10). Begun as a two-story, side-passage or hall-parlor plan, the dwelling was soon enlarged by the addition of a two-story, one-room-plan wing on the opposite side of the passage. The passage could be entered through doorways at either end and the second story reached by way of a winder stair located in the rear of the passage. A second, enclosed winder stair connected the addition's ground-floor room to the chamber overhead. The expanded house included a ground-floor, four-bay facade, composed of a centrally placed doorway into the passage, with two windows illuminating the parlor and one lighting the added dining room.

From the exterior the fenestration of the Huguenot House appears to lack the balance and symmetry of the Georgian style. In plan, however, balance can be found in discrete formal units. The original three-bay core presents an even rhythm of openings relative to the first house as a self-contained unit. The wing that balanced the plan was provided with a single window centered to the addition but not with regard to the whole plan. The existence of such conceptually balanced facades is found in center-passage plans throughout the peninsula and in circumstances of both original forms and additive solutions.[19] In all cases, the symmetry is achieved by solutions that do not strive for total balance. In terms of additive options, these solutions, which simultaneously isolate and integrate formal separations, describe a pattern of building that became dominant between 1820 and 1850. A second house, Hill Island, also built in Appoquinimink Hundred, was first raised early in the eighteenth century as a chambered hall—a full two-story, one-room-plan house. By the mid-1700s it too had been extended into a central-passage-plan dwelling, but with a five- rather than a four-bay facade.

More characteristic of the center-passage, one-room-deep houseplan were dwellings like the Crossan House in western New Castle Hundred and the David Stewart House located in the village of Port Penn. Dating from the 1780s the Crossan House was built as a center-passage, one-room-deep plan (Fig. 2:11). The rooms on either side of the passage are of equal size and are furnished with architectural storage cupboards between the hearth jambs and gable-end corners. The passage is approximately half the width of the principal rooms and contains an open-string stair. On the second floor the stair opens onto a passage connecting heated chambers of equal size and directly over the rooms below. Directly above the

A

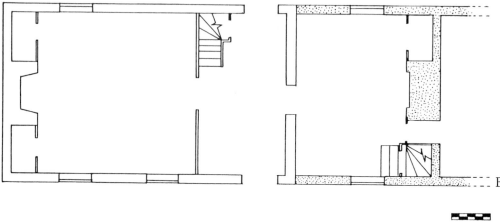

B

Figure 2:10. Huguenot House, Odessa vicinity, Appoquinimink Hundred (built and enlarged mid-eighteenth century). The first-floor plan (B) illustrates the extension of the original house from the right of the door to the left into a center-passage plan; the exterior view (A) shows the resulting asymmetrical elevation. The dotted lines in the plan indicate the continued extent of the addition, possibly to include exterior chimney closets or access into an earlier kitchen wing.

front door, the second-floor passage has been partitioned to create a third, unheated chamber. In several dwellings of this type, this small chamber is further distinguished from the other two by its exposed beams (rather than plastered ceilings) and walls of a slightly rougher finish. By the early nineteenth century, the attics of these houses, which had been typically left as unfinished lofts, were being plastered and used as unheated secondary chambers or storage areas.

While the Crossan House illustrates the formal character of the center-passage, one-room-deep house, the David Stewart House (Fig. 2:12), together with an 1829 room-by-room inventory of it, suggest how the interior spaces were functionally organized.[20] The plan of the Stewart House is nearly identical to the Crossan House—one room on either side of a center passage on the ground floor and a similar arrangement on the second floor, with a small room partitioned off the front of the second-floor stair passage. The ground-floor rooms were identified on the inventory as parlor, dining room, and entry. Both the dining room and parlor had paneled chimney closets. Dining tables were in both parlor and dining room, with an additional breakfast table and chairs in the latter. The chimney wall cupboards of the parlor contained empty bottles, demijohns, and jars, as well as a half gallon of brandy and twenty-three bottles of wine. The dining room cupboards held items related to food service, such as a tea caddy, decanters and wine glasses, and silver sugar tongs and spoons. The entry passage between the dining room and parlor contained three chairs. The second-story rooms were densely furnished. The chamber over the parlor was packed with a bed and trundel bed, desk, chest of drawers, bureau, chairs, and trunk. The other large chamber was similarly furnished. The little room above the entry contained only a bed and chair. Of particular note are the contents of the second-floor cupboards. In the parlor chamber, the cupboards held all the dining service, including glassware, queensware, waiters, decanters, tea sets, and "Liverpool Ware," as well as sets of chessmen and checkers, and textiles for bed and table.

In the instance of the Stewart House, the distribution of objects within the household indicates that the idea of a central passage envisioned as dividing and separating interior space had extended to the entire ground floor. The rooms most lived in were on the second floor and were used in much the same way as were the rooms in John Hales's chambered-hall house of 1723. What begins to emerge in the case of the Stewart House and the other center-passage forms built

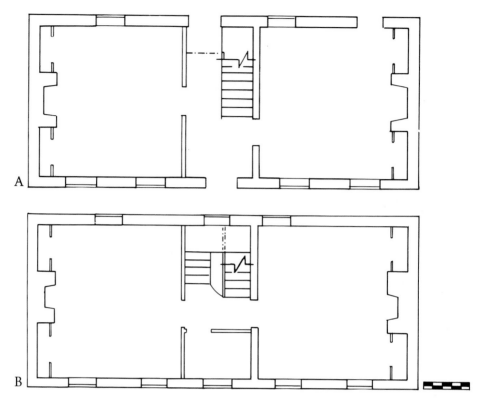

Figure 2:11. Crossan House, Christiana vicinity, White Clay Creek Hundred (late eighteenth century). The first- (A) and second- (B) floor plans illustrate several features associated with single-pile, center-passage plans in the lower Delaware Valley. These include the typical use of built-in cupboards in the parlor (C) and dining room (D), storage closets in the upstairs chambers, and the presence on the second floor of what was called the "little room over the entry."

from the mid-eighteenth century on is a type of dwelling containing more and physically better-defined spaces than before, but spaces that lacked centered or clear notions of domestic functions. Dining rooms not for general dining and parlors not for sitting were both possibilities and realities in an architectural environment that remained basically traditional in the world view it incorporated and progressive in the image of rural life it anticipated.

Not all center-passage, one-room-deep houses conformed to an aesthetic of balance and symmetry. The Noxon House, built in 1740 near Middletown, employed a four-bay facade, but on the interior the center passage was fully developed, with a small enclosed stair located at the rear of the house. The plan also departed from the

C

D

norm by having a large hall or dining room on one side of the passage and two equal-sized chambers or parlors on the opposing side. Stonham, commissioned by George Read around 1780 on the outskirts of New Castle, was erected with a four-bay facade and an entry passage no more than five feet wide (Fig. 2:13). The passage ran the

Figure 2:12. Stewart House, Stewart Street, Port Penn (ca. 1740). The interior arrangement of the first- and second-floor plans parallels the Crossan House (see Fig. 2:11) and is described in an early nineteenth-century, room-by-room probate inventory.

full depth of the house to the rear entry and opened onto a semi-enclosed stair against the back of the north parlor. In essence, the Noxon House and Stonham possess all the spatial qualities associated with the newer entry-passage types, but physically, they present a comfortable synthesis of the old hall-parlor form with the center-passage concept.

Houses designed around an entry containing a stair included a number of two-room-deep forms that were not as numerically dominant as the one-room deep side- and center-passage types. These double-pile houses fall into three categories: center-passage, side-passage, and corner-passage. In each type, the rooms adjoining the passage had a separate hearth, although they might share a chimney pile. Two double-pile, center-passage houses built in the last third of

A

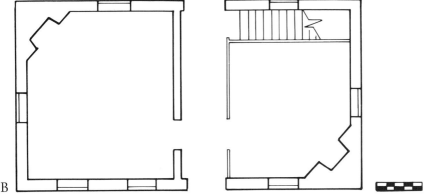

B

Figure 2:13. Stonham, New Castle vicinity, New Castle Hundred (ca. 1780). The acceptance of the center-passage-plan concept (B) did not extend to its articulation in a balanced, tripartite facade (A). Photo: DSA, Richard Jett.

the eighteenth century were William Corbit's dwelling in Odessa and the Andrew Fisher House in Pencader Hundred. At the time they were erected, these structures far exceeded the spatial norms of the area, and the Corbit House came to be locally identified as Castle William (Fig. 2:14).[21] The image of a palatial dwelling is compelling through its suggestion of the degree to which these large

Figure 2:14. Center-passage, double-pile plan: William Corbit House, Main Street, Odessa (1774).

houses stood above their neighbors and the way in which they were viewed by the community. The first full-blown center-passage, double-pile houses were not the florescence of an architectural ideal but the manifestation of conspicuous consumption. In the second half of the eighteenth century, a smallish two-story brick or timber structure might have been considered a mansion house; however, dwellings on the scale of Corbit's dwarfed and reduced such mansions into comparative insignificance.

Smaller in scale than Corbit's mansion were the scattered double-pile, side- and corner-passage houses built in southern New Castle County. The Shannon Hotel built at Christiana Bridge, ca. 1760, began as a corner-passage plan, two stories in elevation, with a three-bay facade (Fig. 2:15). The passage, entered from the outside, contained an open stair and direct access to the front parlor and the room behind the stairs. The rear parlor could be reached through either the front parlor or the room behind the passage. The arrangement on the second floor found a stair leading to the attic and three rooms radiating from the passageway. Later examples of this type, such as the Cann Store at Glasgow, were built in the 1820s and 1830s and used the same general design (see Fig. 7:16).

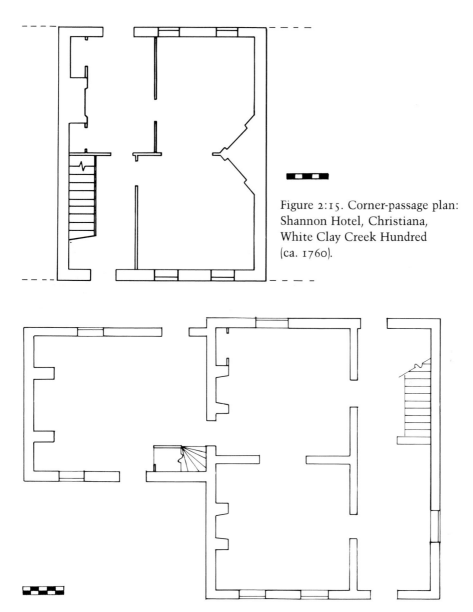

Figure 2:15. Corner-passage plan: Shannon Hotel, Christiana, White Clay Creek Hundred (ca. 1760).

Figure 2:16. Side-passage, double-pile plan: Brook Ramble, Townsend vicinity, Appoquinimink Hundred (ca. 1800). The plan includes an original service wing.

Side-passage, double-pile houses were not built in the region until the late eighteenth century. In these dwellings, the passage runs the full depth of the house, and the stair occupies half the depth. Two ground-floor rooms, often of equal size, are situated to one side of the passage (Fig. 2:16). On the second floor the passage often occupied only the side of the rear room, with the front chamber taking up the full breadth of the house. With two exceptions, the double-pile, side-passage plans are found in or around towns and villages. Delaware City has semi-detached row houses dating from the 1820s, with the entry passages penetrating only half the depth of the house. In rural settings, the side-passage, double-pile form was never widely accepted.

All the notions of architectural space that had come into general circulation between 1700 and 1820 were subject to additions. The forms for additions were either drawn from the general range of concepts of domestic space or conceived as sheds and lean-tos which could only stand as structurally dependent wings. Householders frequently used both. William Weirs, for example, owned a "Publick House . . . one part of which is built with Brick and the other with Frame with two shed rooms joining the whole."[22] Additions based on the image of a discrete, free-standing domestic unit had the effect not only of increasing household space, but also of completely realigning the formal organization of the house. A two-story brick addition to the Dilworth House in the early eighteenth century transformed the dwelling from a hall to a hall-parlor plan, and that transformation created a new house. In the case of John Golden's house (1790), its transformation was completed by the types of furnishings used in the two rooms.[23] Both contained beds, but the "new room" also held the finer furniture, including "six walnut chairs best quality" and all the tea and coffee service, the best china, and the silver. By contrast the "old room" was relegated to common or public usage with less showy furniture, and everyday table and serving vessels of tinware, crockery, queensware, and pewter. In much the same manner, the Huguenot House was physically enlarged and conceptually redefined as a center-passage-plan dwelling and may have had a kitchen wing (see Fig. 2:10). In contrast to new rooms, sheds and lean-tos commonly consisted of an additional one-story storage or work unit shoved up under the eaves or the second-story floor line of the rear elevation, or built against the gable end. While these wings enlarged the square footage of domestic space, they did not alter the character of the house to the same degree as larger additions because they could not transform the spaces within the dwelling.

By 1820, the close of the first building cycle, the range of formal options for dwellings in southern New Castle County had been expanded to incorporate the house-types that would be built again and again until mid-century. The dominant forms were one- and two-room-plan houses that were one or two stories in height. These included houses like William Weir's, described in 1801 as a "New Log Dwelling House twenty six by twenty feet not in Tenantable order having a Cellar under the same not wall'd in consequence of which the House has sunk." or Alexander McMurphy's 1794 "Log dwelling House with two rooms below two rooms above stairs."[24] Nearly a century earlier, small dwellings composed the core of housing in the area. Larger ones were erected, but initially these were simply more elaborate versions of the hall, hall-parlor or an occasional three-room plan. Beginning in the 1740s the so-called mansion houses began to incorporate an unheated entry passage, opening into heated rooms and containing a stair to the upper floors. The introduction of the new configuration had two immediate consequences on building practice in southern New Castle County. The new range of options heralded an increase in building types; and the new forms, with their properties of balance and symmetry, moved the definition of space into a self-consciously formal concern with architectural fashion. Aesthetic needs, no longer satisfied by the ornamentation of structural materials or the overlays of trim, now included the modeling and division of space.

In 1725 the greatest houses of southern New Castle County were the Ashton family dwellings, which were brick, two stories in elevation, built on raised basements, and laid out as hall-parlor plans (Fig. 2:17). Fifty years later the most elaborate house was William Corbit's "Castle," a two-and-a-half-story brick structure designed on a broad center-passage, double-pile plan (see Fig. 2:16). Where qualitative distinctions in matters of finish had served to architecturally rank the members of an earlier rural society, these distinctions were reinforced and extended by a later generation to the very definition of space. The architectural gulf separating the most affluent members of the community from the common farmer or the tenant had become vast. The accessible image of housing for most folks, however, remained constant throughout this period from the meanest tenements, "18 by 15 feet one story high in bad repair," to more substantial yeomen's dwellings with a parlor, common room, and partitioned loft.[25]

By the close of the eighteenth century, there was a distinct relationship between the emergence of well-defined social classes

Figure 2:17. Ashton House, Port Penn vicinity, St. Georges Hundred (ca. 1700).
Photograph: David L. Ames.

and architecture. As Stephen Saunders Webb points out, one of the sources of the intense frustrations that led to Bacon's Rebellion in the 1670s was the inability of newly arrived Virginians to economically and socially improve their position under the government of Sir William Berkeley.[26] In the eighteenth century there was a growing divergence of status in and around urban centers like Philadelphia. In his descriptions of colonial society in the urban ports of Boston, New York, and Philadelphia, historian Gary Nash succinctly outlines the parameters of hierarchial rank and the possibilities for social mobility.[27] Also using Philadelphia as a focus, Sam Bass Warner offers the notion of "privatism" as a partial explanation for the process and mechanisms creating an American class structure:

> Psychologically, privatism meant that the individual should seek happiness in personal independence and in the search for wealth; socially, privatism meant that the individual should see his first loyalty as his immediate family, and that a community should be a

union of such money-making, accumulating families; politically, privatism meant that the community should keep the peace among individual money-makers, and, if possible, help to create an open and thriving setting where each citizen would have some substantial opportunity to prosper.[28]

Southern New Castle County, the back country of Wilmington and Philadelphia, was one setting among many where urban social order had a rural equivalent.[45] Mansion houses were invariably commissioned by men who managed multiple farms, local manufacturers, or merchants engaged in trade and money lending. Whatever their source of income, they were not yeoman-farmers. They were, in fact, the first to advocate scientific agriculture over traditional farming, to keep detailed account books in favor of verbal contracts, and to commission and occupy houses that promoted social separation over customary interaction. The essence of privatism was a combination of achievement and exclusivity—the same values symbolized in the new brick, stair-passage houses of late eighteenth-century lower New Castle County.

3. Matters of Finish

IN THE STUDY OF HOUSEHOLD FURNISHINGS and material status in colonial America, we find that there are two methods by which goods convey social distinctions. First, a hierarchy may be composed based on the number and finish of artifacts in individual households; second, the presence or absence of types of objects in particular dwellings also indicates social rank. Thus, there is an interplay between quantitative/qualitative aspects and typological characteristics. Most one-room-plan houses, for example, were furnished with pretty much the same sorts of objects: three or four beds, six chairs, a couple of chests, a cupboard, two or three tables, two spinning wheels, and a loom. Larger houses contained the same objects, but in greater numbers and of consistently better quality. The best houses, of any size, are also likely to contain one or more typologically distinctive objects, such as a desk or secretary, a bookcase, a specialized dining or tea table, or a sideboard. By using these standards of status and applying them to the manner in which houses are decoratively finished, we find the same sets of qualitative, quantitative, and typological distinctions obtaining.

Architectural finish or ornamentation is the single area of traditional building that students of vernacular architecture have been most reluctant to address. The reasons for this hesitancy are not clear, but may rest in the concept of style and the purposes behind most conventional decorative-arts-oriented studies. In the past, students of traditional architectural history tended to use style to define periods and chronology. Style was based on decorative motifs. In order to bracket these periods historically, various progressions of style—beginning with the *avant garde* (the new) and concluding with the *rétarditaire* (the out of date)—were introduced. Coupled with the emphasis on style was the notion that aesthetic concerns filtered down from the academic taste makers to the lower orders and also moved outward from urban centers to rural areas; according to this approach, stylistic expressions in vernacular architecture were the product of the folk builders' imperfect understanding of complex aesthetic philosophies. In more recent years scholars have begun evaluating vernacular architecture on its own terms, but in so doing they have avoided tackling the thorny issue of style. As in other regions, householders and builders in southern New Castle County used what worked best for them and what was in keeping with local convention and practice. Within that framework, we will examine the decorative elements that were used to convey a stylishness that underscored certain spatial and social separations within the household and the community.

The first step toward unraveling the householder's intention is to determine the decorative focus or orientation within the household. In the first prolonged cycles of durable building (1700–1820) fashion is oriented toward the enhanced definition of both form and fabric. Ornament, when used, is applied either to exposed structural elements such as ceiling beams or to points of passage such as doorways, windows, and fireplaces. The two exceptions to this general rule are the use of built-in, architectural furniture, including corner cupboards and chimney closets, and the decorative elaboration of exterior surfaces, especially patterned brickwork.

Fashion directs movement, both visual and physical, through the house. Through elaborate window surrounds with raised panel aprons, open stairways with turned balusters, and paneled overmantels, decorative elements stress the dimension of the house as a concrete space pierced with openings connecting interior to exterior, rooms to other rooms, as well as incorporating secondary spaces within the whole of a room. Concentrations of fashionable trim emphasize thresholds existing within the house as bridges joining domestic spaces. The internal and external aspects of these thresholds are highlighted through decorative elements, which accentuate and even exaggerate them. Visual reference points project the social values experienced through architectural movement.

Since the predominant areas of emphasis are doorways, we can describe the house as a series of spaces bridged by thresholds. In the most immediate sense the ornamentation is a method of finishing the openings in the neatest manner possible, but, on a deeper level, it is an implicit acknowledgment that the spaces lying on opposite sides of a common wall are different. The decorative elements frame what lies on each side and what passes through them.

The primary thresholds of any dwelling are the doorways to the outside yard and the landscape beyond. Throughout the first building periods in southern New Castle County, the way in which these openings were treated reflected contemporarydefinitions of interior space. Initially, doorways were plainly finished with simply molded architraves and unpaneled reveals. On brick dwellings the masonry surrounding the door was occasionally elaborated with glazed closers, but rarely with the rubbed and gauged brickwork used in Virginia, Maryland, and Pennsylvania. Doorways were frequently equipped with stoop-like porches consisting of a raised wooden platform, customarily lacking a roof, and with rails and board benches built along the sides. The doors were either of raised-panel or board-and-batten construction and swung into the room. Even in the finest pre-1760 houses the primary entry into the house was finished with only a modicum of finery. In many of the earliest durable houses these doors opened into a common room/hall. Conceptually this room was an open domestic space, and within it there was no comparable need to mark public and private spaces. Not surprisingly, there was sparing use of trim around the doorways.

By the 1740s, householders were building dwellings that had centrally located passages containing stairs to the upper levels of the house. While this arrangement signaled a change in the division and potential use of space, it was not decoratively stressed in the trim applied to the main entry into a house. Just as the interior spaces of the new center passage were often used in the old ways throughout the eighteenth century, there appears to have been little desire to emphasize their presence through the application of decorative detailing. The result was that the first generation of center-passage houses did not externally telegraph the message of their interior arrangement.

The first decoratively paneled entries appeared in the 1760s. From that period onward many (but by no means all) of the center-passage-plan houses, as well as a few of the more elaborate hall-parlor-plan dwellings, had doorways surrounded by academically inspired decorative trim (Fig. 3:1). At the same time householders began emphasizing the distance in social function between the passage and the various rooms. Located in and around Odessa and

A   B

Figure 3:1. Paneled entries: (A) Grantham House, New Castle vicinity, New Castle Hundred (ca. 1790); (B) Greenlawn, Middletown vicinity, St. Georges Hundred (ca. 1810).

Middletown and dating from 1769 to 1810, Greenlawn, the Wilson House, Fairview, and the Corbit House were all in the vanguard of the new arrangement. In the village of New Castle and the neighboring countryside the execution of these entries can be attributed to a craftsman, Peter Crouding, who carved the doorways and interior trim for a number of houses. As heavily ornamented doorways came into vogue for private dwellings, they also began to appear on public and religious buildings. A paneled entry similar in design to that on houses remains in place for Old Drawyers Church near Odessa and the court house in New Castle (Fig. 3:2).[1] The same door treatment clearly stated that the interiors of a prosperous house, a church, and a public building were environments distinct from that of the general landscape. The move toward social distancing and the ordering of social relationships revealed by the increased selection of stair-

Figure 3:2. Entry:
Old Drawyers Church,
Odessa vicinity,
St. Georges Hundred
(ca. 1769–73).

passage plans by the most affluent building clients conveys a world view bound and prescribed by certain rules and rituals.

Unlike main entryways, the treatment of secondary exterior doorways and windows remained constant from 1730 to the 1820s. Framed with the jambs tenoned into the sill and the lintel tenoned into the jambs, the construction of these openings was masked by planed trim ornamented with a variety of beads, fillets, and ogee moldings. Window openings in the primary elevation of brick structures were frequently enclosed with glazed or dressed closers and, in the most elaborate houses, capped with projecting cut stone flat arches. Secondary doorways were finished with plain rowlock or segmental arches composed of headers; in earlier buildings glazed brick was sometimes used decoratively to pattern the arches.

In addition to windows and doorways the exteriors of eighteenth-century brick dwellings are marked with vertical divisions—watertables, belt courses, pent roofs, and cornices—revealing the stratified domestic layers within the building. Watertables defined the division between cellar and main floor. Although a tech-

Figure 3:3. Exterior cornice: Mount Jones.

nological explanation for this division is that the cellar walls were necessarily thicker than those above for purposes of support, the ornamental externalization of this division went beyond the matter of technique. Watertables, whether they ran straight or jogged across the facade, were applied only to the main elevation and often incorporated molded brick trim to create a visual plinth for the superstructure of the building. Pedestaled upon their foundations, two-story houses were further divided with belt courses two and three bricks thick. In dwellings built before the 1770s the belt course often served as a weathering strip for pent roofs, but in the later eighteenth century they were primarily ornamental. At the roof line was the final ornamental vertical division: the cornice. Throughout the first building period cornices were cased or boxed with boards and finished with strips of molding, dentils, or modillion blocks—at Mount Jones the blocks are straight sided with ogee profiles (Fig. 3:3). But such detailing was rare and the greatest number of cornices, if they were ornamented at all, were finished with hand-planed bed moldings.

Frame and log buildings typically lacked the same degree of external expression of vertical interior divisions; however, some spatial divisions did find expression on the exterior. For example, the exposed brick chimney-back on the original block of the Christopher Vandergrift House provided an external expression for an internal feature. Due to the low survival rate of early timber framed buildings it is difficult to calculate the prevalence of such features. It is apparent that the degree of exterior ornamentation was related to the choice of building material and that brick, judging from period tax lists, was the material chosen by the most affluent level of society. That brick dwellings should be the recipients of the most self-consciously thought-out decorative elements reflects the social distancing processes also recognizable in the center-passage houses by the same affluent householders.

One area of external ornamentation that falls outside the aesthetic ordering of matters to do with physical and visual passage is the use of gable-end patterned brickwork in which glazed bricks were positioned in an exterior wall to create geometric designs, dates, and initials. Examples of such work are found on both sides of the Delaware River, with the greatest number remaining in southwest New Jersey.[2] The majority of these date from the second and third quarters of the eighteenth century, but scattered instances appeared as late as the early 1820s. Commissioned by wealthy planters, many of them Quaker, the pattern-end houses convey a different sort of progress. In the lower Delaware Valley, initial English settlement was seen as permanent. Durable housing was perceived as an investment in that permanence and was to be achieved as rapidly, profitably, and efficiently as possible. If there are identifiable Quaker qualities in vernacular buildings of the eighteenth century, they do not reside in matters of simplicity or plainess, but in the construction and maintenance of durable buildings. The decorative expression of that achievement was found not only in the general quality of houses raised in the lower Delaware Valley during the colonial period but also in the explicit commemoration—through the practice of dating the structures—of the passage from impermanence to durability.[3] The Liston House in Appoquinimink Hundred, a brick building dated 1739, replaced an earlier post-in-ground-built dwelling. Some dated buildings, like Mansion Farm 1750, were built by non-Quakers and extended the use of patterned brickwork across sectarian lines into a more general aesthetic statement of the transition from initial construction to lasting architecture. By the 1760s the fashion had gained currency to the extent that even non-dwelling units such as the Brick Store, a grain warehouse, were dated through the medium of patterned glazed brickwork.

The lines of social and physical demarcation found in later eighteenth-century thresholds extended throughout the house interior. Windows were finished with molded surrounds and, in some cases, paneled aprons. Interior doorways received the same sort of treatment but, depending on the nature of the connected spaces, could be handled with very different decorative detailing. In the Huguenot House, the threshold connecting the center passage and the parlor was encased in a round-arched architrave and opened as a double door, while the entry into the dining room, made over from the old notion of the hall, was decidedly less ornate (Fig. 3:4). As stairs were brought into the open in center-passage and related dwellings, they initially retained the configuration of winder stairs; they were compact vertical affairs packed against the rear wall of the passage or nestled behind closet doors in the corners of hall and hall-parlor houses. By the 1750s stairs had been opened up and typically ran nearly the full depth of the passage in a straight run to an intermediate landing before turning to the second floor. (Fig. 3:5). Once stairways became more visible, decorative carved spandrels and turned balusters became prevalent. The result was clear to all observers: increased trim applied to these thresholds made the spaces lying beyond them increasingly distinct and distant.

Within the room the hearth walls received the most concentrated decorative detailing. In southern New Castle County a tradition of extensively paneled fireplace walls containing mantels, overmantels, chimney closets, cupboards, and stair closets developed in the first decades of the eighteenth century and continued through the early nineteenth century. The focus of this attention was the hearth, and the decoration around the fireplaces was scaled to meet and occasionally exceed the general degree of ornamentation in the particular dwellings. In rougher buildings the fireplace opening may have been graced only with a beam lintel and possibly a mantel cornice, while those dwellings with pretensions to refinement sported rigidly geometric fields of raised paneling that opened to reveal cupboards designed to display fine silver and ceramics (Fig. 3:6).

Only traces of first-floor interior trim dating from the eighteenth century remain. Indeed not one hall or parlor from the first period of durable building made it through the nineteenth century intact, but similar rooms in houses in Chester County, Pennsylvania, and Salem County, New Jersey, pre-dating 1725, provide some general information as to what the appearance of the best sort of houses must have been.[4] In these structures with hall-parlor plans, the hearth opening in the hall was capped with a mantel cornice

Figure 3:4. Parlor doorway: Huguenot House. The round, arched opening dates to the remodeling of the house, when the plan was extended into a center-passage configuration (see Figs. 2:10 and 3:6).

Figure 3:5. Stair landing: Fairview.

Figure 3:6. Dining room: Huguenot House (see Figs. 2:10 and 3:4).

composed of heavily planed moldings built up from a composite of several individual profiles. The spaces above the mantel cornices were finished only with plaster, while the walls on either side of the hearth were finished with a combination of vertical board walling and raised panels. In one Salem County house the spaces above the doorways and cupboards were fitted with sawnwork grills, while a Chester County dwelling had only a single panel over the chimney closet door. Evidence of similar arrangements appear in southern New Castle County houses. Although stripped and heavily re-modeled in the mid-nineteenth century, scars in the plaster at Nox-on House reveal that the hall had a fully paneled end-wall, with cupboards, a heavy ceiling cornice, and paneled aprons placed be-neath the windows. The Dilworth House still possesses its original openings to the cellar and the second-story stairs. It has a raised panel over the doorway, battened board doors, and red paint with a baseboard painted black. Although the Ashton houses contained no original first-floor finishing trim, the second stories showed the continued use of vertical, beaded-edge board, partition walls, with painted baseboards and a hearth surround composed of bolection moldings and a boxed and molded mantel cornice. Repeated mention in early probate inventories of ornaments on the mantel pieces throughout the house underscores the role such trim played in terms of visual reference and decorative display.

The earliest intact first-floor ornament survives in only the most substantial durable houses built in the mid-eighteenth century. By that date the jumbled appearance presented by paneling juxtaposed with vertical board walling had been solved, and the rooms took on a more formal and uniform appearance which paralleled solutions worked out in the regularization of plan. The new options for ornament, like those for form, were not accepted across the whole range of dwellings, nor did they occur as a chronologically dramatic break with earlier traditions. Instead they occurred at a certain social level as the expression of a group most preoccupied with separating and defining its position apart from the condition and place of its neighbors. Attempts at balance and symmetry and the consciously formulated drive toward an aesthetic coherence among all the decorative motifs fashioned into harmonious compositions were the hallmarks of the new image. Innovation took place in the context of contrivance. The hallmark was artifice rather than a free manipulation of parts. Paneling and ornamentation did not become more complex, they became simpler and more formal, thus befitting the image projected by the spaces they graced.

Paneling in houses with two or more ground-floor rooms gradually came to be more uniform. The aesthetic distinction made between inner room and outer room even in the best hall-parlor houses (Fig. 3:7) was replaced with distinctions made between the front and back of the house. The front-to-rear separations are also contemporary with the earliest center-passage houses, where, despite differences in name and in assigned functions, the rooms split by the stair hall were visually much the same (Figs. 3:8 and 2:11). As the eighteenth century drew to a close the new decorative concerns extended to houses that continued the old formal traditions and still had direct entry from the outside and offered access to upper stories by means of corner stairs—no longer completely concealed by closets. The resulting landscape was one in which architectural detail conveyed values of domestic interaction and social distance that were understood by many, accessible to some, and communicated

A   B

Figure 3:7. (Above) First-floor interiors: Grantham House, (A) hall, (B) parlor. The different interior finishes of the two rooms directly communicate their relative status in terms of access and intended function.

Figure 3:8. (Right) First-floor interiors: Fairview. (A) dining room; (B) parlor. In center-passage-plan houses the visual definition of space through the application of ornament became increasingly subtle. While certain decorative distinctions between dining room and parlor can be picked out in Fairview, they are not nearly as evident as in the Grantham House. A similar decoratively balanced interior is in the Crossan house (see Fig. 2:11).

by a few using combinations of formal, constructural, and aesthetic options.

Interior paneling also included the installation of architectural furniture. The extensive use of such furniture, like chimney closets and corner cupboards, was another reflection of the rapid move from impermanent to durable housing. Unlike the lower Chesapeake Bay settlements of Virginia and Maryland, where the cycle of impermanent housing was protracted over as much as a century, the shift in southern New Castle County came as early as the second generation of habitation.[5] Because ephemeral building practice did not

A

B

gain the time to develop as a lasting regional tradition, the investment in portable-case furniture, such as chests, dressers and cupboards, was less crucial. There was instead a marked preference for built-in-case pieces that were to be as permanent as the buildings themselves. (Fig. 3:9). And not only did this architectural furniture become a significant aspect of local architecture in the principal downstairs rooms, it also was placed in the upper chambers. The best houses seldom had movable cupboards; according to the estate inventories of the period, the owners rarely had any storage furniture larger than a chest. The implication of this is similar to that for the dated and patterned gable ends of brick dwellings; it marks the passage to permanence.

The final ingredient in this progression toward an increased formalization was the gradual abandonment of exposed board walls and ceiling beams. In the first wave of durable housing, partition walls were constructed of exposed beaded-edge boards, and ceiling beams had similarly beaded or chamfered edges (Fig. 3:10). By the 1740s, in new houses, these features were covered with lath and plaster finishes. (Fig. 3:11). In the best dwellings applied ornament included tiled fireplace jambs (Fig. 3:12); at the same time the finest of the structures already standing were updated with applications of plaster and lath. By the close of the eighteenth century even frame and log buildings were adopting plaster finishes to effectively mask the old visual impression, if not the earlier formal images, of the dwelling. The Dilworth House and Vandergrift House, for example, were both erected with exposed and ornamented interior framing elements, but received eighteenth-century additions that were fully covered on the interior. The Kielkopf log house north of Middletown, raised around 1800, was intended from the start to be completely masked on the interior (as was the Noxon House). In other instances only ceilings were plastered over, and in some houses erected as late as the 1770s the original design included open ceilings but plaster finished walls.

One aspect of interior finish about which little is known is how color was used. The majority of dwellings may have been either left unpainted or whitewashed inside. Where whitewash was applied, it was done on an annual basis as part of the general upkeep. Because surviving eighteenth-century houses were dwellings of the best sort, we find little evidence of whitewash in the main living areas; cellars and attics, however, often retain this finish. As the white-

A
B

Figure 3:9. Architectural furniture: (A) The Yearsley House, Congress Street, Port Penn (ca. 1800) incorporates a paneled display cupboard into the hall (or common room) chimney breast. (B) Mount Jones possesses built-in corner cupboards, installed in the hall and in the room behind (see Fig. 2:7).

wash has grown old and scaled off in these secondary spaces, the heavy, multiple coats have been revealed. The better rooms in these houses were painted. Typical color schemes would have been black baseboards and dark red or bright green walls, board ceilings, and woodwork. In at least one instance, a wider variety of color was used: a paneled fireplace wall painted red; baseboards, chair rail, and window trim of yellow; black and grey marbleized plaster wainscot; and whitewashed walls and ceilings. But most houses have been repainted so many times through their histories that it is difficult to identify original color schemes.

Examining the housing stock from the first period of durable building until the second decade of the nineteenth century reveals

A

B

Figure 3:10. Vertical board walling: (A) Christopher Vandergrift House, Port Penn vicinity, St. Georges Hundred (late eighteenth-century addition, see Fig. 7:3); (B) Huguenot House. The board walling in the Vandergrift House partition is fitted around exposed beaded-edged ceiling joists, framed by a planed molding strip. In the Huguenot House dining room chamber, the upper ends of the boards composing the fireplace wall are nailed to the face of a joist hidden from view by the plaster ceiling.

Figure 3:11. Panel finish: Huguenot House parlor chamber. The mantel is a later addition.

Figure 3:12. Fireplace tiles: Mount Jones. Mortared into the face of the masonry fireplace jambs, the tiles in Mount Jones were reserved for use in the best rooms, including the front parlor and front parlor chamber. Compare the hierarchy of finish here with the patterns of interior ornamentation in the Grantham House (Fig. 3:7) and Fairview (Fig. 3:8). The tiles' manufacture date of 1750 to 1770 assists in dating the house.

that the role of fashion was to isolate and communicate strategic points of physical passage and social intersection. Where house form served as a map for interaction, style provided instructive signposts along those paths that were socially traveled. As time and social assumptions expressed in architecture changed during the eighteenth century, the channeled flow of day-to-day interaction could no longer rely on customary usage and common understanding. The thresholds between impermanence and durability, between exterior and interior, between the levels of society as perceived by those who struggled most to separate themselves from their neighbors, all demanded devices that would accent those passages and make them clearly understood by those who lived in the shadow of that order.

4. Other Buildings

THE TYPES OF DWELLINGS ERECTED in the first building period describe only a single theme in the shaping of the landscape. As significant to understanding the order built onto the land is a consideration of the artificially imposed boundaries on spaces surrounding the house, the buildings occupying those spaces, and the larger boundaries bringing farms and villages together in a single community. The importance of outbuildings, for example, is best underscored by the role separate kitchens played in creating functional and conceptual distinctions between houses of the same type. Thus outbuildings enlarge our perception of the household they surround. By the same measure, public buildings, meeting houses and churches, stores, mills and warehouses linked the spaces between the households. A rural countryside interspersed with villages cannot be evaluated as clusters of isolated elements; it is an environment that must be assessed as a social unit bound together by ties of commerce and communication.[1] The spaces extending domestic domains and those larger spaces tying them together represent an enlarged perspective on the contexts of vernacular architecture.

Between 1760 and 1820, farm buildings in southern New Castle County outnumbered farmhouses by an average of six to one. Only a handful of eighteenth-century outbuildings still stand, and only three farm buildings from the first quarter of the nineteenth century remain. The situation is no better for other sorts of eighteenth-century work buildings: one grist mill and one tannery remain. Most pre-1820 barns, corn houses, stables, and granaries were replaced in the course of later nineteenth-century agricultural reforms and architectural renewals, yet the spectrum of outbuildings supporting the activities of house and farm prior to 1820 is well documented in the written records. By piecing together information gleaned from the orphans court, tax lists, and estate inventories, we can mentally reconstruct the diverse array of buildings and lesser structures, from barns to beehives. Outbuildings can be broken down into two groups: those oriented toward household activities and those geared to the working of the land. A vivid portrait of the type and number of both groups of structures is painted in the terse 1775 evaluation of Isaac Billerby's estate—

> one log dwelling house with a shed on the back part and likewise at the end with a seller under said house, one old log kitchen, one brick oven, one meat house, one corn crib, one garden, one cart house, one granary, one log stable, one chair house, one log barn, three barracks, one old granary, one small orchard with fifty trees, one small tenement with an old log house[2]

A breakdown of 48 St. Georges Hundred orphans court property valuations between 1760 and 1820 likewise provides a neat picture of the numbers and types of outbuildings associated with local dwellings. Each farmstead averaged six to seven structures in addition to the house. Most common among these on a farm-by-farm basis were kitchens (83 percent), corn cribs (79 percent), stables (69 percent), meat or smoke houses (66 percent), barns (56 percent) and tenant houses (52 percent). Other common building types included granaries, carriage houses, fowl and hen houses, storehouses, and milk houses or dairies. These buildings were predominantly of log and frame construction. Kitchens and tenant houses were almost exclusively of log construction, whereas barns were most often timber framed.

The number of buildings per farmstead in St. Georges Hundred was more than double that of other contemporary Delaware farms in central Sussex County to the south, which averaged three outbuildings per estate: kitchen, smokehouse, and either a barn or corn house. Two other important facts emerge from these figures: first, buildings in southern New Castle County were generally in better repair than elsewhere in the state, and, second, farms had a conspicuous lack of wooden fencing. The absence of fencing may relate to the amount of land under cultivation. In southern Delaware more than 50 percent of all listed lands were unimproved or forested; in St. Georges Hundred only 16 percent of usable lands were unimproved. The wooded areas in this hundred seem to be intentionally set aside, with wood lots designed to provide firewood and other necessary timber for the farm. Thus, the farmsteads of southern New Castle County, with the exception of the poorer lands in the southwest corner of the district, were set on fields divided by hedgerows and not wooden fences.[3]

Predominantly log or frame, the farm kitchen was a free-standing, one-room building of one story plus a loft. On farmsteads where kitchens were associated with one-room-plan houses, there was little difference between the house and kitchen, although the house was typically larger and more finished. Not surprisingly, the quality of kitchens varied throughout the eighteenth and early nineteenth centuries, ranging from "a new kitchen . . . 18 feet by 16 of logs & hew'd down covered with oak shingles and a brick chimney," to "an ould fraimed kitchen . . . new syled [silled] covered and the south end weatherboarded, and a new chimney built in the south end."[4] During the late eighteenth century, as farmers began to incorporate kitchens into the overall house plan, they joined the formerly separate structures in many different ways. John Murphy had "one dwelling House occupied for a Tavern with a kitchen under the same ruff."[5] In one case an enclosed passage, built as a lodging room, was constructed to connect the house and kitchen. In other cases kitchens were moved (or new ones were built) to abut the main house.

From the earliest mention of kitchens in estate inventories, a clear pattern emerges: kitchens were spaces for rough domestic work—especially food preparation, but also spinning and weaving. Occasionally they housed slaves and servants. Inventories enumerating the contents suggest these were one-room structures containing a cooking hearth, with a bake oven either built into the chimney pile or standing separately in the yard. Joshua Clayton's kitchen in 1798 was also furnished with a pine table, four rush-bottomed chairs, and a wide assortment of pans, kettles, casks, and utensils related directly to food preparation and storage; the garret—containing bedding, barrels and leather—provided a storage area and possibly sleeping quarters for one or more of Clayton's nine slaves.[6] Similar records as late as the 1820s show the persistence of the same general arrangement. The ground floor invariably contained a table and chairs of little value, a hearth or stove, and cooking utensils; bedding and most storage items were consigned to the loft. Farming implements, spinning wheels, and weaving looms were used in the earliest kitchens, but about 1800 were typically moved to the barns, sheds, and the upper rooms of the house. With the development of specialized domestic space in the eighteenth century, kitchens, which had once been the common rooms—as in John Hales's 1720s household—came to be designated as spaces used exclusively for preparing food and for housing servants.

Tenant farmers resided in smaller houses, whether in the shadow of the owner's house or off by themselves. These dwellings were nearly always of log construction, and it was the tenant's responsibility to keep them in a reasonable state of repair. Contracts between farm owners and tenants from the late eighteenth century onward customarily specify the owner's responsibility to provide a sufficient dwelling, a garden plot, a share in the harvest, and sometimes even washing and mending. Dr. Thomas Evans's 1790s contracts may be typical:

> [March 1793] To rent for the little house you live in part—[the tenant] agreed to pay 0/7/10 for the house and little field next year, he is to cut & put up the log[s] of a shed adjoining house he is to roof it & hew the logs down & to floor it at his own cost, & I am to find the boards for the floors.

> [August 1793] My agreement with Christopher Jones with respect to building the house he lives in, he was to have it at $5.00 per year til he was paid the cost of building it, it commenced March 25, 1791.[7]

In a 1799 listing of all his country and urban properties John Dickinson, historically remembered for his role in composing the United States Constitution, described two tenant farms in St. Georges Hundred. Both were one-story-high frame dwellings; each had a one-room plan and had a small log kitchen. Tenant Isaac Vandergrift's 22-by-17-foot house had been enlarged with a 12-by-17-foot frame shed attached to the gable end. Samuel Smith's was simply a 24-by-18-foot house without any addition. The interiors were lit by two windows each, on the front and back elevations; Smith's house also had a gable window, and had two more in the shed. These, however, were substantial tenant houses; some of Dickinson's tenant houses in Kent County had so little value they were not worth taxing.[8]

A further architectural distinction between farm owner and tenant was the number of outbuildings. Tenants' houses had considerably fewer support structures than the farm owner's average of six to seven. For obvious reasons tenants were unwilling to construct a barn or stable on land they did not own and from which they could be evicted at the owner's convenience. Tenants who did maintain a number of buildings were usually living on a farm that had been developed by one owner who sold it to another established farmer. In these cases the tenant benefited not from a landlord's largesse but from his business dealings.

Smoke or meat houses, used for the curing and salting of ham, bacon, beef, and fish, appear in estate appraisals almost as frequently as kitchens. Although there were brick examples, most smokehouses were built of more flammable framing or log. The few that have survived are gable-roofed structures, usually no more than fifteen feet square (Fig. 4:1). The roof frame was open, and iron hooks, ropes, or leather cords hung from the rafters, tie beams, and shingle lath; to these the meats were attached. Fires for smoking were kindled on brick or earth floors or on raised masonry and iron hearths. Although Chesapeake Bay region smokehouses had multiple tiers of tie beams, increasing their capacity, similar features are not found in lower New Castle County. These houses were also used for curing meats. Waist-high work benches lined three walls, and, in the spaces beneath, casks packed with salted meats were stored. Smoke and meat houses were not used solely to preserve meat, however; inventory takers found them containing everything from fence rails to farm tools.

In close proximity to the dwellings, kitchens, and smoke-houses were household gardens. They were enclosed with post-and-rail or vertical board fences, and these garden palings were constantly in need of maintenance, as a 1793 appraisal notes: "twenty four pannel of pailing is wanted for the garden in the southeast end of the old house."[9] Some gardens were large and included as many as 150 peach, cherry, and apple trees. The draw well was usually located within the garden. Often lined with brick or stone, but sometimes framed in or of barrel construction, the well and its superstructures required occasional repairs. The other typical component of gardens was beehives (bee caps as they were called in one inventory). Fixtures rather than structures, they were stored in the smokehouse or a shed when not in use.[10] Beehives, fencing, the mechanism of wells, and the gardens themselves were the most ephemeral sorts of constructions. Whether the wells used long sweeps or windlasses to lift buckets of water, or whether beehives were of board construction or coil basketry is information which has simply failed to survive.

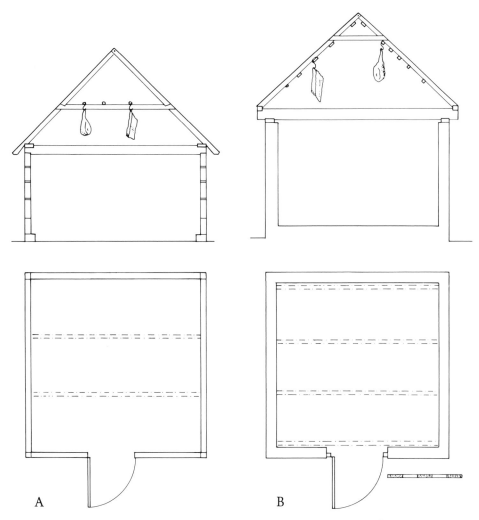

Figure 4:1. Smokehouses: (A) Kanely House smokehouse, Middletown vicinity, Appoquinimink Hundred (late eighteenth century); (B) Corbit House smoke-house, Odessa (ca. 1780). Tie beams, collars, and lath-like strips nailed to the underside of the rafters provided the anchors for hanging meats. In length, depth, and height (from floor to ridge) these two structures were twelve-foot cubes.

Descriptions of other work structures for the first building cycles in southern New Castle County come down to us almost solely in the written record. With the exception of a single barn and a combination cornhouse/granary, stables, granaries, cribs, bar-racks, barns, and similar structures dating prior to 1820 have vanished. Despite such a near-total lack of architectural information, the court records document the general appearance and functions of these buildings.

The most frequently mentioned farm buildings in the orphans court valuations are stables, barns, cribs, and granaries. Stables were commonly of log construction, seldom larger than 24 feet square—the size required for sheltering a team of work horses or of oxen—and could be as small as nine feet by eleven feet. Some stables were of extremely insubstantial construction, consisting either of a shed made by setting posts in the ground and covering them with a clapboard roof or of a rough log structure capped with a thatch. Others were solidly built of logs, well roofed with wood shingles, and raised on wood blocks, masonry piers, or foundations. Many were not free standing but were lean-tos such as ". . . an Old Barn with a stable at each end," or incorporated with other functions as in a "Stable and Cart Shed under one roof."[11] What the layout and design of most stables were is purely conjecture.

The documentary record on the design and layout of late eighteenth-century barns is supplemented by one structure that survives in southern New Castle County and two from Kent County to the south. A composite portrait of the common eighteenth-century barn type can be pieced together from the orphans court records. The barns were rectangular, sometimes as large as 44 by 24 feet, of either log or frame construction; and they frequently sat directly on the ground without benefit of foundations, blocks, or piers. The interiors were tripartite: a central threshing floor and flanking mows and mangers were laid out in an arrangement that corresponds to so-called Yankee or English barns found elsewhere in the eastern United States.[12] In a few later instances, where the terrain permitted, the barns were cellared or banked, and stables were placed on the downhill ground-floor level. More commonly the flat Delaware terrain encouraged farmers to add stables as shed additions or as a separate nearby structure. David Thompson, however, took drastic steps to incorporate stabling in his old barn. His "was to be clap-boarded, and sufficiently supported by pillars of brick; a cellar to be dug under the barn and converted into a stable for horses; a shed to be erected over the front part of the same, ten feet by the length of the barn, for the purpose of sheltering horned cattle."[13] The result was a bank barn resembling those common in southeastern Pennsylvania in the same period.[14]

New Castle County's sole surviving early barn, Retirement Barn, was built by the Vandergrift family sometime between 1790 and 1810 (Fig. 4:2). Roughly 24 by 36 feet, it has three nearly equal-sized bays. The central bay was entered through tall double doors (known as folding doors in the eighteenth century) located on each side of the structure, allowing that bay to serve as runway, wagon shed, and threshing floor. The bays on either side stored hay and provided stabling. Although much of the original interior has since been changed, what evidence remains indicates that both bays were vertically subdivided by movable joists and loft flooring to maximize storage spaces. The eastern bay was studded in on the lower level to create livestock pens. The only other local visual evidence for this form of building is in a 1798 portrait of a Middletown farmer (Fig. 4:3).[15]

Probate inventories yield little information on the contents of barns, for even the most painstaking room-by-room listings of households became less detailed as the appraisers moved further from the house. As late as 1832, the barn of Isaac Cleaver contained hay stacked in the north and south mows, and seed and potatoes

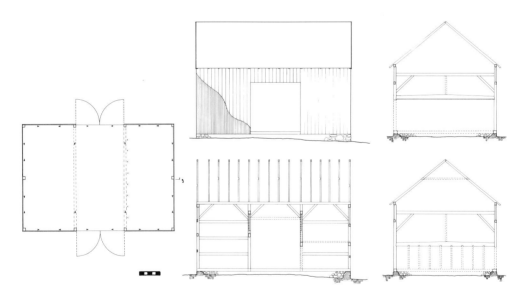

Figure 4:2. Retirement Barn (1790–1810), Biddles Corner vicinity, St. Georges Hundred. Drawing: Historic American Buildings Survey (HABS), Melinda Fike, William Macintire.

Figure 4:3. William Frazer's farmyard. Detail of a portrait showing the farmyard at Rich Neck Farm, Appoquinimink Hundred (ca. 1798). From left to right, the structures are a barn, hay barrack, fodder stacks, post-and-rail fence, and stable. The view is a detail from the background of William Clarke's portrait of Frazer. Photograph courtesy of the Historical Society of Delaware.

stored elsewhere in the building.[16] It is generally apparent that most barns had hay piled in the mows and stacked either in the open area adjacent to the buildings or under the roof of an unsided barracks built of posts set in the ground or on mudsills. The barracks typically had pyramidal roofs that could be raised or lowered according to the size of the haystacks they sheltered. One exceptional barrack was built with an elevated floor to allow space for a cart shed beneath it.[17] In addition to hay, barns stored sowing and harvesting tools: flails, screens, and fans for threshing and winnowing the chaff from the grain; ploughs, harrows, cultivators, and marsh rollers (to aid in cultivating wetland meadows). The barn of David Ross also held a "Mill for grinding Horse Food"; John Alrich's barn doubled as a carpenter's shop, having a sawhorse and a "Lot of boards & Work bench," and held ladders for reaching the tops of the mows and cutting boxes for chopping fodder.[18] Farmers also stored other crops in barns, such as flax (which could be broken on the flax breaks and processed for linen on the spinning wheels found in the houses), oats, clover hay, and corn fodder. Adjacent sheds housed additional tools, carts, rigging for plough teams, and occasionally stabled the livestock.

Smaller barns, also common throughout the eighteenth century, were designed for storing grain and for limited threshing activities. Alexander Chance's "new log barn . . . twenty feet by twenty five" was of this type.[19] These barns were divided into only one or two interior compartments and lacked flexible working spaces. With small barns, the unsheltered storage spaces in the yard around the barns became especially important. Here excess hay, oats, and corn, or other crops awaiting cutting and storage were stacked, wagons and sleighs were stored, along with boxes of tools, ploughs, harrows, shovels, hoes, and scrap iron that could not be shoved up under the eaves of the buildings. In harvest time the barn yard was also used for treading out grain with horses and for threshing with flails.[20] Although the inventory evidence is scant, the amount and type of yard storage varied with the size of the barn. Where larger barns, sheds, or tool rooms were present, the clutter of the yard was correspondingly reduced; and in inventories where all the tools and implements are listed in individual structures, the only items in the yard are surplus haystacks and penned livestock.

As significant as the barn to the landscape of the farmstead were the corn houses, cribs, and granaries that are repeatedly mentioned in the orphans court records prior to 1820. Corncribs were either long narrow structures with slatted or lath sides (one was described as "six by twenty-four feet") or small rectangular log structures approximately eight to ten feet on a side.[21] Although no eighteenth-century corncribs remain standing in southern New Castle County, similar structures survive in southern Delaware (Fig. 4:4).

Granaries were square structures of log or frame construction, sealed with weatherboards. In the eighteenth century, because the majority were framed directly on the ground, rot and insect damage required constant repair to and even replacement of sills and joists. Eventually many were raised onto wooden blocks (called pillows), posts, or masonry piers. This shoring up process is well noted. In 1779 the court directed a guardian to supply "covering, weatherboarding," and to have the granary "raised from the Ground."[22] In

A

B

Figure 4:4. Farm buildings: (A) corn house, Hardscrabble vicinity, Sussex County, (early nineteenth century); (B) granary, Cross Keys vicinity, Sussex County, (early to mid-nineteenth century). Smaller-scale agricultural buildings dating to eighteenth-century farming practices in southern New Castle County have failed to survive into the present. Parallel examples based on period descriptions, however, can still be located in Delaware's southern counties.

1810 a "Granary of sawed logs was going rapidly to ruin for the want of pillows under the cils, and for the want of weatherboarding."[23] By 1800 combined granaries/corncribs and corncribs/carriage houses were being built under a single roof. These multipurpose buildings possessed gable-end doors, a large square central runway space, and long narrow corncribs along the sides.

Although early examples of the combination corncrib and granary are found throughout the lower Delmarva Peninsula, only one example remains standing in southern New Castle County. Built by Richard Mansfield about 1820, the Achmester farm granary has two plank-floored log pens. The building was entered through the gable end, and doorways from the threshing area opened into the sides of the pens (Fig. 4:5). Overhead, the open loft had grain bins walled with tightly fitted horizontal boarding that was nailed to studs fitted under the eaves and to the gable-end studding. A ladder-like stair rising to the rear corner of the ground floor central bay provided access to the loft.

Like the contents of the barns, the objects in the granaries reflected their use both for harvest activities and for general storage. The granary of John Cleaver contained wheat, corn, sacking, bushel measures, a grain shovel and cross-cut saw, while those of David Ross and John Alrich held chains, coils of hemp rope, and a block and tackle.[24] The corncrib of Edward Congo, a black carpenter who died in St. Georges Hundred in 1811, held a small amount of grain, a general assortment of tools including "maul rings & wedges, Post spade, Hominy mortar, Grind stone, wheel barrow, mowing scythes & fork, shaving horse and Cultivator."[25] Less than a decade later Jacob Fariss's granary contained much the same sort of "Lumber" (as odds and ends were called), a bookcase, and a desk.[26]

Just as the organization and use of space within a house and a farmyard constitute individual linkages to the larger landscape, the places of work, worship, public meetings, the routes of transportation, and the spaces in between them compose a countryside built upon constant social and economic commerce. The eighteenth- and early nineteenth-century roads to church or mill were well traveled by local residents and strangers alike, and the paths they traced describe a widely held sense of community structure.

All rural roads eventually led to nearby towns, and these villages were the sites of most specialized activities. John Janvier resided in the riverside village of Odessa and worked as a cabinet

Figure 4:5. Achmester Granary, Armstrong Corner vicinity, St. Georges Hundred (ca. 1820). Photograph: HABS, David L. Ames.

maker, producing a variety of furniture, coffins, and clock cases.[27] Duncan Beard, who manufactured the mechanisms frequently found in Janvier's clock cases, lived well outside of Odessa in rural Appoquinimink Hundred. Their customers were residents of the town and the country, and their dealings bridged whatever gap may have existed between village streets and country crossroads. In a similar fashion, wheelwrights' shops, smithies, storehouses, weavers' shops, cooperages, taverns, and wharves connected individuals across a sprawling countryside made up of farms, townhouses, and country residences. The degree to which people traveled is indicated by the daybook Richard Mansfield kept during the 1820s.[28] Alongside entries on crops and contracts with tenants are comments on frequent trips made by Mansfield, his family, servants, and tenants to Wilmington, Annapolis, Auburn Mills, and other places in a seventy-mile radius of his farm north of Middletown. The points of connection illustrate the sphere of nonagrarian occupations in the area and important gathering points. The courthouse in New Castle, the churches near Middletown and

Odessa, and the scattered mills and tanneries were places for social discourse as well as business.

Mills and tanneries were the most plentiful across the landscape. Information on the mills was collected as part of a federal industrial survey published in 1833.[29] The mills responding to the survey were typically old and worked on the "old process" principle characteristic of eighteenth-century flouring methods. In addition, Daniel Corbit, a tanner at Odessa, compiled brief descriptions of eight working mills in the region. Most were generally run-down and in need of extensive repairs. Each of the mills was powered with a water wheel and ran two sets of millstones. Several of the mills also possessed attached sawmills, and some had other equipment such as machinery for processing clover seed. All the mills were custom mills employing one or two men to grind corn meal and flour from area-grown grains. Their market was strictly local. Although the mills were capable of functioning as the sole business of the miller, they were invariably set up in conjunction with a working farm. Millers (like carpenters, blacksmiths, surveyors, physicians, and local merchants) tended to practice two trades: one industrial and the other agricultural. The buildings that distinguished their farms from others included not only the mills but also storehouses and additional corncribs and granaries. As with most rural industries, the area around the merchant mill and miller's house was the site of a small hamlet, complete with tenant houses, tavern, and cooper's shop.[30]

The custom grist and flour mills situated along St. Georges, Appoquinimink, Drawyers, and Blackbird creeks did little business compared to the large merchant mills along the Brandywine Creek near Wilmington.[31] Where those northern mills manufactured flour and meal worth $20,000 to $40,000 annually, southern ones averaged $3,000. But shipping manifests indicate farmers living in lower New Castle County marketed their crops up and down the coast and into a transatlantic trading triangle linking Europe, the West Indies, and South America with the Delaware Valley. While merchant mills such as Andrew Fisher's in Pencader Hundred supplied that trade in the eighteenth century, by the early nineteenth century the rural mills of the lower hundreds served wholly local markets.

The millers in the lower half of the county were hampered by a lack of water power; so where they chose not to rely on wind or tidal forces, they built earthen dams across the sluggish creeks to raise the water levels and create a usable water flow. This entailed an often complex arrangement of dams, gates, and races, and also required constant maintenance. Upkeep was something which some court-appointed guardians were reluctant to supply, as in the case of "a Grist mill with two run of stones dirt dam and wooden gates the mill stones and gears & all in bad repair," or the mill in need of "a sett of new drains at the flood gates and a new safe gate with two new braces or more if necessary at the flood gates."[32] The two sets of stones found in most mills were used to grind wheat and corn separately and thus to prevent the oils of one grain from saturating and discoloring the other. Typical of the shift from an eighteenth-century merchant mill to a custom mill in the early 1800s was the Noxontown Pond Mill built in the mid-eighteenth century (Fig. 4:6). Although mechanically altered in the nineteenth and twentieth

Figure 4:6. Noxontown Mill, Middletown vicinity, Appoquinimink Hundred (ca. 1740).

centuries, the structural fabric of the mill, which has massive framing members, remains intact.

The water-powered mills of southern New Castle County were customarily one- or two-story structures whose interior was divided into three main levels: a basement containing the drive system, a first floor housing the grind stones, and a second floor or loft holding the bolting machinery used to sift the flour. In larger operations a bag hoist was installed in the attic level, lifting sacks of grain to be screened and fed down through the building to the grinding floor. The mill operated by converting and intensifying the vertical movement of the water wheel into a horizontal motion that turned the millstones. Wood gears, mounted to a husk frame in the basement, increased the waterwheel's eight to twelve revolutions per minute into the millstone's a hundred or more revolutions. On the main floor, each set of stones was held in place by the upper reaches of the husk frame, and each set had a separate drive shaft, making it possible to run one set without the other. In each set the bottom (bed) stone remained stationary while the top (cap) stone mounted on an iron spindle turned. Both the upper and lower surfaces of each stone were cut with grooves called furrows which rose at an angle to raised faces known as lands. Around each set of stones was the skirt, a barrel-like device, and atop that was a cradle supporting a square, funnel-shaped hopper. Grain poured into the hopper fed directly into the eye, or the center of the top stone. The entire process was based on a simple combination of centrifugal force and a sheering action. As the beveled faces of the millstones drew the grain in between the stones, it was ground into progressively smaller bits that were gradually pushed out toward the edges. The grain was cut into flour, not crushed. Once pushed out to the skirt, the flour or meal was fed down a narrow chute into a bin or onto some sort of conveyor. Corn meal and feed were sacked or barreled immediately; flour had to be sifted with screened bolters to create a uniform product. In some flour mills the residue that failed to filter through the bolting screens was ground a second time.

Tanneries were also a significant element in the pre-1820 rural economy, and at least four were in full operation in the latter half of the eighteenth century. Like the merchant millers, most tanners bought their raw materials locally and sold the finished products outside the community.[33] The Phillip Reading Tannery, built circa 1790 on the easternmost edge of Middletown, was a brick structure

Figure 4:7. Phillip Reading Tannery, Middletown vicinity, St. Georges Hundred (ca. 1790). The building was converted into a barn in the mid-nineteenth century. During renovation, one of the arched doorways was filled in, and much of the interior framing and partition detailing was removed.

over a hundred feet long, "including under the same roof a Tan House, Currying Shop, bark House and Carriage House with a Tan Yard containing thirty seven vatts in pretty good condition" (Fig. 4:7).[34] Reading also had a two-story log tenement on the thirty-acre lot he rented out.

Tanners' responses to the same 1832 survey of manufacturers described the operations, volume of business, and marketplace of the tanneries. In the early 1800s tanning had declined due to the increased expense of raw materials, in particular the bark from Spanish oaks as well as the hides themselves. As one Wilmington tanner noted, "The amount of tanning done in this place has been much diminished within fifteen or twenty years past; at the same time it has been increasing in the adjacent county."[35] No wonder, when tanning bark commanded double and triple the cash amount in New Castle County that it brought along the Susquehanna River thirty miles to the west! Daniel Corbit, who had operated a tannery in St. Georges Hundred for at least thirty years, processed $3,850 worth of leather annually in the early 1830s. His tannery purchased an average of 900 cow hides and 700 calf skins from local farmers and sold the finished leather locally and to nearby urban markets. (His Wilmington counterparts had to purchase South American hides.) Corbit employed two laborers (at $16 a month for a man and about $10 a month for a youth) and nine horses. Like most workers, Corbit's two employees worked sunup to sundown.[36]

Tanning was a nasty, malodorous business.[37] The raw hides were brought into the tannery, washed, crushed with heavy stones, soaked in lime water, and allowed to putrify. These actions cleansed the hides, made each pliable, and loosened hair, cuticle, and flesh so that each could be manually scraped off with a round-bladed knife. The scraped hides were then soaked in a progression of vats containing an "ooze" of tanin (made from oak bark) graduated in strength from mild to harsh. After a year or more of soaking, the leather was removed, rinsed, and softened by beating or by passing it through rollers. The tanning vats were out-of-doors in a tanyard, but the other facilities were housed in a long, low, barn-like structure. Reading, like many tanners, also operated a currying shop for dressing the leather for use in shoes, harnesses, and other leather goods. At Reading's tannery, the finished hides and leather, loaded onto wagons that had entered the tannery through large, paired, round-arched bays, were either transported to nearby landings on the tributaries of the Chesapeake Bay and Delaware River or sent north to Wilmington or New Castle.

The southern New Castle County tanners were comparable to millers in the sense that they operated farms in conjunction with their manufactories. Reading, for example, also owned two nearby plantations. One, his own farm, contained a large brick house and kitchen, granary, stable, corncribs, and barn.[38] The other was a tenant farm with fewer structures. By maintaining his farm, Reading daily escaped the stench and filth of the tannery. Corbit, likewise, occupied a dwelling house upwind of his tannery on nearby Appoquinimink Creek.

One indicator of the amount of the county's external trade is the numerous storehouses mentioned in the eighteenth-century records. Jonas Preston owned a wharf with three storehouses at "the landing place" in St. Georges Hundred; Thomas Coombs owned "one new log wheat storehouse standing on a new wharf by the creek side" elsewhere in the county.[39] The most elaborate eighteenth-century storehouse was Brick Store along Duck Creek (Fig.

4:8).[40] With the date 1767 announced in glazed brick on its main facades done in Flemish bond, the store served as a commercial threshold across which grain grown in southern New Castle County passed and was loaded into the holds of ships bound for distant ports. The storehouse had three large, whitewashed rooms on the main floor and a second-story loft partitioned with rough board walls into bins. But by 1810, about forty years after it was built, the storehouse was converted into a dwelling: interior gable-end chimney piles were added, and the ground-floor rooms were finished with lath-and-plaster ceilings and paneled hearth walls. The fate of the once-important Brick Store reflects the gradual centralizing process of the early nineteenth century: most manufacturing and trading activities were brought into the orbit of the towns.

The several small towns scattered through southern New Castle County were as much a part of the rural scene as barns and mills. In the definition of the landscape from 1760 to 1820, towns and villages became increasingly significant focal points. Middle-

Figure 4:8. Brick Store, Smyrna vicinity, Blackbird Hundred (1767). Built as a three-bay, waterside grain storehouse, Brick Store was converted into a dwelling before 1810. Drawing: HABS, Charles Bergengren and William Macintire.

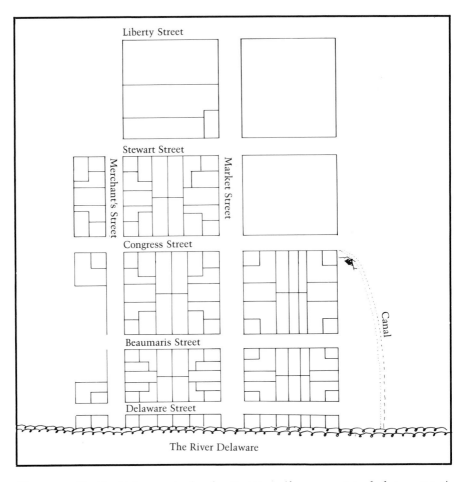

Figure 4:9. Dr. David Stewart's plan for Port Penn (from an original plat ca. 1790). Stewart's town never approached even the modest scale suggested in his drawing. Delaware and Beaumaris streets, as well as the lower edge of the Congress Street block, are still marshland. Drawing: CHAE, William Macintire, after manuscript original (Stewart Family Papers, DSA).

town and Glasgow began as line towns strung along the crossroads running east to west and connecting the Chesapeake Bay and Delaware River.[41] Odessa and Noxontown developed in a similarly random fashion. By the 1760s, however, the first planned town designed as a trading center was laid out by Dr. David Stewart opposite the sheltered anchorage between Reedy Island and the mainland in St. Georges Hundred.[42] Partitioning his farm into blocks and lots, Stewart envisioned a flourishing city named Port Penn that would be financed and built through profits culled from the West

Indies trade (Fig. 4:9). Although the town had only achieved a population of approximately three hundred residents at its height in 1800, ten years after Stewart's death, his neat grid plan and a scattering of first-period dwellings survive. More importantly, Stewart's plans illustrate the external orientation and ambitions of southern New Castle County merchant society. The town was intended as a commercial way station, the economic funnel through which riches would flow directly into the region, challenging established ports such as Wilmington and Philadelphia further up river, and thereby creating fortunes for the local population. The presence of a favorable anchorage and a federal customs house, however, was not enough to attract urban commerce to Port Penn.

The towns were an integral part of the countryside. Landed farmers throughout the district maintained village dwellings for themselves in addition to their farm houses. The pattern of possessing a country estate and town residence was common to affluent colonial Americans. With the exception of water-powered mills, where the lay of the land dictated setting, the majority of meeting and business places were found in or around the towns by the late 1700s. Odessa, for example, developed around a landing on the Appoquinimink Creek, and, as a transportation center, contained a variety of buildings devoted to economic, secular, and spiritual purposes.

The road to Odessa came from the watershed of the Chesapeake Bay through the back country and down to the town's wharves. At the east end of town on the creek was a frame tide-mill, and on fast land along the bank sat both frame and log storehouses filled with wheat and corn. On the southeastern edge of the village along the creek stood the Corbit family tannery. The inhabitants of the town lived in dwellings arrayed on either side of the road that ran down to the landing. Ranging from brick mansions to one-room, hewn-log houses, each dwelling possessed outbuildings that typically included a stable and carriage house, smokehouse, and kitchen. Interspersed among the outbuildings were the shops of local artisans and merchants, as well as taverns providing lodging for travelers and spirits for all. At the west end of town was the Quaker meetinghouse (1785), and just a little over a mile to the northwest was Old Drawyers Church (1769–73). Farmers came to town frequently. On business trips and market days, for the sustenance of the spirit offered by church or tavern, to tally accounts and gain news, people traveled to Odessa, Glasgow, Port Penn, Middletown, and other towns and hamlets. And, with business done, they went home again. From houses surrounded by farm buildings, down roads, rivers, and creeks to crossroads, church, mills and villages, the inhabitants of lower New Castle County fashioned a landscape and created a local community geared to the movement of a larger world.

5. Matters of Construction

I F THE CREATION AND DEFINITION of private and public space
became the medium for one aspect of social change, the
treatment of architectural fabric charted another shift in prevailing
attitudes concerning architecture in eighteenth-century southern
New Castle County. Architectural form is known through its construction. While certain options may remain consistent across
broad periods of time, the way in which those forms are articulated
and the manner in which they are made fashionable communicates
a great deal about the changing society that produced and used those
spaces. Except for the mid-eighteenth-century introduction of the
stair-passage plans, the formal qualities of houses evidence little
change prior to 1820. But in matters of construction, several building periods emerge in the eighteenth century. These periods are not
chronologically exclusive, so although they may be identified as
general movements in the area's building history, it is difficult to
bracket them with dates.

Before turning to the technological developments and practices, it is necessary to consider the building materials available in
the eighteenth century. In the tax records and orphans court descriptions, we find that those buildings noted by their fabric, are predominantly of wood construction. Within the broad category of
wood buildings, there is a division between frame and log. Primary
dwellings and barns were most often raised as joined timber frames.
Tenant houses, kitchens, smoke and meat houses, and stables, on
the other hand, were usually log. Granaries and carriage houses
appear equally in both media. The choice of materials was an important one; those available (in descending order of expense) were brick,
frame, and log. All three walling materials were readily available

throughout the 1700s. The manner in which materials were prepared and assembled informs us not only of the technology of construction, but also of the economic range of the builder.

The first phase of building activity, up until circa 1740, focused on the construction of impermanent architecture—temporary houses intended to endure from a few years to a decade or more.[1] These buildings were built of posts set directly in the ground, with sills connecting the posts and providing the seating for floors, wall studs, and bracing. On the upper end of the posts rested the timber members for the base of the roof framing. These earthfast structures were common across the Chesapeake Bay and lower Delaware Valley landscapes and were even a part of William Penn's promotional literature: "There must be eight trees of about sixteen inches square and cut off to Posts of about fifteen foot long, which the House must stand upon."[2] Although no earthfast buildings remain standing in lower New Castle County, recent archaeology has identified several sites. One such dwelling fronted the Delaware River at Liston's Point.[3] Partial excavation has revealed the existence of the first one- or two-room dwelling, framed on posts set into the ground, with an irregularly shaped plank-walled cellar and a chimney made of posts interspersed with wattles and finished with clay. The building was abandoned in 1739, when a brick house was built adjacent to it.

The impermanent nature of buildings such as the Liston Point house was not inherent in the materials and methods used in their construction so much as in the minds of the builders who erected them. A substantial number of impermanent dwellings were built by newly arrived settlers who expected to replace them with durable houses within the span of a generation. But durable architecture was achieved at an uneven rate. Individuals such as Robert Ashton could afford to build a substantial brick house by 1704, while others remained in houses described as no better than huts. Some householders continued to build impermanent dwellings even in the early nineteenth century, but by the mid-eighteenth century these structures appear to have fallen to the lot of the poor; the more affluent moved on toward grander building schemes.

Not all impermanent architecture was of frame construction, nor was it restricted to houses. The orphans court valuations contain numerous descriptions of log houses, several of which lacked wood floors or glazed windows (even in houses in good condition), or chimney piles. As the appraisers assessed the buildings, one of the most common improvements they specified was the repair of sills and joists that had deteriorated to the point of endangering the structure. But log buildings were constantly in want of repair, such as Joseph Hart's kitchen, whose "roof decaying a new one of Cedar to be put on when necessary and the said kitchen to be raised from Ground."[4] While roofs were being repaired and sills replaced, chimneys also often needed to be rebuilt and special attention given to sagging jambs and broken hearth backs.

Outbuildings remained the most characteristically impermanent structures throughout the eighteenth century. Built of logs or frames set directly upon the ground or on timber blocks, they constantly required raising so that new timbers could be inserted to carry the walls and floors. In numerous cases, the buildings had deteriorated beyond the point meriting further investment and were either pulled down or left to rot. If the buildings were demolished, the court suggested some of the materials be salvaged and reused: "the old log kitchen we allow to be taken down the duftails cut off and put up anew covered with oak shingles one upper floor to be laid with pine boards and a brick chimney put therein"[5] Frequently, timber buildings with sills laid on the ground were made more durable by raising the structures onto brick or stone piers, thus protecting them from ruin generated by rot and by insects like termites. Roofs, however, were a continual problem, as reflected in the prevailing generic complaint, "the roof wants covering."

The earliest built of the structures surviving to the present are houses made of durable materials such as brick or timber and set on full foundations. All the known buildings extant from the pre-1750 era are of brick construction and are one-and-a-half to two stories in elevation. The brick was made of locally dug clay, tempered with sand, and burned in brickyard kilns or on the site in temporary kilns known as clamps.[6] One result of the firing process was the reaction of natural salts in the clay with potash released from the oak used as fuel. This produced a blue-black glaze on the headers or butt ends of bricks set nearest the fire (Fig. 5:1).[7] These glazed bricks might be culled from the kiln and used to create geometric patterns, dates, and initials in the walls of the houses.

The first methods for laying brick were Flemish bond, which alternated glazed headers and stretchers in each course for the facade, and English bond with alternate rows of unglazed headers and of stretchers for secondary exterior walls and foundations (Fig. 5:2).

Figure 5:1. Flemish bond brickwork using glazed or vitrified headers to produce a decorative finish.

By the 1730s common bonds, alternating multiple courses of stretchers broken by courses of headers, had come into general use for foundations and secondary exterior walls. The bricks were cemented into the walls with a mortar made of lime from burned oyster shells, clay, and sand, and they were finished with tooled or struck joints. A house's brickwork was commonly enhanced by offset watertables beveled in from the foundation at the first floor

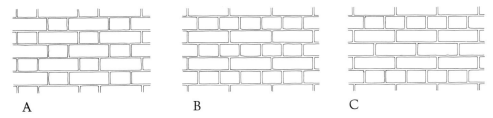

A   B   C

Figure 5:2. Brick bonds of the eighteenth century: (A) Flemish bond using alternating headers and stretchers in a single course; (B) English bond composed of alternating courses (rows) of headers and stretchers; (C) three-course common bond. Drawing: CHAE, William Macintire.

Figure 5:3. Watertable: Mount Jones.

line, and by belt courses, two to four bricks deep, used to flash pent roofs between the first and second floors, and also by pilastered chimney stacks (Fig. 5:3).

On the interior, brick buildings were framed with timber joists, rafter systems, and board partition walls. As the building went up, joists were set into sockets left in the masonry walls and were leveled with wood shims. Flooring was laid atop the joists. In some instances, a timber pad or sill was laid and worked into the masonry at the first floor level, where it provided support for the joist framing. While joists were sometimes logs with only the upper faces hewn flat, all other lumber was square-hewn, adzed, planed, and either pit sawn or mill sawn.

As each story was added, the front and rear walls became thinner, and ledges needed to carry the joist ends were set in the masonry. In two-story dwellings built through the mid-eighteenth century, the second-floor joists frequently extended eighteen to twenty-four inches beyond the wall and supported a pent roof. These shallow pents are a common and a distinctive regional feature on brick buildings. At the base of the roof line, a plank plate was laid atop the masonry walls. The attic floor joists, projecting eight to twelve inches beyond the wall, were set on edge on the top of the plate.[8] The wall was then completed with an additional two or three courses of brick to bring it flush to the upper surface of the joists. The house was finished with a timber frame roof, footed onto false (raising) plates laid over the ends of the joists (Fig. 5:4).

In brick structures, the chimney piles were built along with the overall structural fabric of the house and bonded into the walls to prevent any sort of separation or sagging. In houses that had cellars, the chimney base was supported on vaulted relieving arches (Fig. 5:5), but in uncellared structures the weight of the pile simply rested on a broad pad of brick or rubble fieldstone construction.

Although a number of brick dwellings survive from as early as the second generation of settlement, with few exceptions, the remaining log houses and frame houses date from near the close of the eighteenth century. While the orphans court valuations indicate a gradual movement towards dwellings of durable construction, the tax lists for 1804 and 1816 reveal that the bulk of the architectural landscape was still dominated by wood houses.[9] Although these frame and log houses have suffered a much higher rate of attrition than their brick counterparts, enough examples remain to provide a general impression of how at least the better sort of timber houses were built.[10] Where building materials were specified in the early nineteenth-century tax records, houses of log construction clearly outnumbered their frame cousins. All log construction was not qualitatively equal, and it is clear from the written and architectural evidence that a wide variety of techniques and finishes were used throughout the period. Descriptions of log structures often specify hewn, sawn, "skelpt," and round timbers, and special mention is made of dovetailed corner notching, corner casings, exterior wall coverings (for both houses and work buildings), and replacement of logs within the walls. The individual logs composing the walls were called "rounds"—a term analogous to "courses" in brick and stone construction.[11] The pattern of log construction that emerges from the records of the 1760 to 1820 period is of a building technique employed for everything from stylish two-story houses to chicken coops. Sawn and dovetailed corners were used on buildings of above-average quality, while round logs, scarcely a step beyond their condition as felled trees, characterized structures at the lower end of the scale. Log houses of more refined construction, as well as

Figure 5:4. Roof-framing detail: Dilworth House. Shown here is the relationship between the rafter foot, board false (or raising) plate, and the attic-floor joist. The strip of wood nailed across the outer face of the rafter is a strip of lath (or nailer) used for attaching the roof covering.

granaries and corncribs requiring a sealed enclosure for grain storage, were the log buildings most commonly finished with weatherboard or shingle.

The type of log construction most often mentioned in specific terms was that using sawn timbers fitted together at the corners with full dovetail notching. Sawn logs could be reduced to the size of heavy planks three inches or less in thickness and up to a foot wide. Once sawn, the logs used in house construction could be planed down to a smoother and more finished surface. The Vandergrift House near Port Penn is an example of sawn-log construction at its finest (Fig. 5:6). The logs used in the building of the original one-room-plan house were sawn on all four sides to an average size of three by eleven inches, and then planed. They are tightly pieced together with sawn dovetailed cornering. The amazingly small interstices between the logs were caulked with oakum—an easily spread compound of pitch and plant fiber that was normally used for sealing the planked hulls of wooden boats.[12] Like most buildings of sawn logs or planks, the walls were stabilized with wooden pins driven into the upper and lower edges of the planks.[13] Although the

Figure 5:5. Relieving arch: Liston House. The arches are often listed in probate inventories as containing items ranging from crockery to casks of salted herring.

Figure 5:6. Plank-walling detail: Christopher Vandergrift House (mid-eighteenth century). Drawing: CHAE, William Macintire.

Vandergrift House has lost its original cladding, examples of similarly built structures elsewhere in the mid-Atlantic region retain exterior finishes such as riven clapboard, sawn beaded-edge weatherboard, vertically boarded or cased corners with strips of riven lath nailed over the spaces between the planks, and exposed walls. Indeed, colonists repeatedly mentioned cladding sawn log structures with some sort of siding or, at the least, boarding over the corners as a means of preventing decay.

If sawn and dovetailed log construction was of the best kind, hewn log walling was the most widely used.[14] Yet few of these latter buildings survived the nineteenth-century rebuilding cycles of southern New Castle County; although those that remain represent the best of log building technology. Hewn log structures were normally composed of logs worked flat with a broad axe on the two vertical or wall sides, and the upper and lower edges left in the round. In some instances hewing extended to all four surfaces. In yet other cases, the degree of shaping was minimal, leaving the logs in not much more of a worked condition than if they had been left undressed in the round. The variety of notching and cornering techniques used in raising hewn log buildings included dovetailing, V-notching, and mortise-and-tenon joints (Fig. 5:7). Although examples of all these techniques survive from the 1800–20 period, in most structures the walls have been covered with siding. In the sided buildings, the logs were not tightly fitted together, and, if they were not immediately covered over, the spaces between the logs were filled with a chinking of rubble stone or broken brick plastered over with clay and a finish coat of lime-based mortar. With the logs in place and the gaps between them filled, the exterior walls were customarily whitewashed or clapboarded.

Log walling at its meanest level consisted of logs left in the round, frequently unbarked, and laid up with only minimally worked corner joints. As a rule, buildings of this quality were relegated to rough farm usage, often serving as fowl houses and stables, but seldom as dwellings. No eighteenth-century examples survive, although documents prove that this form of log construction was widely used.

A number of buildings were framed with logs or sawn planks hewn to a thickness of three to four inches and tenoned into corner posts that ranged from seven to nine inches square (Fig. 5:8). In some cases the spaces between the framed planks were chinked with brick, clay, or mortar, but in others the interstices were left unfilled because the planks were immediately covered with shingles or clapboards. The Wilson dwelling, standing on the outskirts of Odessa and dating from the second half of the eighteenth century, reveals how finely executed such plank-and-post construction could be. Built on a hall-parlor plan, the house is a full two stories in elevation, shingled on the exterior, plastered and partially paneled on the interior. The four-inch-thick sawn planks are tenoned into eight-inch-square corner posts, which are covered over with beaded casings that match the beading run on the ceiling joists in the rooms.

The interior framing of log buildings presented builders with a number of options for setting in floor and ceiling joists, partitioning walls, and framing the roof. Most log structures were raised atop a heavy timber sill that rested on a masonry foundation. The sill extended from three to six inches inside the walls and was cut with open mortises into which joist ends were placed. If the house lacked sills, the ends of the joists either rested on a masonry ledge extending inside the bottom log or, rarely, were tenoned into blind mortises cut into the inner face of the lowest log. The ceiling joists for the topmost floor were lapped over the top (plate) log and, as in brick structures, carried a false plate on which to foot the roof framing. No false plate system was employed in dwellings with a half story; the base of the roof frame came down directly on top of a log plate. Joists for second and half stories were supported on the external walls of

Figure 5:7. Log-walling detail: Achmester Granary. The logs, joined at the corners with V-notches, were originally covered with vertical board siding. The practice of using a fully joined sill supporting the log walls is unusual.

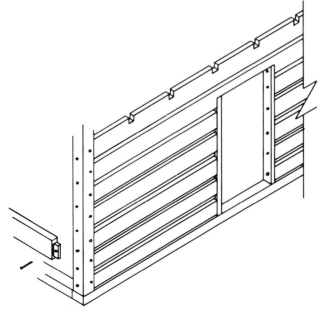

Figure 5:8. Sawn-plank construction: Donoho House, Clayton vicinity, Blackbird Hundred (early nineteenth century).

the building by the builder's cutting open, mortise-like sockets into the logs topping the first floor and starting the second. The dressed ends of the joists were then bedded into the wall. Partition walls were commonly of vertical board construction, with the upper edge nailed to the side of an exposed ceiling joist and the base fixed to the floor with a nailing strip or baseboard.

Although the Swedish origins of log construction in the lower Delaware Valley have been vigorously defended in some quarters, it is more probable that the stock of pre-1820 log buildings in southern New Castle County ultimately stems from the general diffusion of pan-European log construction.[15] In Delaware, settlers with British antecedents quickly adopted and modified log walling techniques as a means to raising affordable, presumably durable, and techno-logically efficient housing and work buildings. There are European counterparts for the cornering techniques using notching and wall-ing treatments that are found throughout the mid-Atlantic region.[16] Distinct from Old World types is the sawn log building with tightly joined corners and walls. Such buildings appeared in localized pockets or as isolated structures, and were used for everything from houses to barns in New England, the mid-Atlantic, and the upper South. Their appearance makes little sense in terms of historic set-tlement patterns; sawn log structures have been located in settings as different as mid-eighteenth-century Pennsylvania German settle-ments and in nineteenth-century rural southeastern Virginia.

Frame buildings were raised throughout the eighteenth cen-tury, but were less numerous than log structures. Few pre-1820 frame dwellings and work buildings survive, and of these only one, Noxontown Mill, dates as far back as the mid-eighteenth century. Despite the lack of architectural data, the basic construction of timber framed buildings can be generally described, and within the limitations of the sample, regionally recognizable patterns of house carpentry are suggested. Like eighteenth-century timber-framed buildings elsewhere in the Anglo-American settlements of the east-ern United States, the structures in southern New Castle County were erected on a principal-post system, with heavy corner timbers and regularly spaced intermediate posts.[17] Tenoned into sills, the principal posts supported the major structural timbers for flooring and attic framing. Secondary members, such as studs, were set be-tween the principals and fitted into sills, wall plates, and girts. The roof framing was erected on top of the attic joists, and the whole building was covered with weatherboards and shingles on the outside and paneled or plastered on the inside.

Built around 1800 in the village of Port Penn, the Yearsley House incorporated a number of timber-framing elements that were revealed in the course of its demolition in 1981 (Fig. 5:9). Two stories in elevation and built on a hall-parlor plan, the house was framed with four heavy corner posts resting on timber sills. The building of the house began with the tenoning of the gable end sills and first-floor joists into the front and rear sills. The corner posts were then fixed to the wall plates, and mortises for the stud walling were cut into the underside of the plates and girts. The principal framing for the facades, having been assembled on the ground, was then raised to meet the second-floor girts already in position atop the first-floor gable-end studs. As the tenons of the corner posts were slipped into open mortises that had been cut into the top corners of the sills and as the tenons of end girts were fitted to the corner posts, the whole of the structure was secured with wooden pins. With the fully framed and studded front and rear walls standing, and the gable ends framed to the top of the first story, the second-floor joists were set in place, resting on edge and not secured to the rest of the frame. At this point the second-story gable-end studs were inserted, the end girts dropped into place over the tenoned tops of the corner posts, the attic floor joists laid, and a board false plate for the base of the roof nailed into place. In the final stage the builders raised the roof framing, constructed the brick chimney within the frame, and laid the floors. On the exterior the building was covered with a heavy, bevel-edge wooden siding and roofed with cedar shakes.

The Yearsley House and its contemporaries were little more than braced, framed wooden boxes. In most cases the principal posts were left jutting into the corners of the rooms. While these projecting structural members were most often encased with planed, beaded-edge boards, occasionally they were left exposed and finished with molded edges. A visual exaggeration of support was conveyed by flared, or "gunstock," posts—more ornament than structural necessity. A number of frame dwellings were also finished with nogged walls—the spaces left between the members of the timber skeleton were filled with low-quality brick, fieldstone, or rubble, and cemented in place with a clay-based mortar. Used as a method for sealing the walls of the house, nogging could be employed for the full elevation of the structure, as in the first frame

A

Figure 5:9. House framing: Yearsley House. (A) The frame exposed during demolition; (B) detail of the corner framing, showing the basic parts of a lower Delaware Valley stud-walled house.

addition to the Vandergrift House, or only to a height of two or three feet above the sills, as was the practice at the southern end of the Delmarva Peninsula. The exteriors of the buildings were covered with riven clapboards or sawn weatherboards (Fig. 5:10). Riven siding was split from four- to five-foot lengths of white oak and finished with feathered upper edges to allow the boards to overlap one another. Sawn weatherboards with beaded lower edges lapped or rabbetted together were used on the better-quality houses. At the Vandergrift House, the weatherboards were fitted bottom to top with rabbeted joints, nailed in place, and painted red. On the Yearsley House, plain flush siding was used instead of weatherboards.

Once the log or frame walls were in place, a masonry chimney pile was built inside the house, rising to four or five feet above the ridge of the roof. In structures with full cellars, the relieving arches that supported the chimney pile were not bonded into the basement

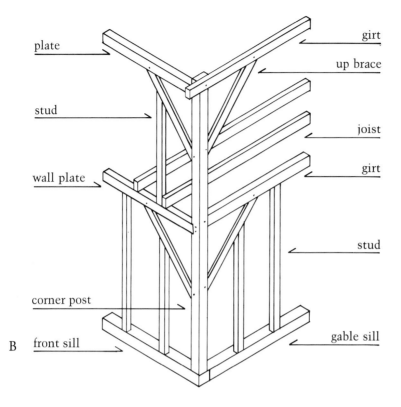

plate

girt

up brace

stud

joist

wall plate

girt

stud

corner post

B   front sill

gable sill

walls; in some cases, the arches were of brick construction abutting rubble fieldstone walls. (At the Yearsley House, the back of the brick stack was built flush with the outside walls.) With the chimney pile in place, the exterior walls were sheathed and the roof covering applied.

Barns and other large agricultural buildings were framed differently from dwellings. In Retirement Barn, once the sills were in place, the walls were raised in a series of four bents that consisted of four pairs of principal posts joined by heavy tie beams (Fig. 5:11). The bents (structural units composed of principal uprights and the beams defining spatial units known as bays) were aligned at the bottom and top on continuous sills and plates. As each of the four sections of the building was pulled into place, the light timber rails were tenoned into the sides of the posts. Lacking a floored loft, barns and granaries were frequently built without false plates for the roof

A

B

frame. Once erected, the frame was sheathed with vertical board siding that could be left with open spaces between the boards or finished with either tongue-in-groove edges or battens nailed over the joints between the individual boards. Principal-post and stud-work buildings are exemplified in the Noxontown Mill, which may be contemporary to the 1740 Noxon House. In this small-scale industrial structure, the principals carry the major elements of the wall framing, and a timber girder that spans the length of the build-

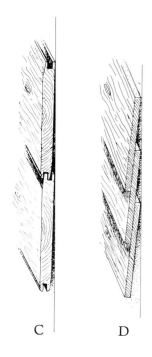

C   D

Figure 5:10. Exterior siding: (A) riven (split) clap-board; (B) riven shingle; (C) sawn lapped-groove weatherboard, (D) sawn lapped weatherboard. Drawings: CHAE, William Macintire.

ing and which is supported at mid-point by a decorated chamfered edge post and pillow. Builders set studs between the principals, and nailed the first skin of horizontal weatherboard to their outer face.

In matters of construction, a considerable amount of variation is apparent even within the most restricted building technologies.[18] The choice and creative use of brick bonds to produce glazed-header patterns or to emphasize particular elevations, or the manipulation of log corner-notching and braced-frame technology are both proof of an architectural tradition coherent in its overall pattern, but significantly variable in details. Because building could be done with several walling methods, it is instructive to turn to the single feature all the methods hold in common—timber framed roofs. In roof construction, the play of logic and variation within a limited arena can be more fully explored.

Once the walls of a house, barn, mill, or granary were in place, the structure required covering. In some instances a shed roof sufficed, while in others only the most elaborate and fashionable roof would do. Between the extremes, however, lay a middle ground of simply framed, common-rafter roofs, most of which were built as gabled or "square," but a few of which were raised as gambrels or "hipped." The span of these roofs seldom exceeded twenty-five feet

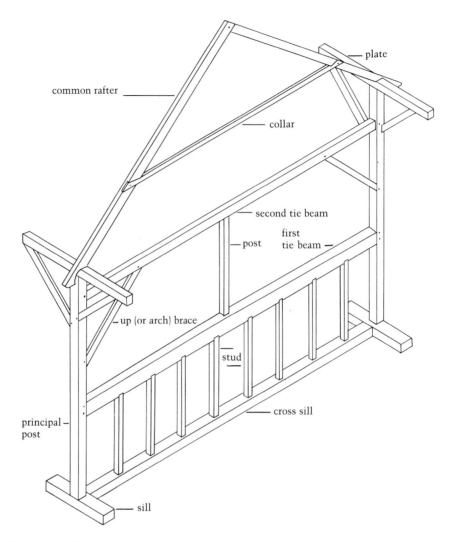

Figure 5:11. Framing: Retirement Barn.

from end to end. Since common-rafter gable roofs were most numerous we shall focus on them. The features that gable roofs have in common, beyond the need to cover a given span and securely foot the framing to the tops of the walls, are the use of equal-sized rafter blades spaced on more or less equal centers. Roofs covering double-pile buildings average a pitch of 35 degrees. Those over one-room-deep structures hover around 45 degrees, unless the span was unusually broad in which case the pitch could be as flat as 35 degrees.

The organization, layout, and construction of roof framing is quite logical and is based on the relationships of the framing elements within the total structure and the methods through which they were joined. Once this is understood we can comprehend the range of complex variabilities open to builders in what superficially looks like a simple building problem. Of equal importance is the understanding that in even the most mundane aspects of vernacular architecture there are multiple solutions for a single situation common to a host of dimensionally equivalent buildings—and the realization that any and all of these solutions solve the same set of problems.

The basic common-rafter roof design for a dwelling of the eighteenth century consisted of a timber plate affixed to the top of the walls and over which were lapped the attic-floor joists (Fig. 5:12). In frame buildings the plates were tenoned into the sides of the principal posts just below where the uprights joined the gable-end girts, or they were mortised to the tops of the posts and the girts lapped over the ends of the plates. Plates in masonry buildings were heavy planks mortared into the last two or three courses at the top of the brick wall, and they ranged from one to three inches thick and six to ten inches wide. In log structures, plates were the top logs in the front and rear walls. Where there were floored lofts, joists were laid on edge over the plates and extended six to twelve inches beyond the exterior face of the wall to form the framing for a cornice.

Once the attic joists were in place, a false plate—a light timber or board—was fastened to the upper edge of the joists at either end. The false plate, often composed of several pieces laid end to end, ran the entire length of the building and provided the seat for the rafter feet. With base framing for the roof in place, the rafters were brought up to the loft floor and laid out in the sequence of their raising. Prior to being hoisted to the attic, all the rafters had been prefitted, trimmed to size, and numbered with roman numerals often, but not always, indicating their position and raising order. Once in the attic, the rafters were reassembled flat on the floor and then lifted into position. As they were raised, nailing laths for shingles were used to stabilize the pairs of blades until the roof could be finished. The rafters themselves were generally three to four inches thick and four to six inches deep. In all instances, the depth of the rafters tapered from the base, which could be six inches thick, to the ridge, which might be only three inches thick. At the ridge the blades were

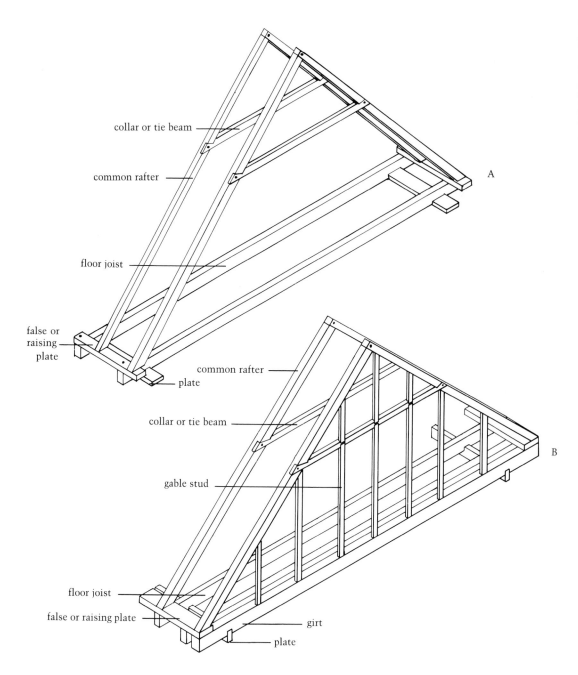

collar or tie beam

common rafter

floor joist

false or
raising
plate

plate

A

common rafter

collar or tie beam

gable stud

B

floor joist

false or raising plate

girt

plate

Figure 5:12. Common-rafter roof framing: (A) Clearfield Farm, Smyrna vicinity, Blackbird Hundred, early eighteenth century; (B) Hickland House, Christiana Hundred (1720–30). The Hickland House roof (B) clearly illustrates the pattern of studding in gable walls common throughout the region in the eighteenth century.

pinned together with a wooden peg driven through either a mortise-and-tenon or a lap joint. In some roofs, collar beams were used to tie the rafters together and provide tension that prevented the rafter feet from kicking out at the base. The additional advantage of a collared roof was that it also offered a secondary storage area at the very apex of the house.

Plates, joists, false plates, rafters, and sometimes collars—all the structural elements most often found in eighteenth- and nineteenth-century roofs throughout the Delmarva Peninsula were known and used from the first durable buildings onward. Within the mechanical task of assembling framing elements, however, was latitude for considerable individual variation and innovation. Where the joists were laid over the plates, for instance, they were sometimes trenched to fit around the plate or sometimes just balanced on top of it. In one early eighteenth-century example, several of the joists were reused from another structure, but because they were of insufficient length for the new building they required an extension of nearly eighteen inches. To resolve the problem, new ends were spliced with lapped scarf-joints to one end of each joist and were trenched over the plate. The combination of a self-locking joint and the fulcrum of the plates countered the stresses that otherwise would have torn the ends off the joists.

The construction of false plates exhibits even greater variation, ranging from boards nailed across the joist ends to squared scantling trenched into the upper end of the joists. In several roofs, the rafter feet are finished with extended heels that catch the inside edge of the false plates and prevent the roof base from scissoring outwards. For the most part, false plates were nailed to the joists, but, where heavier squared timbers were employed as false plates, the entire assembly was pinned together. By the late eighteenth century, composite false plates had come into use. One solution was to nail a board to the joists with a squared timber fitted to the top of the first false plate.[19] As false-plate systems developed through the first building period, the positioning of the rafters changed. In the earliest houses, rafters were aligned with joists, and the false plate sandwiched between them served to maintain the spacing of the joists and to provide a nailing strip for spiking the rafter feet into position. By the 1730s though, the alignment of rafter foot to joist end had been abandoned, and, while joists and rafters remained equally distanced, they were set on independently variable centers.

Although the reasons for this shift are uncertain, it is clear that the false plate had moved from the perceived position of a simple cushion or pad to that of a load-bearing structural member.[20]

Some structures did not have false plates, but used the wall plate itself as the seat for the rafter feet. Buildings of this sort either lacked lofts or attics and consequently needed no upper-level joists to carry a false plate, or were a true story-and-a-half in elevation, with the joists set into the walls well below the top of the wall. Log structures, barns, and granaries compose the bulk of buildings without false plates. In the case of log buildings, the rafters came down directly onto the wall plate; a heel locked the underside edge into position, while the upper face of the rafter continued in a tail beyond the face of the building to form a protective eave. Frame and masonry structures lacking false plates relied on a slightly different system: the rafter heels came down on the plate and were fixed in position with a heavy wrought-iron spike, while the tail projected beyond the plate to form the eaves.

Collar beams that bound the rafter blades together were frequently used to reinforce roof frames. Collar beams were not always uniformly used within a single roof. Where they were employed, collars were dimensionally similar to the blades of the rafters they tied together in an A-shaped configuration. To hold the collars, a half-dovetail open mortise was cut into the side of each blade well enough above the floor to allow for adequate head room. At the ends of the collar beams half-dovetailed lap tenons were fashioned. These were equal to no more than half the thickness of the rafter. When set in place, the collars were pinned to the rafter with the half-dovetailed joint splayed upwards to prevent any settling at the bottom of the roof frame. In some buildings, collars were used on only every other pair of rafter blades, while in others they were distributed throughout the roof. In the case of the Brick Store (1769), two collars were attached to each set of rafters at heights of seven and eleven feet above floor level (Fig. 5:13). The Naudain House (ca. 1735) used collars that were fully tenoned into the tops of common rafters to construct a hipped roof surmounted with a flat deck, and dwellings like the Noxon House (1740) employed no collars at all. In gambrel roofs the collars supported kerb plates that acted as the base for the next tier of rafters.[21]

Conspicuous by their absence from common-rafter roofs of southern New Castle County are purlins—horizontal timbers ei-

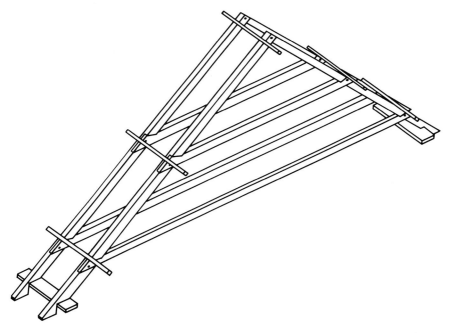

Figure 5:13. Roof framing: Brick Store. Common rafters footed directly onto a plate laid over the uppermost course of the brick walls, with double tiers of collar beams and light through-purlins trenched across the backs of the rafters.

ther lapped over the backs of rafters or butted up and tenoned between them. Only one instance of their use is found in the area: in Brick Store. As commonly found in early New England and Pennsylvania roof framing, purlins ran parallel to the ridge of the building and were spaced at regular intervals with the result that they created a laterally stable framing system and the base for the application of cladding.[22] In the middle-Atlantic region, purlins are most often found in principal rafter roofs on double-pile buildings, where they are tenoned into the sides of the principals and bedded into the masonry or framing of the gable ends. There are instances, however, of purlins carried on upright struts and trenched into the underside of the principals, or of purlins bedded in the gables with no intermediate principals. In all cases, the purlins support the common rafters across their outward facing side, or carry halved common rafters tenoned into the upper and lower face of the purlin.

In Brick Store, two sets of two-by-three-inch common purlins were lapped over the backs of the rafters on each side at the level of the collars. At the ridge a single purlin ran the length of the roof, alternating from side to side of the ridge line. With only an inch of the common purlins rising above the rafter backs, it is apparent that their purpose lay in maintaining the line of the roof, and that once shingle lath was applied to the rafters, they would serve a double function as additional lath.

In the majority of remaining common-rafter roofs, the use of shingle lath across the outer face of the rafters produced the desired rigidity for the roof structure, but in at least one instance scantling was also applied to the underside of the rafters in order to tighten the span where four sets of blades crossed over an attic stairwell. Although no examples survive in the area, roofs originally sheathed with clapboards achieved the same lateral stability found in lathed and shingled roofs.[23] In these buildings the backs of the rafters were weatherboarded in much the same way as the exterior walls of a frame or log building, and the joints between the individual boards sealed with tar or paint.

Not all variation was the product of choice. Poor workmanship, inferior materials, structural repairs, and accidents of construction produced a number of spontaneous variations. The roof of the Newry, erected in the mid-eighteenth century and repaired before 1800, incorporates a number of these features (Fig. 5:14). Built on a common-rafter system without collar beams or a secure footing onto its board false plates, the Newry roof immediately began to fall apart. First one of the middle rafters cracked through, and scantling was scabbed on to either side in an effort to prevent the break from snapping the timber in half. Two other sets of rafter blades further down the roof did not hold together, and they had to be replaced. The effort expended in that repair was minimal; instead of neatly sawn rafters, roughly hewn timbers cut from oak saplings were used. The green oak warped, and shims had to be nailed to their backs to level the roof so that it could be relathed and shingled.

The logic of construction principles governing the shaping and fitting together of building materials such as roofs was not dissimilar to that used for producing socially appropriate space. In the general movement toward durable housing in the 1730s, both building types and elements of building technology were advanced and manipulated through common practice in the formation of a regionally identifiable architectural landscape. As in New England and the Chesapeake Bay country, the buildings that were erected in southern New Castle County drew on some basic patterns of small-scale

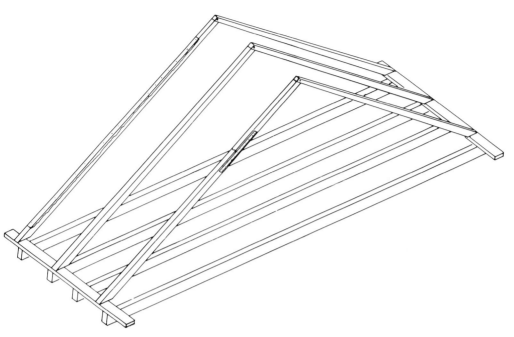

Figure 5:14. Roof framing: Newry, Christiana vicinity, White Clay Creek Hundred (ca. 1740). The flaws of a common-rafter roof without collars or other bracing methods are apparent here, where eighteenth-century repairs include the scabbed-on brace stiffening the cracked rafter blade in the foreground, and the complete replacement of the rafter pair in the background. The middle pair survives as erected.

domestic building customs of the British Isles.[24] But the structures that were actually built were more than fundamentally American; they were basically regional, and in some cases local.[25] The timber-framed roofs of the first periods of durable housing in New England are dramatically different from those of the lower Delaware Valley. Those of the Chesapeake are somewhat more familiar, employing common rafters and false plates, but they differ in the nuances of detail.

In the framing of roofs in southern New Castle we are able to see parallels with other aspects of local vernacular architecture. As with house plans, we are able to classify the frames by types and subtypes. Within a restricted type, though, there is considerable variance in size and finish. The range of subtle differences among roofs of the same type describes a process whereby basic concepts are constantly tested by practice. The idea of a roof type composed of common rafters seated on raising plates and braced with the beams still allows for considerable variation in details, such as the way in which the rafters feet are joined to the raising plate. We can identify the type through its form; to attempt our identification through detail would be difficult at best. In our examination of the construction details of individual roofs assigned to a particular type, we can begin to question our notions of the concept of tradition. Tradition in vernacular architecture is a process by which builders must both draw on a traditional body of knowledge from the past and reconcile it with the exigencies of the present, the specific economic means, availability of materials, or technological limitations. Identifying types of construction based on the relationships between multiple elements, we discern the breadth of their knowledge; and by examining the range of possibilities found in detail, we begin to appreciate the flexibility expressed in putting that knowledge to use.

6. Architecture and Agriculture

Although discussed as a single protracted building period, the time from the first permanent settlements in the late 1680s to the eve of the agricultural reform movement and the advent of the rebuilding of southern New Castle County around 1820 is actually composed of several cycles in building activity. The rise and fall of these cycles overlap to a considerable degree, and together they coalesce into one movement shaping a now-familiar architectural landscape. Throughout the nearly one-hundred-fifty-year period, a repertoire of form, fabric, and fashion was developed and remained constant through the late nineteenth century. However, the details of architectural production and usage, together with the particulars of appearance, changed gradually as the meaning of architecture changed.

The peaks of building activity in the colonial and federal periods echo several significant developments: the shift from impermanent to durable housing, the introduction of stair-passage plans, and the initial redefinition of the types and placement of domestic and agricultural support buildings. At the time of the 1816 tax evaluation, the majority of dwellings were of log or frame construction; a significantly lesser number were built of brick. Earthfast houses had largely vanished from the landscape, except for those occupied by the very poor; and stair-passage-plan dwellings had come into a more general acceptance among the most affluent members of the same society.

As we have seen, until the 1730s, the majority of housing throughout the region and across social and economic lines remained impermanent. The insufficient archaeological data makes it impossible to describe these buildings adequately. By 1705, the first durable buildings began to be erected. The Ashton Houses, the Dilworth House, and possibly one or two others were standing and occupied before 1720; however, they were decidedly grand and unusual mansions for their time and place. The dramatic increase in the number of durable buildings for yeoman farmers began to gain momentum in the late 1730s. At this juncture, farmers began to replace a number of impermanent dwellings with structures intended to endure through the occupation of succeeding generations. The Liston House, Newry, McDonough House, Vandergrift House, and others were raised, using the plan options of one-, two-, and three-room forms. As the movement toward durable housing accelerated, regionally identifiable characteristics in construction and decoration were established.

As the pace of durable building continued, the idea and use of unheated stair passages gained currency among the more affluent members of society. Although the earliest dated center-passage houses may be pinpointed to the 1740s, their appearance did not become more general at the upper economic level of building until the 160s. The very first examples of the new form were less concerned with external symmetry than with simply working out and cramming in all the requisite spaces. By the 1750s, fully developed center-passage plans, with balanced five-bay facades, had made their debut. As the new idiom was accepted into more constant use, it became better defined in terms of balance, exterior ornamentation, and interior trim—particularly in the progressive elaboration of the stair from its first cramped position at the rear of the passage to its expanded station occupying nearly the full length and half the width of the same space. Three social ramifications of the new form were that, for many who occupied such dwellings, the center of domestic activity remained in one or two rooms; also the former common room or hall was supplanted through a more specific designation and furnishing scheme such as the establishment of a dining room; and finally the form remained the property of the wealthy and did not filter down through society.

The final cycle of building activity toward the close of the eighteenth century occurred outside the house. Domestic functions such as cooking were sporadically removed from separate buildings and annexed into wings built off the rear or gable ends of the houses. At the same time, farm buildings slowly became the focus of more permanent construction practices. Barns and granaries, most of which had been framed on the ground, were raised on masonry foundations; more attention was given to better walling and roofing materials. As farm buildings were commissioned with an eye toward durability, they also became larger and functionally more diversified structures. The tendency toward houses and farm buildings with appreciably more and functionally better-defined interior spaces was to hold a particular significance for the next building cycles. In the decades marking the close of the first building cycles, these structures communicated the sense of ideas that had been worked out in architectural terms, and yet not fully verbalized.

Although the building cycles charting the shaping of the land take place in a temporal sequence, they do not chart an architectural progression, but rather the broadening of the tripartite and mutually interdependent melding of form, fabric, and fashion. As the volume of options grew, the process of selection did not necessarily become more complex, just more calculated to the circumstances of individual building projects. Architectural expression as an affirmation of class standing, for example, was the worry of those who had the luxury of time and money to fret over their place in society. Tenants and laborers had little means to invest in building as more than shelter; for them the social aspects of housing were not a pressing concern. By the 1820s some people continued to occupy impermanent structures, and others were building permanent dwellings that ranged from one-room to center-passage, double-pile plans. The net effect of all building activity was the emergence of a regionally recognizable architecture. This architecture was not self-consciously formulated and adopted by all the builders in southern New Castle County, rather it was achieved through a process of selection and default. Those with access to capital were able to negotiate the financing of extravagant buildings. For members of the same society who were unwilling or unable to invest in architecture, the perceived order of things proposed by those who did build came to be an inherited reality. The consequence of that legacy was an architectural layering whose sponsors made and received their own bequest. The architectural shaping of southern New Castle County's pre-1820 countryside brought the area across the threshold of a profound change. The superficial cause of this was a conscious drive toward a general, agricultural reform, but an underlying cause was an emerging popular image of rural economy and domestic life. The agricultural reform movement brought cohesion, direction, substance, and even a guiding philosophy to rural living. The first traces of that transformation are seen in the houses of individuals like William Corbit and David Wilson who shared a similar economic stature and world view.

At the time of the 1816 tax assessment, of which St. Georges Hundred offers a good case study, the majority of buildings in southern New Castle County were of wood construction.[1] There were 567 taxable heads of households and 170 dwellings. Only 5 percent lived in brick dwellings, and 22 percent lived in houses built of frame or log. The housing of the remaining 73 percent was unspecified. Because a tax assessment is generated as an inventory for public revenues, the housing of the less affluent simply may not have been considered worthy enough for valuation. However, there are other explanations for their not being mentioned, which appear in mid-century manuscript censuses.[2] In the counting of mid-century households, tenants and laborers are often listed at the same residence as the owner of the farm. Indeed, single fieldhands and domestic servants were often housed in the kitchen or upper reaches of the main house, but a substantial number were provided with separate quarters. So were tenant families. But tax assessors only occasionally enumerated support buildings such as barns, granaries, and storehouses by name and took little note of tenant houses and quarters. Of equal significance is the fact that only 37 percent of 567 individuals designated as taxables in 1816 owned land. The demographic and economic facts are clear: at the close of the first building periods only a little more than a third of the taxables owned their own land and possessed houses meriting a tax evaluation.

A key to the architectural importance of the situation is the number and ownership of brick dwellings. Of the 29 persons (5 percent of the taxable population) who owned such buildings, 28 owned land and 26 owned more than a hundred acres. Twenty-seven of these 29 individuals were among the richest 20 percent of the population (Fig. 6:1). At the same time only 10 owned slaves and just 3 possessed more than two. Within the larger group defined as slave holders, only 11 percent also owned brick dwellings. The pattern is particularly striking when we note that approximately half of the brick dwellings listed in 1816 still stand, as compared to less than a tenth of the wood dwellings. In short, the eighteenth-century vernacular housing surviving in southern New Castle County is that of

Deciles	Number of cases	Percent of cases	Cumulative percent
Top 1	20	69.0	69.0
2	7	24.2	93.2
3	1	3.4	96.6
4	1	3.4	100.0
5	0	—	—
6	0	—	—
7	0	—	—
8	0	—	—
9	0	—	—
10	0	—	—

	1816	1850
Mean number of acres per farm	235	198
Mean number of improved acres	160	184
Mean number of untilled acres	75	14
Improved acres	68%	93%
Untilled acres	32%	7%
Total	100%	100%

Figure 6:1. (Left) Distribution of owners of brick dwellings in the wealth decile distribution for St. Georges Hundred (1816 tax assessment, St. Georges Hundred). Table: CHAE, Rebecca S. Siders.

Figure 6:2. (Right) Changes in the proportion of improved acres per farm in St. Georges Hundred (1816 tax assessment, 1850 agricultural census manuscript returns, St. Georges Hundred). Table: CHAE, Rebecca S. Siders.

a minority of the population who had wealth, land, and a preference for tenant or day labor over a chattel work force.

More specific to the landscape and the status of building in 1816 are the facts that nearly two-thirds of the total taxable population were landless, living in other people's dwellings, and inhabiting houses unworthy of notice. These individuals and their families labored in the employment of an affluent minority. They worked in fields, tanneries, storehouses, mills, and shops in which they held no vested interest. The thoughts of this majority on the subjects of housing and labor are unknown, but their presence and availability were central to the local rural economy. When the economy came upon difficult times in the early 1800s and then underwent a dramatic recovery in the second quarter of the nineteenth century, their place on the land was subject to a critical reevaluation by those who owned and controlled the countryside.

The 1816 tax list for St. Georges Hundred also provides information on an average farm size. The mean farm contained 235 acres, of which 22 percent was woodland. The smallest farmsteads contained only 25 acres, while massive estates, composed of as much as 2,000 acres, were undoubtedly divided into several farms supervised by farm managers or leased to tenants. By the time the 1850 agricultural census was taken, average farm size had decreased by 37 acres, and the proportion of untilled acres had dropped to 7 percent. Most of the land that could be put into production was in use by mid-century (Fig. 6:2).

The 1850 agricultural returns for southern New Castle provide invaluable insights into farm economy. With the sole exception of the poorer soils in the southwest, the district was dominated by large farms cultivating wheat, corn, and oats, and raising cattle for dairy products, slaughtered goods, and hides. In an overview of the state of agriculture in 1850, historian Jack Michel has described St. Georges Hundred as the heart of the Delaware wheat belt. The farms were by far the largest in the state, and the average farm of 198 acres yielded in excess of 500 bushels of wheat annually. Farms in the area kept three-quarters of all tilled land in hay, oats, and corn, with the average corn yield at 1,300 bushels. Unlike wheat destined for urban markets, corn, oats, and hay were grown as feed:

> Hay production, by contrast, was relatively de-emphasized in the large farm hundreds. . . . Large farms had the largest absolute number of animals, and it seems clear that animals here were grain fed, and that hay was used as a dietary supplement, presumably for dairy cattle.[3]

The farm animals, and especially the beasts of burden, further distinguished the agricultural estates of southern New Castle County:

> . . . with some exaggeration, but not much, it might be said that the divide between the world of the peasant and that of the modern is the divide between the horse and the ox. . . . The ox is stronger and more durable. With him the peasant could till even the poorest soils. For heavy work, he was unmatched. He thrived on pasture grass. But the horse was faster. On average soils he could cover two acres in the time it took to plow one with an ox. In 1850, in Delaware, an ox might be had for as little as $12. Horses cost at least $20, and a good plow horse might run the farmer $50 or more. A horse needed oats if he was to survive in good working health. He was more fragile and required more care. . . . In the cultivation of wheat (where planting and harvesting seasons lasted two weeks or less) and in the mowing of hay

(which needs to be done before it rains or the hay goes sour) the horse possessed every advantage but cost over the ox.[4]

The horse was the work animal of southern New Castle County. A three-animal farm in the large farm district was a three-horse farm. Even on five-animal farms, oxen appear only infrequently, reserved for the heaviest work. The preference for the horse related directly to the cultivation of wheat.

Coupled with their dependence on the speed of the horse, a growing reliance on farm machinery, further distinguished reform-minded farmers. Mechanical cultivators were common and marked a shift from the old process of growing corn in hand-hoed hills to doing so in machine-cut furrows. To operate the machinery and drive the horse, the farmer required a constant pool of day laborers. The potential productivity of the land exceeded technological capabilities in 1850. To increase production, farmers bought more machinery (often sharing costs and machines with their neighbors) and hired more laborers to operate their machines. As labor on the farm increased, the landowner lost the ability to supervise his operations directly and thereby came to the point of relying on individual farm managers who worked the farm, summarized expenses and returns, and brought only special problems to the owner's attention. The result was, by 1850, a class of farmers who did not till the soil but rather observed the annual cycle of planting and harvest by meticulously recording the business of agriculture in leather-bound ledgers and day books.

Raising cattle was also quite important to the agricultural economy. A herd of seven to eleven dairy cows typically generated a thousand pounds of butter yearly. Other cattle were kept for slaughter, and farmers would sell the meat to nearby villages and urban markets. The hides, in the early nineteenth century, were sold to local tanners in Odessa, Middletown, and Glasgow, and by mid-century to leather manufacturers in Wilmington and Philadelphia.[5]

The type of agriculture on these, the largest and most valuable farms in Delaware at mid-century, produced a predictable demand for building large barns for milk cows and hay, stables for horses, cart sheds for machinery, and combination corncribs and granaries for corn and wheat. (These structures are the topic of Chapter 8.) The change in housing, however, is less easily explained. What is the relationship between house types and agriculture? The answer, it seems, lies not in technology or crops, but in the economy and sociology of farming. In his summary of Delaware agriculture in 1850, Michel concludes that in the intensive reliance on contract labor and technology, "we can read finally the psychological concomitant of capitalist agriculture: namely the drive for income."

> Farmers in St. Georges and other large farm hundreds, used more labor relative to machinery . . . not because it made them more efficient, but rather because it allowed them to increase their income. As capital, this income would allow them to expand further in coming years. As money, it allowed them to begin a very different revolution in Delaware rural life—as they became the State's first rural middle class.[6]

A significant percentage of farm income was invested in new housing and new outbuildings, especially between 1830 and 1860. As capital expenditures, the new houses increased the value of the farms as property. As an expenditure of money, the new houses rose as monuments to economic and social success. Aspirations to social class would be worked out in brick, lumber, plaster, and paint; the social revolution would become an architectural revolution.

The principals in these changes were the agriculturalists, the landed farmers of 1816 who became the agricultural businessmen of 1850. Change had been in the wind before the measure of it was taken in rural economy and architecture. The earliest advocates of the agricultural revolution that would bring them money, land, and social power were the founders of the county agricultural society. The first formal paper presented to the society served notice of their ambition.

In 1819 the Agricultural Society of the County of New Castle was formed. The membership was made up exclusively of landowners. At the first meeting of the new society one of the members, Samuel Henry Black, a progressive farmer living in Pencader Hundred, read a paper entitled "An Essay on the Intrinsic Value of Arable Land."[7] Black's essay, published the following year in the Baltimore-based *American Farmer*, had two goals: to describe the state of agriculture in New Castle County, and to prescribe a method of improvement in the future. Black began:

> Whatever diversity of opinion may prevail on the subject of farming and on the value of land, that both at present amongst us, are in the most melancholy and wretched state of depression, will, I think, be

readily admitted by all; that crops of every kind have, of late years, almost totally failed; and that, to the laborious husbandman, scarce a single hope seems left at which he can grasp to encourage him to new efforts, needs no argument to prove: This gloomy truth is felt, and admitted in every sphere of life, from the pauper in the poorhouse to the most wealthy man in the state. Many, however, attribute this melancholy failure to almost every other than the true cause—the seasons, the climate, the Hessian-Fly, the stunt, the louse, the grub, the clay and the sand, and an endless variety of other imaginary evils, have alternately been cursed as the bane of the farmer. The tiller of the ground has perhaps hardly dreamed, that in execrating the cause of his ill success, he but calls for the vengeance of Heaven on his own head. All these plagues are but the *symptoms*, and not as he may have supposed, the cause of his misfortunes.[8]

The cause of agricultural failure, as Black explained, rested in poor husbandry and pervasive mismanagement. The remedy for these ills lay in realizing the "intrinsic value" of the land—the time when agricultural yields could be maximized to the point where the greatest number of people could be adequately fed from the smallest amount of land. The means to the cure rested in increasingly efficient management of crops and labor, and in improved farming through scientific agricultural methods, including use of fertilizers and manure, crop rotation, and labor-saving mechanical devices and buildings. A deeper ambition ran through Black's treatise, though, and was noted in the introductory remarks of the editor: "It will be impossible for any one to read this essay and possess one drop of farmer's blood, without feeling it start in every vein, and flush him with the expectation of realizing the promise of the essayist; in other words an estate."[9] The goal of realizing an estate was compelling, and the means to accomplishing that end were equated with good government, Christian living, applied science and, most important, a consciously formulated sense of order.

On the symbiotic relationship of agriculture and government, Black maintained that

the nature and operations of our government are so mild, as scarcely to be felt by the people, while the laws of it afford the most ample and secure protection of its citizens, in their persons, their property and their privileges. There is not certainly at this time, and perhaps there has never before been on this earth, a country in all respects so desirable, and so perfectly adapted to the safety, the comfort, and the happiness of mankind, as are these United States, I know not if it be possible to find any real defect in the climate, the soil, or the internal government of this country.[10]

For S. H. Black and his fellow members of the agricultural society the benevolence of such a government left them free to create their envisioned estates as agricultural fiefdoms secure from the turbulence of public affairs. Such an estate could be attained through a combination of the farm owner's agricultural initiative and his ability to control his work force economically and socially. No self-apparent conflict or inequity was perceived in a community where the ability to acquire, hold, and husband the land provided structure to a society separating those who managed the farm from those who worked it.

The evangelical quality of the agricultural reform movement proposed in 1819 came to the forefront in later farming guides used in southern New Castle County. Elder C. Suydane's *The Farmer's Manure System* viewed the farmer's vocation as part of a God-given natural order, "and it seems congenial with the law of nature, that every man should pursue some particular branch of business, not only on account of his own peculiar taste, but also on account of that unerring Providence which directs his course through life, as well as for his own interest and the common benefit of society with which he stands connected."[11] Whether or not society included all who worked the land or just those who owned it was a topic open for debate. There was little disagreement over a providential order of things, but there were differences of opinion concerning just what Providence intended and to whose benefit those intentions were directed.

Regardless of the outcome of such high-minded debates, farming remained an economically class-structured society, where limited opportunities for the poor and unlanded restricted their ability to cross the barriers of social stratification. At the same time, considerable latitude existed for those in positions of affluence either to perpetuate their material well-being or to fall from economic grace. If individuals living in southern New Castle County in the first quarter of the nineteenth century could not readily improve their lot where they lived and worked, they could pack up what they owned and leave.[12] According to the censuses taken from 1800 to 1830, the population of the area declined and did not recover until the 1840 census (Fig. 6:3). In St. Georges Hundred the total popula-

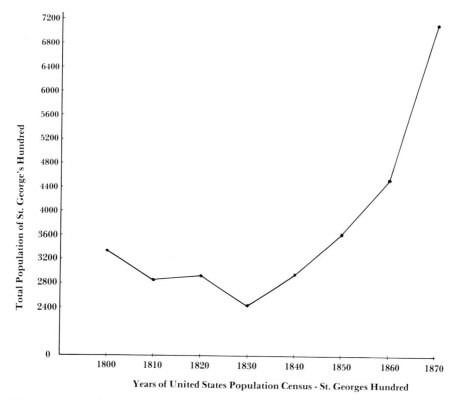

Figure 6:3. Population change in St. Georges Hundred (1800–70). Graph: CHAE, Rebecca S. Siders.

tion dropped by more than a third, by the time Black wrote his essay the catastrophes of poor yields and crop failure were compounded by a diminished labor pool: there were too few to satisfactorily work the estates that were deemed the natural birthright of those who owned the land. The old providential order of things was quite simply not satisfactory for everyone.

In the eyes of some, the panacea was the creation of a new order. The often-repeated motto for the new scheme of things—from the organization of rural society to the place of tools in the workshed— became "a separate place for each thing, and every thing in its place" (Fig. 6:4).[13] What this mandate required was a large-scale self-evaluation of the community as a part of the agrarian mid-Atlantic region.

To better understand the self-conscious pursuit of putting everything in its place and of creating a new order of architecture, we

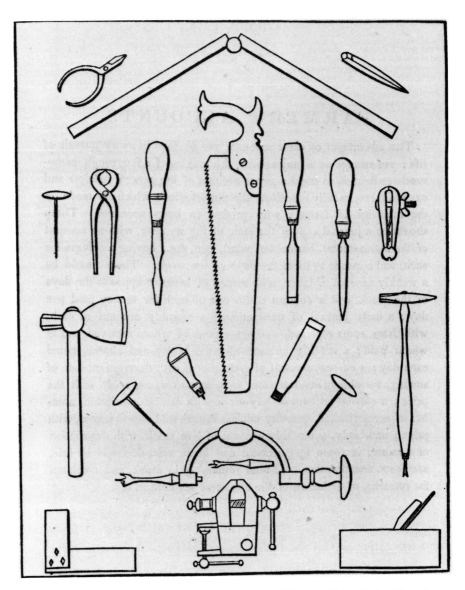

Figure 6:4. "A Separate Place For Each Thing, And Every Thing In Its Place," From *The Farmer's Book and Family Instructor* (1845). The pegboard design offered to the readers of this agricultural manual symbolized an increasingly self-conscious concern with imposing order on all aspects of rural life.

turn to written records of farms. The first annual volume of *The Farmers' Cabinet*, published in Philadelphia in 1836 and with a readership in southern New Castle County, presents numerous suggestions for maintaining farm accounts, ledgers, and day books:

let every farmer carry in his pocket paper and pencil, and as soon as anything requiring early attention occurs to him, which cannot be done immediately, let him make memorandum of it, and thus in a short time he will have a list of whatever is necessary to be done.[14]

From pocket memoranda, the farmer was to compose nightly lists, and from nightly lists, develop weekly work schedules. Another correspondent transmitted his own techniques:

> 1st. I make, on a sheet of drawing paper of good size, a map of my farm, drawing lines to designate fences—(then let a little girl paint these lines after the fashion of an engraved map)—number every field or division of the farm, and let these numbers be the only names by which the fields shall be designated.

> 2d. Every evening before retiring to rest, in a regular account book procured for the purpose (called day book), I charge for expenses of the day to the field or fields where the work has been done that day, and with the same care and precision as a merchant charges his goods, with such remarks on the description of the work and the weather as I may think of consequence.

> 3d. During the long evenings of the fall season, I put all these accounts into a Ledger of suitable size, kept expressly for farm accounts, and no other. By the close of the year I will have my accounts all posted up and footed. Then,

> 4th. Carry these footings, with descriptions, results, &c. forward to "the last leaf of the Leger" for that year, and I have, as will be seen, the kind of crop on each field, the expense of cultivation, the amount of the crop, the profits of each field, and the profits per acre, &c.[15]

Although few if any agriculturalists of southern New Castle County drew the suggested map of the farm, many did keep detailed accounts on labor, production, seasonal tasks, debt, contracts, and income.

The two most common entries in the accounts recorded farm production and farm labor. Richard Mansfield of St. Georges Hundred listed daily who was working, what was sown, and what was harvested. Sereck Shallcross, Mansfield's neighbor, did likewise. Samuel Townsend of Appoquinimink Hundred on the southern edge of the Levels kept his accounts organized by the name of workers and clients. Under each name, he noted by date what services they performed and what goods were bought and sold. In Townsend's accounts, and those of his contemporary Benjamin Biggs of

Pencader Hundred, ledger entries provided an easy reference to economic control. Laborers were kept in perennial debt, owing money for sums borrowed and goods purchased from the farm owner and being docked pay for even minor infractions. But in an agricultural economy where day labor was indispensable to the profitability of the farm, laborers were not without some power. While they might be docked for going to weddings, burying their dead, drunkeness—". . . to 1/2 day lost at a wedding, drank so much whiskey that he had headache next morning, laid in a granary"—or for debts owed to the farmer's "company store," they were seldom dismissed.[16] More often, the laborer would absent himself from the neighborhood. Debtors' departures were not always mourned. Benjamin Biggs wrote in 1855: "This account is made and kept for one of the meanest of Negroes and after impudence cleared him out when he went to New Jersey where he ought to stay."[17] Maintaining a steady level of debt contributed to keeping everything in its place. Without indebtedness laborers were free to move (although illicit movement could be welcome). For the farmer, order provided flexibility to conduct business; for the farm worker, order restrained all social, economic, and physical movement, except flight.

The process of creating a place for everything extended to the naming of farms. The consolidation of land into large tracts that were then redistributed into smaller farms supervised by sons or tenants created a need for literally dividing and labeling the land. The architecture of house and farm continued to communicate the course of social interaction and of distancing that had been first expressed in the mid-eighteenth century. The architecture also worked out the tensions between accepted practice and self-proclaimed innovation. Still, buildings alone could not express the new territoriality that defined the landscape of the nineteenth century. Although big houses stood on well-kept grounds, surrounded by fences and hedgerows, and although farm buildings came to be clustered in courts behind the main house, the farmsteads of the reform era could not be distinguished from one another in the sameness of the economic and social relationships they housed. As a result the landscape was not only rebuilt but extensively renamed. The renaming of the farm parcels is significant because "naming systems are one of the chief methods people use to impose order on their experience."[18] The practice of naming plantations and large tracts of land in southern New Castle County can be traced back to the earliest settlement periods. By the beginning of 1800s, naming single farms had became a more general practice. One contemporary architectural writer advised "the application of some distinctive name to every detached country house, however small, since it cannot be distinguished by a number, as in town." The name should be, "suggestive of some fact connected with the house, its owner, or its location, and should be original, or at least not copied from any in the vicinity." Farmers in southern New Castle followed the spirit of the recommendations.[19]

D. G. Beers's *Atlas* of 1868 lists over 200 farms by name in the lower hundreds. Many of the names evoked picturesque images of siting such as Fairview, River View, Marsh Mount, Hill Island, and Summit View. Others used names that were common throughout the eastern half of the United States including Mt. Pleasant, Cherry Grove, and Woodlawn. A few celebrated historic places—Gettysburg, Bunker Hill, and Mount Vernon Place—and far away places—Australia, California, Devondale, Rolling Prairie, and New Canada. A substantial number of names called to mind a world of agrarian prosperity with names like La Grange, Cornucopia, Wheatland, Eden Farm, and Peach Blossom. As a whole, the names chosen for farms were aggressively pastoral in the images they conveyed.

The fact of naming is not unusual nor, given the prevailing agricultural economy and world view, are the names that were selected. What is significant is when and where the naming process occurred. With very few exceptions, the incidence of named farms in a given area corresponds directly to the level and intensity of rebuilding activity there. Farmsteads and houses erected on the poorer lands of the county were likely to have only the owner's name; wealthier farms occupying prime farmland had more elaborate or fanciful names. The process of naming farms in nineteenth-century southern New Castle County was tied in with the passion for new architecture. As the landscape was architecturally reshaped, it reflected the transformation of social and economic interaction, and of the community's relationship to the land itself. While houses internalized patterns of changing domestic behavior and farm buildings embodied the resolution of conflict inherent between old and new, place names pinned down the direction of those relationships. Names put gloss on the ideas set forth in buildings, and they underscored the images treasured by the inhabitants of the area. Prosperity was measured in yields of grain, fruit, and dairy products;

image was measured by names. The process of renaming the land was not a consequence of the architecture, but it was a necessary concurrent activity for a society that had self-consciously reordered itself through architecture.

In the fifteen years following Black's speech, three major events occurred that perceptually reordered the place of southern New Castle County in the lower Delaware Valley. All three events became highly influential in the redefinition of the region. The first event was the completion and opening of the canal connecting Chesapeake Bay and Delaware Bay in 1829; the second was the introduction of peaches as a major cash crop by Philip Reybold on his farm near the village of St. Georges around 1835;[20] and the third was the establishment of a railroad line to the north. The first two events had a less immediate impact on Delaware farms: commerce between the Delaware and the Chesapeake was already well established across New Castle County, and large productive fruit orchards were in full growth certainly as early as the 1780s. The third event, however—the coming of the railroad in the 1850s—had a dramatic impact. It enabled farmers to drastically alter farming methods and grow new types of crops.

Construction of a canal connecting the head waters of the Chesapeake Bay to the lower Delaware River began in the early 1820s and was completed in 1829. Cutting across southern New Castle County, with locks at Summit, St. Georges, and Delaware City, the limited-access canal linked the regional urban marketplaces of Baltimore and Philadelphia by way of Wilmington.

Contemporary with the opening of the canal was the first cultivation of peaches and other orchard produce as large-scale cash crops. Although fruit orchards had been common in the eighteenth century, the beginnings of the peach boom in southern New Castle County are attributed to Reybold's farm in Red Lion Hundred on the north bank of the canal. Reybold, like S. H. Black and many of their land-owning neighbors, was caught up in the excitement generated during the first years of the agricultural society. While he continued to derive the bulk of his farm-related income from the cultivation of grains and livestock husbandry and from a brick yard he owned and operated, Reybold was also among the first to realize the cash potential of perishable crops.

The two primary marketing factors common to peaches, as well as plums, pears, strawberries, and other fruits grown later in the nineteenth century, were their rapid rate of spoilage and their inability to travel well. In the 1830s and 1840s, only farmers and merchants with ready access to water-borne transportation and excess capital for more venturesome agricultural marketing endeavors were in a position to experiment with peach cultivation, the success of which depended upon getting the perishable crop quickly to market. Thus grain, butter, and leather goods remained the mainstays of the local farm economy, however, the markets to which they were sent were being redetermined by emerging local and regional trade routes. With the opening of the railroad in the mid-1850s, peach and fruit cultivation became a significant element in the economy.[21]

The railroad's impact was economically immediate. As a right-of-way was developed, farmers and town fathers alike petitioned for sidings and depots. High-speed transportation created new agricultural possibilities and new rural trade centers. The railroad provided the economic focus for Middletown to grow rapidly from a crossroads village into a large and fashionable town, and for Samuel Townsend to develop a town named after himself. The presence of the canal maintained the economy of Delaware City, and, by 1868, a new spur route had been proposed to link the eastern terminus of the canal with the main north-south line. Less fortunate were riverside villages like Port Penn and Odessa—they sank gradually to the status and condition of backwater landings.

We can best trace the impact of the canal, peaches, and railroads on the richest agricultural lands of Delaware: the Levels. This stretch of the flat lands west of Middletown across parts of St. Georges and Appoquinimink hundreds, contained twenty to thirty large farms which in 1850 had an average size of 375 acres, nearly double that of rural estates in rich St. Georges Hundred, and almost four times greater than in poorer Appoquinimink. Compared to the farmers of St. Georges Hundred, who owned an average of $226 worth of machinery and five horses, those of the Levels owned $475 worth of farm implements and eight or nine horses. They grew 56 percent more wheat and 79 percent more corn than their neighbors in St. Georges Hundred. They received additional income from sheep (wool) and swine and cattle (slaughtered goods), but they earned $100 less from the annual sale of butter (despite the fact that they owned the same number of milk cows). In relation to available improved land, the ratio between income from grain and dairying is much greater on the Levels than in St. Georges Hundred. Architecturally, by 1860 the Levels were more improved than the rest of St. Georges Hundred. For example, the Cochran family commissioned at least five new houses and thirty new barns and outbuildings, plus new tenant dwellings, between 1830 and 1860; William Wilson who owned a half dozen farms, furnished each with new barns and houses, and remodeled his own eighteenth-century family house, Homestead Hall. Everywhere new houses went up, and the few old dwellings that were kept were remodeled inside and out.

Twenty years later, in 1870, the Levels produced the same amount of wheat, but corn had decreased by 66 percent and oats were down 90 percent. There were fewer cows and half as much butter. The new source of income was in orchard products—$2,255 per farm as compared to an 1850 average value of $9. Only the impact of the railroad, which dramatically reduced the span of time from farm to market, could have provided the mechanism for such a shift in farm produce. Next to the cultivator, which was introduced in the early decades of the nineteenth century, the locomotive became the most important machine in the farm economy. The railroad brought no revolution but only increased the possibilities for markets, and hence for income. The new prosperity, which saw farm values on the Levels (and in all of St. Georges Hundred) double in the twenty years between agricultural censuses, was short lived. By 1880, western wheat had usurped local grains in a national marketplace.

The importance of the cultivation of peaches for market is a recurring theme in local histories of nineteenth-century southern New Castle County. Locally, the Italianate country houses around Middletown are called "peach houses," however, the introduction of the fruit as a large-scale market crop did not take place until well after these dwellings were built. Howard Pyle's article in *Harper's New Monthly Magazine* in 1879 provided one such description:

> Peaches, peaches everywhere—in baskets, in crates, in boxes, in wagons. . . . Along the roads in all directions rumble the peach wagons, each in a little cloud of dust, like a miniature thunder-storm, each wending its way and converging to a centre represented by the nearest railway station.[22]

The Delaware peach season could last as long as two months each year, during which time both resident and migrant labor harvested the delicate crop. By 1860 as much as a third of some farms was given over to orchards. But peach trees required even more intensive efforts in soil improvement and maintenance than had the crops cultivated earlier in the century. The life of a producing orchard was only twenty years—and even that required enormous investment and constant care. As the trees grew old, their ability to produce fruit declined, and they became increasingly subject to a variety of blights and insect infestations. The peach grower, however, had a worse enemy: "Scarcely less dreaded by peach-growers than a failure is an overcrop, when the superabundant fruit ripens too fast to be plucked, when the overcharged markets return but a pittance to the producers, sometimes not even paying for the expense of shipment."[23]

Despite the profits made in 1860, the combination of disease, mortality, and market worked against the continued investment in peaches. While the farmers of Kent and Sussex counties continued to plant and replant peach orchards, the agriculturalists of the Levels and surrounding neighborhoods had abandoned peach growing by 1870. The 1880 agricultural census returns depicted a landscape in decline. Farm values had dropped back to their 1850 averages, and farm laborers' wages and investments in agricultural implements had eroded by 25 percent. Even more significant are the shifts in the average annual produce. Corn, which had declined by two-thirds from 1850 to 1870 as orchard cultivation took over, was in 1880 only 50 percent below 1850 highs. The increase in corn correlates with a 90 percent decline in orchard harvest; however, corn yields remained comparatively low. In contrast, hay had increased 90 percent over 1850 averages. All evidence indicates that the corn-fed animals of a generation before were now fed with fodder. Thus in 1880, the Levels, like the surrounding farm lands, looked noticeably less well off. Agricultural malaise stunted the architectural growth. The generation building from 1830 to 1860 had revolutionized the look of the Levels; the one that followed spent the next thirty years in economic, agricultural, and architectural retrenchment.

The nineteenth-century rebuilding of southern New Castle County antedates the economic boom with which many historians have associated it. Architectural projects in the rural areas of the lower hundreds have pre–Civil War origins, with the majority dating to the years between 1840 to 1860. Peaches and orchard crops did not become a major economic factor until about 1860. The canal, fruit cultivation, and railway were not causes for the shifts in marketing practice and the closing down of a rural world view. The causes for those changes and the emergence of an increasingly refined architectural order were bound to a deeper process; they were part of the changes in social structure initiated in the mid-eighteenth century.

The pattern of change manifested itself first in the houses of the wealthy over a generation before the changes in market, crops, and agricultural practice. These early householders believed in the virtues of an orderly rural economy. By 1819 agricultural decline and a diminished rural labor force all but demanded the industrialization of the farm and the marshalling of a class of farm workers not unlike mill workers. With all the available land in the possession of a few, the goal of a new economic and domestic order for these farmers was near at hand, and its architectural realization just beginning. From 1830 to 1860 architectural renewal would run its course and scarcely a single farm house emerged unaltered; most were significantly enlarged or replaced.

To understand the relationships between agriculture and architecture, we must also look at the larger phenomenon of rebuilding. American rebuilding cycles have been identified in different regions at different times: middle Virginia reportedly rebuilt much of its architecture at the time of the American Revolution; on the Eastern Shore of Virginia (the lower Delmarva Peninsula) rebuilding occurred between 1790 and 1830 and again between 1880 and 1920; New England rebuilt toward the end of the seventeenth century and again in the mid-eighteenth century; and German settlements of rural Pennsylvania rebuilt their architecture between 1830 and 1870.[24] First recognized in the British Isles, the occurrence of cycles of building and rebuilding activity has been identified as a pattern recurring at intervals usually paralleled by significant social and economic changes that produced both the reason and the means for widespread building projects.[25] Rebuilding cycles reveal the role structures play in expressing cultural beliefs; furthermore, they reveal performance, memory, and knowledge as significant factors in the production and presentation of domestic architecture.[26]

Social changes periodically reorder architectural landscapes, and this reordering can involve the remodeling of existing structures or the erection of entirely new buildings. This is somewhat different from established English notions of rebuilding as a transition from impermanent to durable architecture. In the British concept, rebuilding cycles are perceived as the manifestation of a unified architectural theme across a span of time that is defined by a group's having access to the capital necessary for substantial building projects. Thus rebuilding occurs at different times for each of the different economic strata of society. In that context rebuilding has been used to define vernacular architecture as part of a triad—durability, traditional design, and local practice. Accordingly, rebuilding cycles have provided an index to the way in which architecture is used to contain and direct social and economic interaction.

Just as a means of communication functions as a collection of signs transmitting a multitude of messages that can be read by both occupants and observers, so different types of architecture may communicate a variety of information in similar ways. Or they may convey similar meanings in very different ways. In most societies they do both and thus reinforce each other. Over time and use, media—and sometimes the first layer of information—become devalued. Indeed, although the values of a society may remain stable, the way they are expressed may not. At once fluid and constant, expressive forces are always subject to a reordering process that provides a combination of immediacy, cohesion, and relevance.

In the sense that buildings communicate the structure and values of a society, they are subject to two modes of reinterpretation: first, the actual buildings may remain physically unchanged but become invested with new sets of meanings more in line with the needs of society; second, buildings may be physically altered or replaced in order to shape or fit changing canons of interpretation. The first form of revaluation is comparatively rare in traditional settings and is, in fact, usually confined to the production of architecture as art. The second alternative is as common as building itself. The historical process of revaluing the architectural sign takes place through layers of building and rebuilding.

Rebuilding cycles differ from general building periods in that they do not necessarily represent an enlargement of the architectural options, but rather the manipulation and the proliferation of sets of existing options in such a way that the building both redefines, and is redefined in, the values emphasized by the society. For a rebuilding cycle to begin, there must be sufficient economic resources as well as a stimulus to spark the general movement toward a new architectural order and its social consequences. Once underway, a rebuilding cycle is manifested in three ways: the replacement of one structure by another on the same site, the transformation of an existing structure by remodeling and enlargement, and the erecting of new structures on new sites.[27] All of these elements—financial means, a catalyst, and the three types of rebuilding activity—were present in southern New Castle County throughout the middle decades of the nineteenth century. Since architecture is a consequence of temporal movement, it may be archaeologically read by examining its layers or stratification. The base level is the initial act of building—the construction of a building from the ground up. The second, third, and later period changes do more than simply modify the initial statement made by the building—they create a new structure, using the existing one as a starting place. Although the house emerging on the other side of these changes may still contain recognizable elements of its first appearance, it has become a new dwelling, with different spatial and aesthetic characteristics on one hand and a different social dimension on the other.

The key element in diffusion theory—that one can observe, trace, and discuss the movement or exchange of ideas or goods—has been demonstrated by historians, geographers, folklorists, anthropologists, linguists, and others.[28] Yet how those ideas or goods are exchanged is another matter. We cannot assume that societies are somehow broken into givers and receivers, that the givers are haves and the receivers have-nots. Diffusion involves a constant level of communication throughout society. The acceptance or rejection of ideas is contingent upon a knowledge of their suitability and accessibility. The viewpoint claiming that architectural ideals and innovations diffuse downward through society from an elite (usually defined in terms of literacy and wealth) to the folk (oppositely defined by illiteracy and poverty) is faulty because it ignores the reality of day-to-day commerce in a rural world and the complexity of community organization.[29]

Those who commission architectural projects may provide specifications and even designs gleaned from published sources, but more commonly they turn to buildings in the community in which they live and work. Material expression cannot be so foreign to the mainstream of a society that it is appreciated by only a wealthy, well-read minority. To succeed, architectural statements need to be both appropriate and accessible in the situations where they function, and, as a consequence, these statements must resolve any inherent conflict between abstract thought and meaningful realities. To this end, academically inspired rural architecture typically incorporates established patterns of vernacular architectural usage. The houses commissioned by the local elite are customarily built by local craftsmen, even if the contractor or an architect is imported from outside the community. Surviving contracts between craftsmen and client are usually phrased in accordance with mutually understood agreements of what is or is not sufficient, and are qualified by phrases like "in a workmanlike manner" or "in such a manner as agreed with my workmen."[30] In sum, rural and village architecture are based on compromise—compromise between externally introduced ideas and local patterns of expression and behavior.

Without cultural balance and coherence, buildings can become too radical, can fail to convey the message they were designed to communicate, and may even confound the social interactions they were intended to channel. The members of society who traditionally wield the bulk of economic and political power are the most resistant to those changes that they failed to anticipate or could not control. The elite possess the advantages of money and position and are the members of society who have the most to lose in the wake of change. Consequently, they rely on seemingly innovative building design and practice to conserve an established order rather than to introduce a new one. The qualities of individualism, the distancing of public and private space, the addition of ever more functionally specialized rooms within the households of southern New Castle County and elsewhere in the eastern United States are a conservative revolution designed to consolidate in housing the importance of landed and monied social power.

Throughout the eighteenth century the architectural shaping of southern New Castle County involved successive stages of building activity and resulted in an identifiably regional landscape. The development of localized construction methods (such as common rafter roofs without tie beams or purlins), the increased concern for the precise allocation of space, and the manipulation of fashionable detailing highlighting and visually directing movement within the house were not unique to the area. In New England and Virginia similar transitions have been charted from first settlement through the mid-eighteenth century.

However, regional peculiarities in detailing, construction, and styling are also apparent in southern New Castle County colonial housing. These differences reflect the way in which ideas and building techniques are traditionally practiced and learned. In ports or other communities through which settlers or itinerant craftsmen skilled in the building trades passed, the potential for innovation was different but not greater than in places generally off the beaten path.[31] The builders who shaped southern New Castle County were a mixture of locally established craftsmen, all of whom practiced their trades in much the same way. Trained through apprenticeship and influenced by style books and technical manuals, they worked within a system premised on the adaptation, rather than the exact replication, of generally understood methods to particular situations defined by the clients' desires, budgets, availability of materials, and the limitations of their own talents. As a certain way of doing things was found to be easier, cheaper, or more desirable to the client, the builders accommodated themselves to the market.

Methods of construction, for example, changed only superficially in the mid to late nineteenth century. Although balloon framing was developed in the Midwest in the second quarter of the nineteenth century, New Castle County carpenters continued to use the principles of mortise-and-tenon construction in both houses and work buildings until at least the 1890s (Fig. 6:5). Timber was no longer hewn or manually sawn, but rather trimmed and finished on mechanical up-and-down or circular saws. Wood for framing and siding was no longer produced on the farm, but shipped in from outside the county from lumber yards such as "Bond Bro. & Co." in Port Deposit, Maryland, or sold through local merchants like George Hukill of Middletown or H. G. Whitlock of Appoquinimink Hundred.

Weatherboard was also shipped in and frequently consisted only of dimension-cut milled boards instead of the beveled, rabbeted, or feather-edged sidings of the previous century. By the mid-1840s rafters were no longer joined and pinned at their apex, but nailed together either directly or with a ridge board. In the mid-nineteenth century, stud-walled partitions completely supplanted the use of vertical-board partitions. Further, these partitions were often stiffened with unusually long tension braces running diagonally from near the top of the posts at the ends of the wall to nearly a third of the length of the partition. Also, while braced frame joints remained in use, they were more frequently secured with heavy iron

Figure 6:5. House framing: Craven House, Biddles Corner vicinity, St. Georges Hundred (mid-nineteenth century). The carpentry, visible under the roof of an original ell, shows the continued use of mortise-and-tenon timber-framing techniques at least twenty years after balloon framing had been developed in the Midwest.

spikes or large nails and, in farm buildings, wrapped with iron bands, rather than pegged together with one or two wooden pins.

Log walling continued in general use for small domestic out-buildings like smokehouses and for dwellings in the poorer neighborhoods of the county. Log construction, however, also underwent some changes in the first half of the nineteenth century. Carpenters introduced unusually complicated joining techniques, such as walling in which the principal posts have dovetail cuts on opposing faces at the junction of a main wall and a partition wall (Fig. 6:6).

Brick continued as the preferred material of more affluent householders, but the textures and methods of walling changed. English bond had dropped out of general use by 1760, and common bonds had been brought into general circulation as the basic technique for building foundation and secondary walls. While the brick employed in secondary elevations remained rough and gritty, those used for the primary facade were increasingly smooth and deep red in color (Figs. 6:7 and 6:8). Manufactured in permanent commercial brickyards, these bricks were formed in water- or oil-lubricated metal molds and heavily fired. When laid up in a wall, they were tightly fitted together in running, stretcher, or garden bonds and fixed in place with a lime-paste mortar applied in extremely narrow "butter" joints. To secure the facade to the gable ends of the house, the masons created a structural quoining by extending the brickwork of the facade around the corner of the building at regular intervals (Fig. 6:7).[32]

Stone continued to be used almost exclusively for foundations, basements, and basement walling. As in the first series of building cycles prior to the 1820s, stone walling could be coursed or uncoursed rubble, cemented with thickly applied clay, sand, and lime mortars. One rare, large center-passage-plan house and its original service wings in Appoquinimink Hundred east of Townsend was built entirely of rubble stone which was stuccoed over and scored to visually convey the impression of ashlar masonry. Although found in occasional farm buildings, stone was generally unavailable for domestic building purposes, and, other than being used in foundations, it was generally limited to trim. Marble slabs were imported for door and window dressings, for mantels, and for thresholds and exterior steps (Fig. 6:8). Granite was also brought into the area for occasional paving around the house and for splash blocks at the base of rolled tin downspouts.

Figure 6:6. Post-and-plank detail: William Eliason House, Blackbird vicinity, Appoquinimink Hundred (1830–50). In the mid-1800s sawn-plank buildings continued to be raised but often using innovative applications of existing technologies. The practice of lapping the plank ends into the outer face of corner and intermediate posts combined principles of log walling with timber framing.

Figure 6:7. Pressed brick: Hall-Dunlap House, Delaware City (ca. 1830–40). This corner detail illustrates the method employed for joining a pressed-brick primary elevation to a common-bond second elevation.

Figure 6:8. Stone trim: Bank, Main Street, Odessa (mid-nineteenth century).
Imported marble and granite were used for the window trim, watertable and
foundation.

The process of rebuilding was remarkable in its total extent. Whole towns were reordered. No eighteenth-century dwelling emerged unaltered, and older farm buildings were replaced wholesale with newly designed structures. All this bespeaks a total revaluation of an environment.

Questions remain about why such a general rebuilding cycle took place. Why was there such an intensive investment in building activity? Who were the builders and who were the clients? What was the net effect of the rebuilding in social and cultural terms? The answers to these questions go a long way to making sense of a particular material legacy which we know solely through architectural, written, and archaeological sources. Beyond the scope of a single geographical area these same answers may be applied to what was a general phenomenon in the eastern United States. To evaluate the depth and significance of this change it is necessary to turn to the journalistic questions: who, where, when, how, and lastly, why.

As we have said, the individuals who commissioned the new architecture of southern New Castle County were primarily agricultural entrepreneurs controlling large tracts of the richest farmlands, which were subdivided into several independently supervised farms. Although the larger farmers were the beneficiaries of the prosperity and rebuilding, even the less affluent farmers cultivating marginal land along the lower edge of New Castle County were tied into the economy, and, although working on a lesser scale, they rebuilt their environment with much the same intensity as their wealthier counterparts. The image the gentlemen farmers presented was a paradox of high-minded reform and deeply entrenched conservatism, and it found its strongest outlet in the houses and barns they designed and contracted to be built. Household order became spatially constricted through more and more precisely defined spaces. Domestic improvement was associated with the disappearance of multifunctional rooms. Settling estates, inventory takers increasingly adopted a system by which they numbered rather than named rooms. The same sort of behavior is evident in the design and use of farmbuildings: ostensibly new, streamlined, multifunctional barns were raised only to be clustered together in the eighteenth-century tradition of a farmyard composed of many functionally segregated structures.

While farmers and landholders may have been designers using popular and easily accessible architectural guides as sources for inspiration, they were not the builders. Although there were established families working over a period of years in various construction trades, the majority of carpenters, masons, and other builders were itinerants or short-term residents. The manuscript census returns from 1850 to 1880 reveal a large influx of builders and construction workers into Red Lion and Delaware City between 1850 and 1860, as part of a large federal building project to repair and enlarge Fort Delaware on Pea Patch Island. The total building population in the southern hundreds increased 16 percent from 1850 to 1860. Some of the builders, particularly single men, boarded in local houses, but the majority show up as heads of complete households who are present for one census but gone by the next. The total population of builders declined 27 percent from 1860 to 1870 and dropped an additional 2 percent from 1870 to 1880 (Fig. 6:9). The sharp decrease in individuals employed in construction anticipates the dramatic fall in farm value recorded in the same area between 1870 and 1880. As an occupational group, the builders can be divided into two sub-groups—long- and short-term residents. For the southernmost hundreds 40 percent of the builders listed in the 1860 census show up again in 1870, by 1880 only 20 percent are still in the area.[33] Short-term resident craftsmen were more likely to be single, born outside of the state, and poorer. Long-term residents involved in the building trades tended to live in towns, own property, board their apprentices, and have sons engaged in their fathers' occupation, who set up separate households near their parents.

While it is possible to construct a general profile of individuals involved in construction, it is nearly impossible to associate names with specific projects. Richard Mansfield noted in 1829, "Settled with Robert McFarlan for Carpenters work, he and Willis having worked for me 102 day together at $1 a day," and "settled with John McFarlan for carpenter work and paid him off"; yet it is not possible to know what it was the McFarlans and Willis actually built.[34] References to the Rose family laying the brick work for the new church in Odessa do survive from the 1850s, and several other buildings are attributed to their efforts, but this represents a singular situation.

In rare cases we find builders noting their work. Three roofers in 1880 both signed and left a pencil sketch of their handiwork. William W. Rose, house carpenter and contractor in Odessa, left a note in a house he was building in 1850 and updated it in the course of repairs eight years later:

William W. Rose in closed this on November 25th 1850. On the night of the 23rd of the same month, Josiah Ridgeways dwellinghouse and storehouse & wheelwright shop was burnt down on the corner And this frame suffered from the same fier. With difficulty it was savd. I in close this that when this house is wore out the reparier will [k]now how long it was bilt. James Stevens had this house bilt. He was a Blacksmith by trad the best ax man that time.

William W. Rose was the bilder.

They said James Stevens died May the second Sunday—

1855—did not finish the house. The said house being sold by the heirs. William W. Armstrong being one of the heirs by marrage to the said Stevens daughter Addaline. The said William W. Armstrong bought the the house & lot & all the apertinance containing theretoe & fnisht the house with this portico as an addition with other improvements August in the year of 1858. The above note was deposited in the cap over the front door when the cap was removed for this portico. This with addition is deposit in this box in the seelin of the portico.[35]

A similar message to future generations was left by Robert N. Higgins in the roof of the house where he lived as a tenant:

I think it expedient to drop a few lines to those in years to come or those may read when I wil be among the ded. Whoever may find this is to give it up to the owner of this property, this roof put on Oct. 20, 1879. Carpenter John Jerrel assisted by George C. Deakyne and John Hartup, the old roof taken of was 75 years old shingles 2 feet 6 in long 6-1/2 wide made of hart sedar.[36]

What follows in Higgin's letter is a history of the property, an account of damage done by a hurricane the year before, and a list of local notables, including the postmaster and constable. Few people were as avid in their recording of local life and building activity as were Rose and Higgins. The more common sources for information on builders and their trades are tax lists and federal census returns.

Abel Isaacs, a carpenter working in Red Lion Hundred, completed the census of manufactures in 1870. During the previous year he had worked on four major building projects—a chapel, dwelling house, barn, and stable. Between contracts he spent time "jobbing"—doing small tasks such as repairs, sub-contracts, and occasional day labor. His stock of materials included oak, white pine, and hemlock, bricks, hardware, lime for mortar, stone, and wood

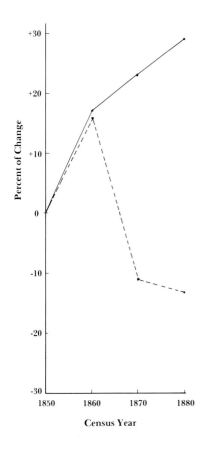

Figure 6:9. Population change in the building community of southern New Castle County compared with total population trends (1850–80). The building community is defined by individuals listing occupations such as house carpenter and brick mason. Graph: CHAE, Rebecca S. Siders.

shingles.[37] In 1867, Jacob Wells, a house carpenter living in Appo-quinimink Hundred, went to work for Samuel Townsend. Although the nature of his commission is unstated, Wells and his brother, David, worked on the project for the entire month of November. The Wells brothers had previously worked for Samuel Townsend in 1864 and 1865. Townsend recorded the 1864 project as "Money that I paid to the Wells Boys for Building a house for me . . . " at cost of $64 expended from mid-November to early January of 1865.[38]

Other carpenters and builders working in the southern New Castle County area were John Calder in Red Lion Hundred and John Hall in Delaware City.[39] Both men had been working in the community at least since 1850. John Calder was born in Maryland in 1822. He had built structures in oak and pine, had employed three men at $30 a month, and completed five houses valued at $6000 in 1870. John Hall, twenty years Calder's senior, had lived in New Jersey until he moved to Delaware around 1820. His family in 1850 was composed of his wife, daughter, and four sons, two of whom worked with their father in the building trades. The household also included two additional young carpenters—William Tucker aged twenty-two from Pennsylvania and twenty-four-year-old, Delaware-born James Holbert. Hall prospered in Delaware City, building eight frame houses with his crew of four in 1850 and acquiring substantial real estate holdings by 1860. While the Wells brothers and Abel Isaacs worked as contractors and jobbers, Hall turned to real estate and became a housing speculator, an urban counterpart of agricultural landholders such as William Wilson, George Brady, the Higgins family, and the Claytons.

An unusual glimpse into the expectations and completion of a building contract is found in Hedgelawn, built west of Middletown in 1856. In 1855 the client, John Cochran, took out a front page advertisement in the *Delaware Gazette:*

Notice to Builders and Contractors

Proposals will be received by the undersigned until the first day of March next, for Building a House of the following dimention that is to say the front building to be twenty-eight feet by forty feet with a wing sixteen feet by thirty-four feet; the whole to be twenty-eight feet to the square, and divided into three stories, with porticoes back and front extended up to the second stories with pannel collums, also a plain portico along the back building, the whole to be similar in arrangement and workmanship to the one I am now erecting on an adjoining farm, the frame to be of the best white oak and other materials of best quality to be furnished by the contractor. None need apply only such as can furnish testimonials of good character and workmanship and give good security for the faithful performance of the contract.[40]

Not only does the house specified in the advertisement survive, but the dwelling mentioned as being raised on an adjoining farm also remains standing (Fig. 6:10 and 7:23). In plan, Hedgelawn corresponds exactly to the dimensions stated by Cochran. Local history names the builders who answered Cochran's advertisement as Franklin Stevens and Lewis Miller, house carpenters living in Middletown. Both men were in their mid-twenties when they accepted the contract. Fifteen years later, by the time of the 1870 census, both were well-established members of the community, with substantial real estate holdings and a jointly owned contracting business.[41]

Forty years prior to Cochran's advertisement, Bennett Downs had undertaken the extensive remodeling of his farm in New Castle Hundred. Like S. H. Black's La Grange and Richard Mansfield's Achmester, Downs's house, begun in 1815, represents one of the earliest architectural projects associated with the renewals of the nineteenth century. A careful recordkeeper, Downs entered the cost of labor and materials in his farm account books.[42] These accounts now provide an unusual glimpse into the division of labor involved in building a house and outbuildings. First, Downs contracted with mason John Melvin, who with two assistants molded the brick from local clay, set the kiln for firing, hauled the firewood for firing the kiln, burned the brick, and laid the walls of the house. By the time Melvin had concluded the terms of his contract, he had laid 114,502 bricks and produced many more than that number in the kilns set up on Down's property. While the mason was manufacturing and laying brick, carpenters John Baly and John Rodgers were contracted to erect and finish the wooden elements in the buildings. This included work listed in June 1815 as "framing my house and covering in the house and kitchen and making winder frames and sash and shetters and makin 5 doors and curing and laying floors and partition." Baly and Rodgers were also responsible for tasks as varied as raising scaffolding for shingling the house, trimming the windows, and building beehives for the garden. In 1816 Lewes Curlet was hired to prepare the lath for plastering and finishing the interiors. By May of 1817 the new house, barn, dairy, smokehouse, kitchen, and carriage house had been completed. But, like many new houses commissioned in the early years of the rebuilding cycle, Bennett Down's dwelling was heavily remodeled in the middle decades of the nineteenth century.

Carpenters and masons were certainly not anonymous in their own time, but due to a lack of written information they have become historically removed from their commissions. For example, no specific mid-century houses in Red Lion Hundred and Delaware City can be attributed to Hall, Isaacs, or Calder. Surviving structures from the period indicate that southern New Castle County builders were on the whole well schooled and practiced in their endeavors and competitive in the completion of their contracts, particularly in the construction of elaborately framed farm buildings. Their contractual arrangements with local clients were customarily written down as well as verbally concluded on the basis of cost and labor, in a

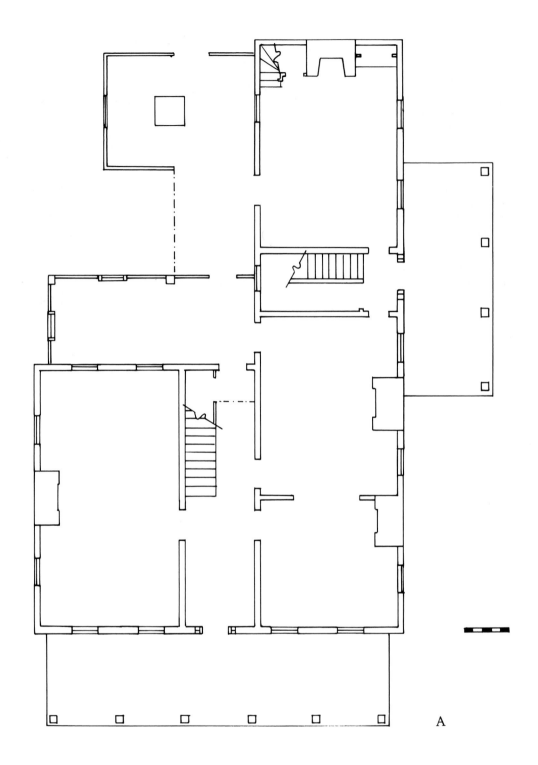

A

B

Figure 6:10. Hedgelawn and Charles Cochran House, Middletown vicinity, St. Georges Hundred (ca. 1856): (A) first-floor plan based on specifications advertised in 1855; (B) Charles Cochran House located across the road was used as the model for Hedgelawn. (See Fig. 7:23 for views of Hedgelawn.)

pattern of contractual agreement common to the Chesapeake Bay country and analogous to other communities in the eastern United States and Canada. The expectations and responsibilities of client and contractor were so much a part of the day-to-day workings of the area that information on builders appears either as an incidental accounting, litigation over a failure in services or payment, or in the terms of a multiple-party contract such as that for a church or public building.

The where and when of the rebuilding are intimately bound together by the nature of building as a temporally specific action. The rebuilding history of southern New Castle County was uniform throughout the area in its degree of pervasiveness and its extended time frame of 1820 to 1890, with the concentration of activity taking place from 1830 to 1860. The first phase of rebuilding began in the 1820s and focused primarily on enlarging dwellings located along the eastern coastal fringe, the region neighborhood in which the most substantial and elaborate houses had been built. By the mid 1830s building projects were more frequently fresh starts and were concentrated in the inland reaches, especially in the wheat belt around Middletown. By the 1860s most activity concentrated in the towns.

Farm buildings were rebuilt and replaced in a much more general pattern. Beginning in the 1830s crib barns and bank barns were introduced as utilitarian and technologically stylish buildings, along with new designs for stables, cart sheds, and granaries. The most popularly accepted farm building came to be the crib barn or granary, with examples built continuously to the close of the nineteenth century throughout the entire district. While significant innovations in size and construction details can be documented, the form and proportional division of space remained consistent. Similarly designed stables achieved the same general circulation, with the arrangements of a large hay loft over box stalls in a pattern not too far removed from eighteenth-century hay and livestock barns. Like crib barns and stables, bank barns were built throughout the area. As a major expenditure in capital they could be afforded by only a few and, where built, they typically underutilized their functional and spatial potential. The bank barns also appear to be the most stylized of agricultural buildings, with several bearing close resemblance to plates published in farming manuals and journals.

The third focus of rebuilding was in the towns and villages that dotted the countryside. Only one of the villages founded in the eighteenth century was laid out in a geometrical grid plan, but by the second quarter of the nineteenth century this tightly organized urban format was laid over existing line towns such as Odessa and Middletown and was used in planning new villages like Delaware City and Townsend. At the same time the introduction of steam power freed rural industries of their reliance on wind, tide, and flowing water. Although several grist and flour mills continued to grind for a local clientele, the majority of local industries and businesses relocated in railroad and canal-oriented towns.

How all of these changes were accomplished is explained by the increased economic capital, the presence of a skilled and competitive pool of local builders, and the emergence of southern New Castle County as an urban-oriented agrarian community. The agricultural wealth of southern New Castle County was extracted from its fertile farmlands and enhanced through its strategic marketing location in relation to large urban centers. Income from agricultural pursuits was substantially bolstered by aggressive land speculation. The presence of a large population of builders provided an extensive skilled-labor pool to which prospective clients had ready access.

Why the architectural landscape of southern New Castle County was rebuilt when and as it was is the most difficult question to answer. We have examined the surface historical character of a particular time and place, and now turn to investigate the actual buildings.

The values the new houses and barns expressed are paradoxical. Dwellings became larger, incorporating more and more specific functions within their walls; but in spite of the increase in space, social and domestic movement became progressively more congested as room use was more narrowly defined. Agricultural buildings were designed and built to streamline and industrialize the production of the farm, but those who commissioned their construction underutilized the new forms, retaining an allegiance instead to the old way of doing things. The drive was to build anew and to architecturally restructure the relationships between man and the land and between the members of the society. The language used by the movement's proponents to describe the process was reform minded, innovative, and progressive. However, the reality they built on the land was the entrenchment and celebration of the way things had already come to be.

7. New Houses

AT THE CLOSE OF THE EIGHTEENTH CENTURY the typical farm-house and village dwelling stood as separate structures un-encumbered with kitchens, food storage areas, or specially desig-nated servants' quarters. All of the working functions associated with the house were nearby in a number of lesser, free-standing buildings. By the time of the 1816 tax assessment though, the first step had been taken toward physically enlarging the house to incor-porate a number of these functions under one roof. Among the earliest surviving dated examples of this process is David Wilson's house in Odessa (Fig. 7:1). This 1769 house was enlarged in 1816 with a brick ell attached to the rear of the main block. The wing added a number of new spaces to the overall plan of the house, including an office or day room, kitchen, smokehouse, and upper-story chambers for both family members and servants. The origi-nal block remained much as it was—a central stair passage flanked by a dining room and parlor on the first floor and second-story bed-chambers above.

The Wilson House expresses the deliberate moves involved in the elaboration and diversification of interior space. Evidence that this pattern of spatial reordering was at first the concern of those who owned the least traditional houses is also found in the Corbit House built in the 1770s. The basement kitchen under the south-west corner office was annexed as part of a rear ell, possibly as early as the 1790s.[1] Similar service wings appeared on other existing houses throughout the area in the 1820s and 1830s, although some structures did not receive them until as late as 1850.

The enlargement of household space was not confined to the addition of rear ells and gable-end service wings. Just as the Huguenot House, begun in the mid-eighteenth century, had been expanded into a center-passage plan within a few years of its first construction, other dwellings began to receive substantial additions to living spaces in the second quarter of the nineteenth century. Geraldsville was increased from a one-room-deep, side-passage plan to a center-passage plan in 1822, and the Christopher Vandergrift House was extended in the same manner from a one-room-plan house prior to 1818. To better understand the nature and significance of these additions at the outset of the rebuilding period, it is best to examine the growth of several of these houses from their original appearance through the 1800s.

Begun in the third quarter of the eighteenth century, Geraldsville started as a two-story, side-passage-plan brick dwelling (Fig. 7:2). With its Flemish bond facade, unheated stair passage, and paneled hearth walls in the two main rooms, the house stood independent from service support structures. In 1822 a gable-end addition, ornamented on the interior with punch-and-gouge-work mantels and chair rails, transformed the house into a center-passage plan; shortly after that, a service wing was added on to the rear elevation of the original block. During the next few decades the service wing was extended with additional wings. By 1850 Geraldsville had evolved from a separate mansion house into a large house with a number of specialized rooms for cooking, storage, and lodging for resident fieldhands and servants. Throughout its nineteenth-century history, Geraldsville displayed a dual emphasis: a dramatic increase in the number of rooms in the house, and a growing sense of functional specificity in designated room use. The number of spaces and their purpose did not describe a larger house so much as a type of dwelling fundamentally different in its organization and orientation. As will be seen, more rooms came to signify more narrowly defined settings for functional and social interaction and consequently conceptually smaller spaces.

The degree to which these changes could be carried out was often quite extensive, and on occasion they swallowed the original building. In several instances rebuildings of an extant structure were so complete that little evidence remained of the origin and physical appearance of the first house. About 1750 Christopher Vandergrift erected a one-story, sawn-plank house. Fifty years later the house received a two-story, side-passage frame addition, which was created by moving an already standing structure up to the gable end of the old house (Fig. 7:3).[2] Between 1825 and 1900, in a succession of

Figure 7:1. Service wing: Wilson House, Main Street, Odessa (1816).

additions and alterations, the plank core was raised to two full stories in frame, the old common room hearth was partially closed down several times to make a parlor fireplace, the exposed ceiling beams were covered with lath and plaster, a shed was added and then removed, twenty feet were added to the remaining original gable end for a two-story frame wing, a bay window augmented a third wall of the plank core, a lean-to summer kitchen was added, and a porch was thrown up on three sides of the structure.

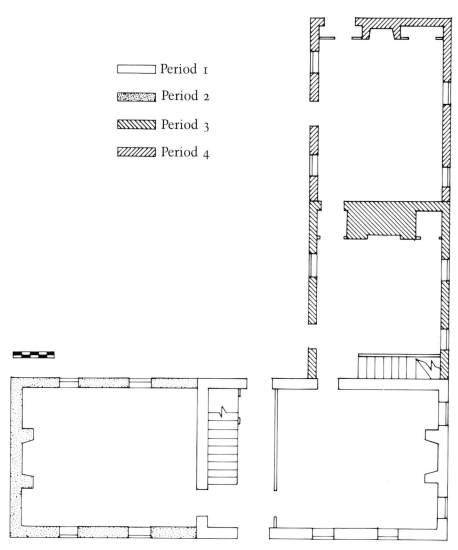

Figure 7:2. Geraldsville, McDonough vicinity, St. Georges Hundred (mid-eighteenth century, plus three phases of nineteenth-century additions).

Equally complex are the histories of McDonough House and George Brady's Greenlawn. From shortly after its construction in the second quarter of the eighteenth century as a brick, two-story chambered-hall structure, the McDonough House possessed a wood, one-story, gable-end addition (Fig. 7:4). By the 1830s, however, the wing had been pulled down and a new two-story, frame one put up in its place. This produced an awkwardly balanced, center-passage-plan dwelling of brick and timber construction, with the dif-

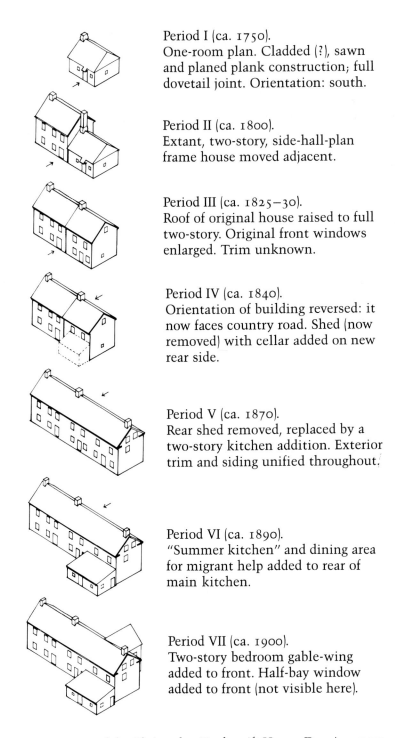

Period I (ca. 1750).
One-room plan. Cladded (?), sawn and planed plank construction; full dovetail joint. Orientation: south.

Period II (ca. 1800).
Extant, two-story, side-hall-plan frame house moved adjacent.

Period III (ca. 1825–30).
Roof of original house raised to full two-story. Original front windows enlarged. Trim unknown.

Period IV (ca. 1840).
Orientation of building reversed: it now faces country road. Shed (now removed) with cellar added on new rear side.

Period V (ca. 1870).
Rear shed removed, replaced by a two-story kitchen addition. Exterior trim and siding unified throughout.

Period VI (ca. 1890).
"Summer kitchen" and dining area for migrant help added to rear of main kitchen.

Period VII (ca. 1900).
Two-story bedroom gable-wing added to front. Half-bay window added to front (not visible here).

Figure 7:3. History of the Christopher Vandergrift House. Drawing: HABS, Charles Bergengren.

Figure 7:4. The Trap, primary elevation. The core of this dwelling was a chambered-hall plan that was reworked through at least four mid-nineteenth-century additions.

ferences in building materials partially concealed by heavy coats of whitewash. In order to even up the elevation of the two units, the roof of the original brick house was raised almost a foot at the cornice line, and a false gable was extended to the rear of the frame wing to create the appearance of symmetry. As service functions were pulled into the house in the mid-nineteenth century, a series of smaller, two-story frame wings were erected against the rear and gable walls of the frame addition. By the 1860s the metamorphosis of the house was complete. All the eighteenth-century, ground-floor fireplace paneling and the original stairs had been replaced with stylish, heavily molded, mid-nineteenth-century trim. The original door opening had been filled with brick, and the attic had been provided with a dormer window and lath-and-plaster walls, converting it to an unheated bedchamber.

The transformations wrought on the McDonough and Vandergrift houses all but concealed the first period buildings. The cumulative additions radically enlarged the domestic space and dramatically changed the very way in which each eighteenth-century house had functioned. At Greenlawn, located near Middletown, the increase in available interior space paralleled that of its neighbors, but the emphasis on redecoration surpassed them both (Fig. 7:5). An unusually large house when built in 1810, Greenlawn's center-passage plan rose a full two stories. The house received a two-story service wing in the 1830s, producing a structure not unlike the David Wilson house. Except for minor changes, Greenlawn remained unaltered until acquired by the Brady family in the 1860s. First William Brady in the 1860s and then George Brady in the 1880s enlarged the house with multiple wings and added a whole new set of domestic outbuildings, including a stable and combination privy-woodshed-smokehouse; then came a full-length rear addition, a conservatory, formal Victorian gardens, and a complete refurbishing of the house inside and out. The changes made were inspired in part by the many popular architectural guides. Authors of these guides proposed buildings designed in accordance with a "natural," or picturesque, aesthetic coupled with concerns about utility, domestic order, and a healthful atmosphere.[3] Yet in their evocation of a natural architectural order they did not deal with nature as a natural state but as a medium susceptible to manipulation. Just as the growing acceptance of center-passage plans set a course toward the spatial control of social relationships, the dwellings and grounds based

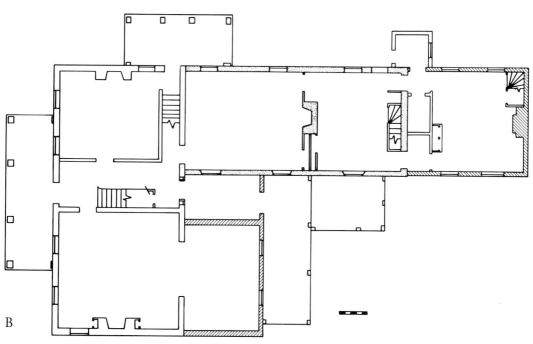

Figure 7:5. Greenlawn. (A) South gable elevation; (B) first-floor plan, both showing the progression of additions from the rear of the ca. 1810 core.

A

Figure 7:6. "How to remodel an old house," (A) The Old House; (B) The Old House Remodeled. From George E. Woodward, *Woodward's Cottages and Farmhouses.*

upon Victorian America's written sources extended the sphere of control beyond the house itself to include the thoughtful manipulation of the overall setting.[4]

Greenlawn epitomized the nineteenth-century approach to architectural renewals. Methods for the enlargement, reornamentation, and landscaping of older houses had been advanced as modernization "in a tasteful manner" (Fig. 7:6).[5] George Brady pursued such methods at Greenlawn to the fullest extent, building a cross-gable addition, porches, a solarium, and a rooftop observation deck. He surrounded the dwelling with beds of day lilies, lilies of the valley, irises, daffodils, and ornamental grasses, as well as with what seemed to be randomly placed clusters of boxwood, ornamental cherries, evergreens, and shade trees. The whole effect—from the moment one entered the yard through a sawn-work picket gate flanked by boxed posts that supported cast-iron urns—was not of naturalness but of contrivance. The intricately arranged expanse of garden, the picturesque detailing, and the neatly finished outbuild-

ings did not summon up images of the natural world, but celebrated instead man's ability to control nature.

Few rebuilt houses display their remodelers' eager embrace of architectural fashion and unrestrained ambition to achieve it to the extent that Greenlawn does. More typical of rebuilding efforts were the changes made at a tenant house near Blackbird Landing, which the Corbit family acquired in the mid-nineteenth century (Fig. 7:7). Begun in the eighteenth century as a hall or hall-parlor-plan log dwelling, the house was enlarged in the second quarter of the nineteenth century with a substantial one-room-plan, weatherboarded frame wing, finished on the interior with a mantel, boxed-in stair, and lath-and-plaster walls and ceilings. The corner posts jutting into the room were encased with beaded boards, and the small fireplace fitted with a wrought-iron crane. By the close of the century, however, the original house had been demolished and replaced with a two-story, frame, Gothic revival farmhouse, which was attached to the gable end of the frame addition. Using materials such as beaded

Figure 7:7. Corbit Tenant House, Blackbird Landing vicinity, Appoquinimink Hundred. The present house is composed of a ca. 1830 addition (left) and the later nineteenth-century replacement of the original structure (right), connected by a small passage that reused timbers from the original dwelling.

ceiling beams salvaged from the earlier log house, the two frame units were linked together with a short corridor and pantry. The pattern of additions and alterations seen in this house was repeated again and again across southern New Castle County (Fig. 7:8).

A different sort of undertaking was the remodeling of Fairview near Delaware City (Fig. 7:9). Anthony Madison Higgins, a progressive farmer associated with the agricultural reform movement, built Fairview as a two-story, center-passage-plan brick farmhouse in 1822. As the house passed through the family it was gradually modified until it came into possession of Higgins's grandson in the 1880s. In 1885 John Clark Higgins, "a gentleman farmer, importer and breeder of Guernsey cattle, and leader of the Delaware Grange," commissioned Philadelphia architect Frank Furness to redesign the house.[6] The changes all but engulfed the original dwelling: a new attic story, a front porch, and extensive service wings, with secondary upstairs chambers.

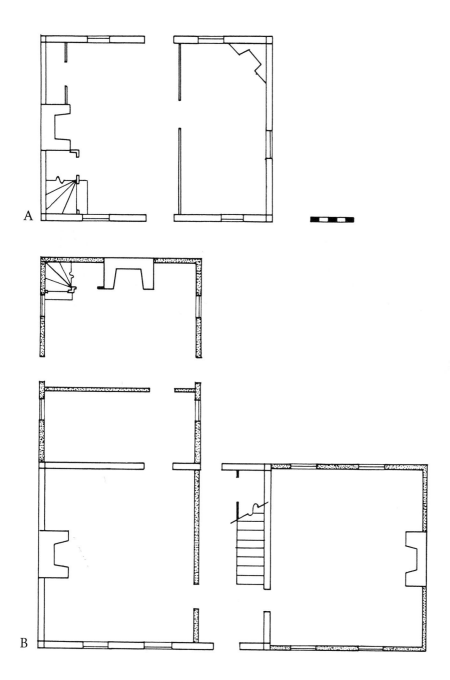

Figure 7:8. C.J. Biggs House, Summit vicinity, Pencader Hundred (late eighteenth century, with additions). (A) First-floor plan as originally built; (B) first-
floor plan as enlarged, ca. 1850. Begun as a one-and-a-half story, log, hall-parlor-
plan house, Biggs House was extended up and out into a two-story, center-
passage plan, with attached service wing.

A

Few of those caught up in rebuilding activities engaged the services of an architect; most worked out their own designs from the pages of popular architectural guides and from local precedent. Houses remodeled through additions, overlays of stylistic elements, and landscaping constituted only a portion of the rebuilding activity. By the 1830s a general movement toward rebuilding the housing stock from the ground up was well underway. The advent of new building emphasizes the perceived non-utility of existing architecture in an area where a substantial, durable dwelling stock already existed (Fig. 7:10). Scores of new houses were begun and completed, and the houses they replaced were abandoned, demolished for materials, or temporarily converted to other uses, only to be vacated in favor of more sophisticated and utilitarian structures (Fig. 7:11). Some of the earlier buildings were undoubtedly recycled as tenant houses, but by the 1840s even that housing was being rapidly improved through a process of total replacement.

Tenant houses fell into two basic qualitative categories: those

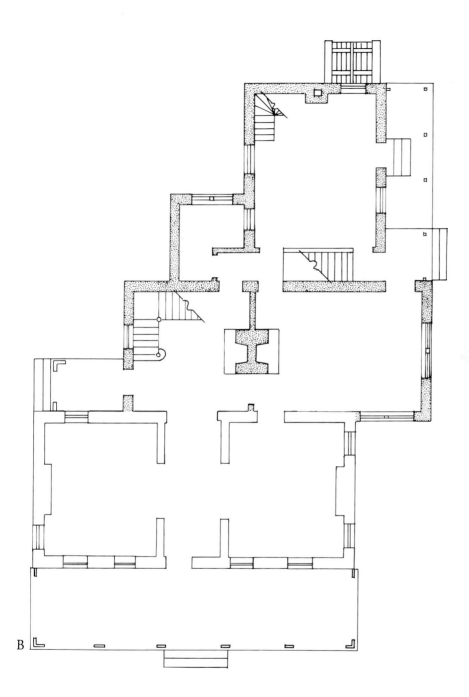

B

Figure 7:9. Fairview (Anthony Higgins House), Delaware City vicinity, Red Lion Hundred (1822, with 1885 additions by Frank Furness): (A) remodeled facade of the 1822 house; (B) first-floor plan, based on the Furness drawings. Drawing: CHAE, William Macintire.

A

Figure 7:10. New houses of the mid 1800s. (A) W.M. Houston House, Mount Pleasant vicinity, St. Georges Hundred (1840–50); (B) Armstrong-Walker House, Armstrong Corner vicinity, St. Georges Hundred (ca. 1870).

provided for farm managers and those for resident laborers. The former were structures typical of the middle range of available housing. Examples such as William Wilson's tenant houses Mayfield and Middlesex are two-story, stair-passage-plan brick dwellings with attached service wings (Fig. 7:12). On the interior they were finished with mantels, baseboards, and other trim generally similar to that in Wilson's house. Laborers typically were provided with smaller, less stylish residences. One of the last surviving examples (recently destroyed) of this dwelling class stood across the road from Cochran Grange, with which it was associated, just west of Middletown. Built as one unit in a row of four, it was a one-and-a-half-story, one-room-plan frame house with a gable-end lean-to against the hearth wall. In form, setting, and construction it was similar to the best single-family quarters provided for slaves and, in some cases, over-

B

seers, on the large antebellum farms located further south on the Delmarva Peninsula and the western shore of the Chesapeake Bay.

Both types of tenant housing could and did coexist on a single farm and occasionally were not far from the main house. At George Brady's Greenlawn there were three: the "mansion house," the "cottage," and the "farmhouse."[7] With its cruciform plan and Gothic detailing the farmhouse (Fig. 7:13) reflected the stylistic concerns found in the main dwelling, but in social terms it was of the same class as Wilson's tenant farmers' houses. The economic arrangements between Brady and his tenants were those of a general sharecropping system using a five-field rotation. The farmer made the basic agricultural decisions, often in consultation with the landlord, and worked the land on halves, putting up labor on his part while the owner supplied both material and capital. Architecturally,

A

B

Figure 7:11. Building materials from pre-1820 buildings reused in mid-nine-teenth-century agricultural buildings. (A) Wheatland granary, Claytons Corner vicinity, St. Georges Hundred, showing hewn corner posts reused as floor joists; (B) Mailley granary, Odessa vicinity, St. Georges Hundred, with crib flooring supported on recycled beaded-edged ceiling joists.

the power imparted to the owner by possession of land, and money in the case of Greenlawn, worked itself out in the stratification of three classes of housing. On most farms, however, the pattern of occupancy was one whereby either the landholder or a tenant resided in a main house, with laborers' dwellings located behind the primary residence or in the back fields. The arrangements between tenant and landholder were not always harmonious. The Wilson brothers of Pencader Hundred had difficulty in getting unsatisfactory tenants off their land in 1874. In a letter to his brother, William Wilson noted his plans for the farm:

> I want the place a year so that I can fence it, I want to put up a porch, a corn crib, a hen house, a yard, and garden. I also want to whitewash and paint some. I wish to make the place fit for a respectable tenant. I will not spend one cent on the place while Hudsons live there.[8]

William Wilson concluded by asking his brother to quickly obtain some fire insurance for the structure.

The houses begun from the ground up in the rebuilding period included the same spaces, construction methods, and ornamentation as their remodeled counterparts. Their facades almost invariably paralleled the roads that ran in front of them, and they were always set back in a yard defined by fences and planted with ornamental trees, shrubs, and flowers. The earliest new houses often continued construction and formal traditions identified in the best rural residences of the preceding century and, as a consequence, were susceptible to extensive additions and other modifications within a decade of their completion. Later structures, however, were erected in a single piece, with all domestic service functions conceived and perceived as integral parts of the whole house. In both instances their designs and execution were compatible with what was occurring generally throughout the region.

Among the earliest buildings associated with the rebuilding of southern New Castle County was Samuel H. Black's La Grange, erected in 1815. Raised in a single build, La Grange incorporated most of the domestic functions characteristic of larger dwellings built thirty years later. Black, who commissioned the house, used the farm as a proving ground for his theories on improved agriculture. The design of his house reflected the same mixture of social conservatism and reform-oriented thinking that Black shared with

A

Figure 7:12. William Wilson's tenant houses. (A) Middlesex, main elevation with original attached kitchen wing; (B) Mayfield, first-floor plan. Both houses date to the 1840s and are located in Appoquinimink Hundred near Middletown. Drawing: DSA, William Butler.

many of his wealthy landholding neighbors. He died about a decade later, leaving the property for his nine children:

> The Mantion Farm having erected thereon a large brick Dwelling, a kitchen, Smoke house &c. also of Brick and in good repair; a Frame stable, Carriage House, &c. in tolerable repair, also a tenant House of log, a Frame Barn, Stables, &c. in tolerable repair, also a large apple orchard of thrifty trees, a small peach orchard on the decline and fencing in tolerable order.[9]

A watercolor dated 1817 vividly illustrates the house set in a yard formally planted with trees and furnished with small frame outbuildings (Fig. 7:14).

Like his affluent contemporaries, Black built in brick on a center-stair-passage plan and embellished the interior with carved mantels and paneled cupboards. The house presents the notion of a front and back separation that came to dominate nineteenth-century architecture. The front of the house, facing the road leading west from

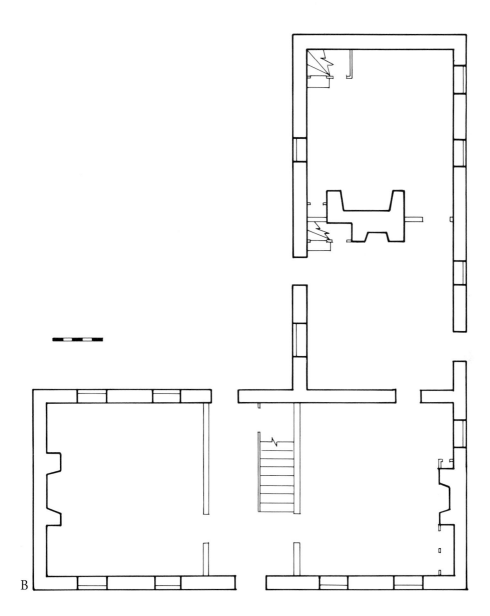

Glasgow and amidst a shady park, was composed of the balanced, five-bay, central entry arrangement that had achieved general circulation by the late 1700s. The central-passage plan, with parlor to one side and dining room to the other, was the formal idiom clung to by those who could afford the social distance they had purchased as part of the emerging agrarian class structure. What is particularly significant about La Grange is what Black attached to the rear of the

Figure 7:13. Greenlawn farm manager's house, Middletown vicinity, St. Georges Hundred (ca. 1870–80).

house. Behind the dining-room wall was a small buttery, or cold room, ventilated with louvered windows and above which was a smokehouse. At the opposite side of the house, behind the parlor, were two smaller rooms one of which was fitted out with book-shelves and served as Black's study. Between the two wings was an area enclosed with brick and frame which may have been either an enclosed porch or the kitchen.

The division of household space and principles of symmetrical design incorporated into La Grange may have been derived from books in Black's library. One of these, William Cobbett's *An Epitome of Mr. Forsyth's Treatise on the Culture and Management of Fruit Trees*, concluded with notes and illustrations for the construction of suitable country dwellings.[10] Cobbett defines farmhouses as fundamentally different from urban residences and claims city dwellings were built for the excesses of city life. Architecturally, these excesses were conveyed by multistoried houses with balanced facades and broad stair halls, which, according to Cobbett, had become the model for the "farmer's modern country house" (Fig. 7:15). The writer's ideal country house, was one story and incorporated

Figure 7:14. La Grange, Glasgow vicinity, Pencader Hundred (ca. 1815). The watercolor view of La Grange painted in 1817 shows the house as completed by S.H. Black. Of note are the post-and-rail fences, garden house, and granary behind the house (see Fig. 8:5).

most domestic functions under a common roof. Black and his contemporaries selectively used both ideas: house fronts built for show, the backs for convenience and service.

The dwelling plan Black pioneered in 1815 provided a house form compatible with an agrarian philosophy based on the intrinsic value of *arable land.* This spatially integrated concept came to characterize local house design for the next generation. The ambitions advanced by the founders of New Castle County's agricultural society contained several key elements: the realization of an estate, improving agricultural practices through scientific methods, and maximizing production and profit through the fullest possible use of available resources. These concerns encapsulated a view of self and society that found expression in architectural terms: the ordering of class distinctions within community, the compartmentalization of household functions, and the gradual wedding of regional and national identity. The architecture of Black's house conveyed the budding ambitions of the generations to come; the facade of his estate expressed a carefully regulated balance and a social retreat.

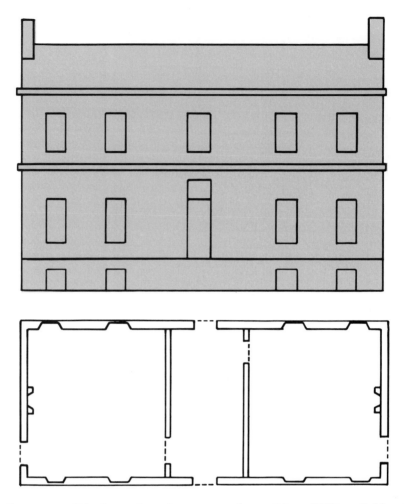

Figure 7:15. "The farmer's modern country house," from William Cobbett's *Epitome*. These designs were used by Cobbett to illustrate the antithesis of his view of the appropriate farmhouse.

Behind that facade the house stood as a machine designed to regulate domestic order. Each household function was connected to another. The synthesis of space repudiated older, but still prevalent, ideas in which space was organized around figurative unities but literal separations.

The social and domestic implications of La Grange did not flash over the lower hundreds. Only in the late 1830s did newly built dwellings that incorporated all service rooms and living spaces under a single roof make their appearance. The Cann House and Store (ca. 1830) in Glasgow was built as a four-room-plan dwelling, plus an adjacent store and kitchen (Fig. 7:16). Similarly Monterey (ca. 1855), near the village of McDonough, Hedgelawn (1856), west of Middletown, and Woodlawn (ca. 1850), west of Odessa—all products of a single build—included servants' quarters, domestic work rooms, and kitchens under one roof as part of their original plan. Other owners developed their houses in a more piecemeal fashion, but achieved in the end the same formal arrangement as at La Grange and its later counterparts. Situated within sight of one another, on opposite sides of the road running from Odessa west to Armstrong Corner, were Achmester and Muddy Branch. Built by Richard Mansfield shortly after his purchase of the farm in 1819, Achmester began as a timber-framed, center-passage, one-room-deep house, finished on the interior with late federal period mantels, ornamental plaster work, and an open string stair (Fig. 7:17). Within five to ten years Mansfield extended the house by adding a one-story frame wing containing a chamber and dining room downstairs and one or two finished chambers in the attic. By 1840 he had extended the house yet again with a one-story frame ell that housed a kitchen and servants' quarters overhead. The final enlargements came in the years prior to Mansfield's death in 1846—a pantry and new stairs to the loft were added at the gable end of the kitchen wing. In his farm accounts, Mansfield noted the arrival and departure of workmen for these building projects but never specified the actual buildings on which they worked.[11] By 1850 the house was surrounded by an expanse of lawn enclosed by a white picket fence with an entry gate of Mansfield's own design (Fig. 7:18).[12] Towering over the property were poplar and cedar trees—one of which has survived to the present. Later in the century Victorian trim was applied, and the two ground-floor mantels were replaced. The house had a range of whitewashed service buildings including a pyramidal roofed smokehouse constructed of logs tenoned into corner posts and covered with board-and-batten siding. In sum, at Achmester, Mansfield had created the farmer's estate as promoted by S. H. Black.

Following Mansfield's death in 1846 the assessors made a detailed inventory of the house.[13] The ground floor had five rooms and a storeroom, and each of these rooms had specific functions. The dining room contained a dozen Windsor chairs, a three-pedestal dining table, and Mansfield's personal library, which included a run of the popular *Niles' Weekly Register*. With such a furnishing schedule, the dining room/library served dual purpose as the room used

A

for formal dining and for the display of current periodicals and books. The other rooms were defined with similar clarity: a ground-floor chamber contained a dressing glass, chamber chairs, bureau, and washstand; the kitchen held a cook stove, utensils, two washing machines, and a lye stand. The large parlor was outfitted primarily with two card tables and a mahogany table as a space for entertaining guests. The small parlor, located on the opposite side of the entry passage toward the dining room, was furnished more as a day room and office, and had a sideboard, workstand, another dozen Windsor chairs, and a sofa. The storeroom, located at the far end of the service ell, stored the best china—Mansfield's 135-piece "Blue Dining Set"—linens, new rag carpets, curtains and assorted baskets and surplus furniture. Given the precise groupings of objects throughout the house, coupled with particular room designations, it is apparent that Mansfield had accommodated himself and his household's structure to the proliferation of domestic spaces identified with the general rebuilding process. By way of contrast we can look back to the David Stewart inventory, taken a full generation earlier, which makes it clear that the bulk of household activity occurred in a

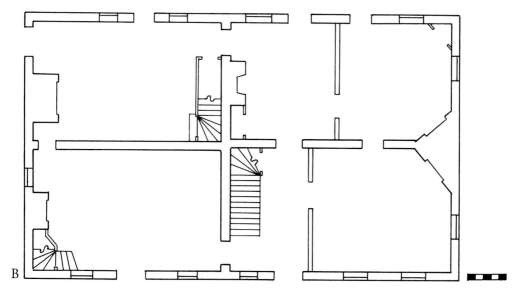

Figure 7:16. Cann House and Store, Glasgow vicinity, Pencader Hundred (ca. 1830); (A) primary elevation with the residence to the right; (B) first floor plan.

single upstairs room designated as a chamber but used as a common room, even though it was surrounded by a series of rooms all of which bore specific names but, as the inventory indicates, lacked distinct functions.[14]

Down the road from Achmester and across a broad expanse of intervening fields and hedgerows stood Muddy Branch, begun around 1830 by the Cochran family (Fig. 7:19). The Cochrans commissioned numerous buildings through the mid-nineteenth century, and several of their family dwellings and farm complexes remain standing in St. Georges and Appoquinimink hundreds. Muddy Branch, like Achmester or any number of other dwellings erected and modified through the period, provides an encapsulated view of the overall process of architectural renewal. The first block of the house was raised in frame as a two-story, five-bay, center-door facade, belying the presence of a hall-parlor plan that lacked a stair passage of any sort. Still, this hall-parlor arrangement was hardly cast in the old image of a general-purpose common room; it centered instead around a newer notion of a parlor and dining room such as that reflected in the David Ross inventory taken in 1818 and

A

Figure 7:17. Achmester, Armstrong Corner vicinity, St. Georges Hundred (ca. 1820 with addition): (A) primary elevation; (B) first-floor plan. Photograph: HABS, David L. Ames.

in the larger houses of the early eighteenth century.[15] Both ground-floor rooms and the second-floor chambers were finished with late federal period mantels. The main room had grained chimney cup-boards, and both rooms had a corner winder stair leading to the upstairs chambers. Around 1855 a major two-story addition was made to the west end of the original house. Built of braced frame construction sheathed with plain weatherboard, the wing contained a stair passage running the full depth of the house and an elaborately finished parlor of substantial size. Overhead, the wing contained two additional chambers and above that a finished attic.

The interior detailing of the wing, with the exception of a man-telpiece, remained intact until its demolition in 1981. The walls of the parlor were covered with a steel-roll-engraved wallpaper with diamond-shaped lozenges containing sepia colored impressions of wildflowers tied into tiny floral sprays. The ceiling was stenciled with pastel colored panels of blue, green, and pink trimmed with geometrically stylized flowers and abstract designs. A molded plas-ter cornice provided a transition from ceiling to wall decorations, with stenciled trails of vines tracing the flat surfaces of the moldings

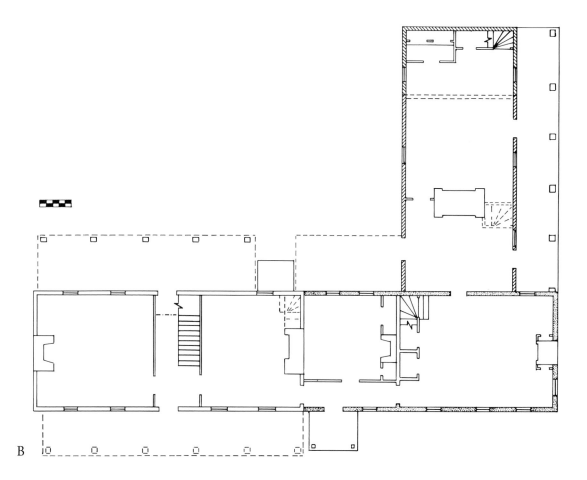

B

and the whole underlined with a brown embossed paper trim (Fig. 7:20). In the center of the parlor ceiling a large, gilded, cast-plaster medallion provided the point for the suspension of a chandelier. Similarly stenciled but less ornate designs covered the border of the stair-passage ceilings and continued to the second-floor landing. The lavish trim and detailing was not unique to Muddy Branch, but a century later it contained the least altered example of such ephemeral interior ornamentation. (A small house built in 1850 on a side-passage, single-pile plan on Congress Street in Port Penn possessed a parlor with a stenciled and freehand painted ceiling and cornice, stenciled trim, a compass motif in the center of the ceiling, and, in two opposing corners, cartouches depicting a pastoral sunset in a mountain valley and a sailing scene on a broad river.) Although cast plaster trim is still in place in houses such as Monterey, Green-lawn, The Maples, and at Marldale (Fig. 7:21), in most houses it was

Figure 7:18. Achmester in the mid-nineteenth century, from a painting completed shortly after Richard Mansfield's death. Collection of Henry Vaughan.

confined to cornices, ceiling medallions and corner blocks of doors and windows.

As the new parlor was grafted onto Muddy Branch circa 1855, a one-room, two-story service wing was added to the other end of the original core. The renovated dwelling had a long facade fronted with broad flat-roofed porches and a multitude of interior spaces, ranging from a kitchen at one end to a formal parlor at the other. Still, Muddy Branch, with all of its additions, did not satisfy its owners, and around 1860 they commissioned a second house, Okolona, directly across the road (Fig. 7:22). In Okolona all the rooms and attendant functions added to Muddy Branch over a generation were created in a single build.

The Cochrans, who commissioned Muddy Branch and Okolona were just one branch of a family of ambitious builders. The principal Cochran family dwellings were clustered within site of each other just west of Middletown. All dating from the middle decades of the nineteenth century (Fig. 7:23). Cochran Grange (1840), Hedgelawn (1856) Summerton (ca. 1850) and the Charles Cochran House (1855) were raised as elaborate two- and three-story mansions incorporating the full range of service, everyday, and formal rooms under one roof. Each was set in a carefully landscaped

A

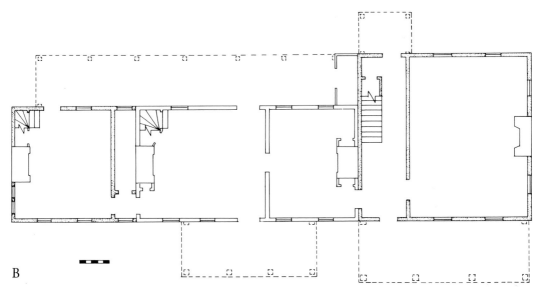

B

Figure 7:19. Muddy Branch, Armstrong Corner vicinity, St. Georges Hundred (ca. 1830, with 1850s additions): (A) primary elevation; (B) first-floor plan. The original hall-parlor-plan house occupies the middle five bays. The additions made in the 1850s include the service wing to the left and the parlor and stair passage to the right.

Figure 7:20. Muddy Branch, interior detail. In this detail of the doorway leading from the parlor to the stair passage, note the classically inspired trim, printed wallpaper, and stenciled plaster cornice.

yard—frequently bordered with a cast-iron fence and gate—and accompanied by ancillary household support buildings, including privies, woodsheds, smokehouses, and milkhouses. Behind the houses stood neatly ranked ranges or open courts of farm building complexes: crib barns, cattle barns, granaries, stables, and threshing barns.

Family settlements like the Cochrans' also appeared elsewhere in the county. The members of the Clayton family built, improved, and occupied farms around a crossroads in northwestern St. Georges Hundred that became known locally as Claytons Corners. The Bradys, who remodeled Greenlawn and owned other farms, lived in some of the finest brick houses, including Weston in St. Georges Hundred and Marldale in Red Lion Hundred. William Wilson, who occupied a farm in western Appoquinimink Hundred, spent considerable money buying up neighboring farms and commissioning two-story brick houses for his farm managers. In the less affluent areas of Blackbird and Appoquinimink hundreds, families like the Deakynes founded communities that were built with log and frame houses.

The houses occupied by the Claytons in the vicinity of Claytons Corners provide an index to several key aspects of the rebuilding process in southern New Castle County (Fig. 7:24). Each of the dwellings, whether for a family member, a farm manager, or tenant farmer, presented the same general five-bay facade to the road. These stately and balanced, center-door elevations announced the center stair-passage entries, balanced on either side with formal parlors, sitting rooms, and dining rooms. Behind these rooms in each house stretched a long service ell terminating in a kitchen or servants' quarters. The lane that led to the front of each house swerved around to the side of the wing and offered access to a progression of less ornate entries, each penetrating a different living area of the dwelling. Behind each house were the farm support buildings, beginning with those most directly related to functions inside the house and ending at the back of the farm lot with the larger barns. At Woodside (Fig. 7:24B), for example, the house faced the public lane through a carefully planted yard. As the private lane ran beside and behind the house, it passed the house and kitchen, then went between the cartsheds, stables, and granary, and finally out to the main barn with its ramped, gable-end entry. The porches which fed into the interior of the house became similarly less ornate from

A

the front to the rear of the dwelling. The Claytons were just one of many families to follow this pattern of building, as we will see later in the discussion of farm plans and agricultural buildings.

As an extended family complex, the Claytons Corners area manifests intriguing patterns as to whose farms were especially named and just who determined the architecture lived in by the average rural family. On Beers's 1868 atlas, only those farms occupied by actual members of the great families were labeled by name. For the Claytons this meant Woodside, Choptank, Choptank-Upon-the-Hill, and East Choptank. These four farms were not the whole of the Claytons' architectural projects, but they were the family seats, and thus symbols of the family's role in that locale. But the Claytons had another role, which the map does not reveal; they and others of their economic class were responsible for commissioning much of the farm architecture during the period of nine-

B

Figure 7:21. Cast plaster ceiling ornaments. (A) Ceiling medallion, Weston, first-floor parlor (ca. 1855); (B) parlor cornice, Monterey, McDonough vicinity, St. Georges Hundred (ca. 1855). Monterey photograph: HABS, David L. Ames.

teenth-century rebuilding. They are representatives of that minority of the total taxable population who possessed most of the arable land. Their financial means and their business ambitions produced the tenant houses that the majority of the population lived in. Thus, as in many other areas of the eastern United States, rural New Castle County's houses were actually the expression of a small segment of the population who, through the raw power of land, money, and others' indebtedness, determined the sort of housing suitable for the economically immobile majority.[16] Their concepts of organi-

Figure 7:22. Okolona, Armstrong Corner vicinity, St. Georges Hundred (ca. 1860).

zation and separation of spaces in both utilitarian and social terms, their naming of farms and landscapes, their acquisition of land and labor, all these were forces of class distinction and social control.

On the less fertile and commercially marginal lands of southwestern New Castle County along the Kent County line, the rebuilding activity kept pace with that in the area around Middletown. These farmers tended to build hall- and hall-parlor-plan dwellings of weatherboarded log or frame, generally with detached service structures (Fig. 7:25). While many of the houses bore the imprint of prevailing attitudes and practices, only a few followed the stylistic concerns prevalent in the wealthier districts. Nonetheless these small houses, less than a generation later, were modified by the insertion of stair passages, large gable-end additions, and attached kitchens and other service rooms.

Indeed, having ascertained the dates of the buildings through

A

B

Figure 7:23. Cochran family farms built west of Middletown: (A) and (B) Cochran Grange (ca. 1840); (C) and (D) Hedgelawn (ca. 1856)—see Figure 7:12; (E) and (F) Summerton (ca. 1850). Cochran Grange photograph: HABS, David L. Ames.

C

D

ARCHITECTURE AND RURAL LIFE IN CENTRAL DELAWARE, 1700–1900

E

F

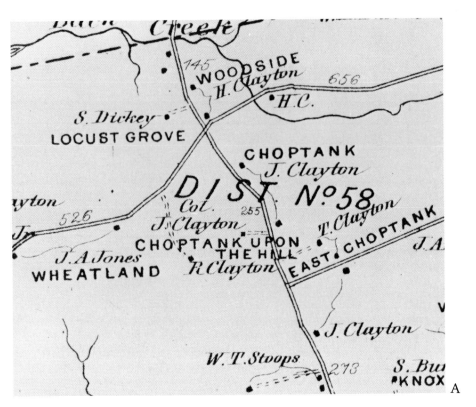

Figure 7:24. Clayton family settlement in St. Georges Hundred: (A) detail from Beers's *Atlas* (1868), showing locations of family members' farms; (B) Woodside (ca. 1850), H. Clayton's house. The Dickey farm, Locust Grove, shown on the map (A) was also formerly owned by the Claytons. Compare the architectural details and general appearance of Woodside to the Cochran family houses (Fig. 7:23).

studying architectural detail and documentary sources, we have found no temporal lag between the best and the worst during these decades. Everyone in a position to build and with the inclination to do so commissioned houses as best as they were able. At one level building fashionable architecture was a means of announcing one's attainment of an elevated social position. In the areas where agriculture failed to generate the capital sufficient for large-scale projects, people tended to rely on qualitative rather than formal distinctions in the social scaling of architecture. As the nineteenth century progressed, the builders in these poorer areas slowly began to adopt the plans that had come into general usage in more affluent lands just to the north.

B

Given the intensity of building and remodeling projects in southern New Castle County during the mid 1800s, our understanding of furnishing patterns and room use in the new dwellings becomes especially important. In terms of access, houses began to be erected with two or more doorways opening into different areas of the house. These multiple entries were not primary, secondary, or tertiary in nature, but channeled specific types of traffic in and out of the dwelling. The house and its immediate environment were organized around shared assumptions about spheres of interaction—household work, entertainment, storage, sleeping, and the daily tasks of farm, mill, or village. Each activity had its own patterns of movement and social discourse, and each spoke to the sense of order that emphasized a place for every activity and every activity in its place. The decision to bring service functions into the house through wings and ells produced large rambling dwellings containing myriad patterns of domestic movement through a multitude of rooms. Yet alongside such big houses were smaller structures where functions were less fragmented.

Schemes for laying out household space reflected changing

A

community activities toward the allocation of interior space, and the larger agrarian world as presented in agricultural publications. One of these journals, the *Illustrated Annual Register of Rural Affairs* from 1857, which was read in the area, contained a chapter on "Farm Houses: The Art of Planning Them."[17] The introduction to this provides a clear statement of attitudes about the need for careful planning, and a set of rules for laying out, building, and using interior space:

> When a farmer is about to erect a house, he should in the first place make two leading inquiries, 1. What are the accommodations I want? 2. What is the amount of means for providing them? In order to to assist in answering these questions properly, it may be well to classify houses, from the most simple and cheap, to the most expensive and complex. But it is necessary in the first place, to examine which of the

Figure 7:25. New houses in the poorer agricultural districts of southwestern New Castle County: (A) Carter House, Clayton vicinity, Blackbird Hundred (ca. 1830–50); (B) D. Clayton House, Townsend vicinity, Appoquinimink Hundred (mid-nineteenth century). Photograph: DSA, Marcia Jarrell.

apartments of a dwelling are most indispensable, and which are of various degrees of secondary importance.

Now, going back to the two leading inquiries already mentioned, let every one about to build, ask himself: How many of these different rooms will be indispensable for me; and 2, what can I expend in procuring them? We suppose that no man, even with quite modern means will be satisfied without:

1. Kitchen and small pantry;
2. Parlor;
3. Nursery or bed-room on the ground floor;
4. Small entry;
5. Bed-rooms with closets above stairs;
6. Cellar.

The cost of a house containing all these, will of course depend much upon the nature of the materials, their cost, the size of the rooms, and the cheapness of the finish; but with a plain frame or wooden house, they could be had from six to twelve hundred dollars.

A larger and more complete farm-house, costing two thousand or more, would contain,

1. Kitchen, pantry, store room, and iron closet;
2. Dining-room, and china closet;
3. Parlor or drawing-room;
4. Nursery or bed-room below stairs, with ample closets; and with bath-room attached;
5. Bed-rooms above stairs, with closets to all;
6. Office or library—which may be simply a small business room, for keeping account books, settling with workmen, making bargains, &c.; or a more complete library, with book-cases and newspaper closets, and even cases for minerals, dried plants, shells, stuffed birds, &c., according to circumstances.
7. Verandas;
8. Cellar.

After the greater or less number of these rooms has been fixed upon, according to wants and circumstances, the next step is to arrange them in the most convenient and economical manner. This is a difficult task to a person of inexperience, but it may be greatly assisted by observing the following rules, and by an examination of published plans. such for instance as we are about to give in the present number of the Register, or which have been furnished in the former numbers.

1. Let the kitchen (the most important apartment) always be on a level with the principal floor—and for strong light and free ventilation, it should have, if possible, windows on opposite sides or nearly opposite sides.
2. The pantry or dish-closet should be between the kitchen and dining-room, and easily accessible from both.
3. There should be a set of easy stairs from the kitchen to the cellar, and also an outer set into the cellar for admitting barrels, &c.
4. More attention should be given to the arrangement and convenient disposition of such rooms as are in constant use, than those but occasionally occupied. Hence the kitchen and living room should receive more attention on the ground of convenience, than the parlor.
5. Every entrance, except to the kitchen, should be through some entry or hall, or prevent the abrupt ingress of cold air, and for proper seclusion.
6. Let the entry or hall be near the center of the house, so that

ready and convenient access may be had from it to the different rooms; and to the too common evil of passing through one room to enter another.

7. Place the stairs so that the landing shall be as near the center as may be practicable, for the reason given for the preceding rule.

8. Let the partitions of the second floor stand over those of the lower, as nearly as may be, to secure firmness and solidity.[18]

The rules for building advanced in the essay, like the recommendations contained in other manuals written for nineteenth-century American society, were simply codifications of existing practices. Stair passages as buffers against weather and public society, multiple entrances into different activity areas within the house, and the concept of a spatially stratified household order—all had made an initial appearance in southern New Castle County in the 1780s and were in general use by the 1830s.

The dwellings that were commissioned in the nineteenth century included some or all of the rooms in this prescriptive literature. Their builders, like S. H. Black, typically eschewed the exact prescriptive arrangement, massing, or detailing. The interior division and subdivision of space were more often within the customary arrangement of rooms rather than the new plans suggested in published sources. No architectural writer rigorously promoted the concept of a main house with long service appendages, yet that was the common idiom most local builders adopted (Figs. 7:5, 7:8, and 7:17). The idea of a separate kitchen died hard, and its demise was softened by linking it to the main block as a semi-detached wing or by putting it at the far end of a long string of intervening rooms. While all of this was occurring, houses came to have a definite front and back, laid out in accordance with commonly understood and externally reenforced concepts for ordered and orderly domestic spaces.

One question remains. How did the occupants actually live in these dwellings? Room-by-room probate inventories from the mid-nineteenth century indicate how the inside of the house was scaled in economic terms (based on the average value of furniture in individual rooms) and how the front of the house became separate from the rear according to the types of furnishings each room contained. On the ground floor the most valuable rooms were consistently identified as parlors and were distinguished from dining rooms, "setting rooms," downstairs bedrooms, entries, and kitchens.

A

Figure 7:26. Kitchen hearth and cooking range: (A) Mount Hope, Summit vicinity, St. Georges Hundred (1840–50); (B) Woodlawn, Odessa vicinity, St. Georges Hundred (ca. 1850), masonry range with cast-iron cooking surface and inset cauldrons.

Thomas Janvier's possessions are typical of the parlor contents and included (in 1856) a safe, bookcase, marble-top table, six chairs, and looking glass. Thomas Alrich's parlor of 1865 had a piano, six walnut chairs, two divans, sofa, marble-top table, rocking chair, and a "Ladies easy chair."[19] The second most valuable room on the first floor was the dining room, which generally contained a table or extension table, two or more chairs, and a cupboard and contents. Where the ground-floor room division was tripartite, the quality of the parlor remained unaltered, dining room fixtures were pieces related to eating, and the sitting room served as a less formal parlor. David Craven's 1862 estate enumeration follows this pattern: sofa, two tables, eight chairs, and rocking chair in the parlor; two tables, work stand, lounge, eight Windsor chairs, and a rocker in the sitting room; and lounger, six chairs, and extension table in the dining room.[20] In some households the terms dining room and sitting room and the furniture for both were interchangeable. William Cleaver's

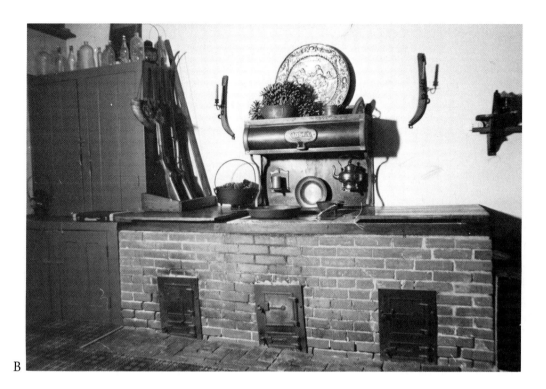

B

sitting room held an extension dining table, four chairs, two rocking chairs, silver, and tableware while the dining room was furnished only with a table and three chairs.[21]

Some pieces of furniture were not limited to one particular room; secretaries, desks, and work stands might be placed in any one of the front rooms of the house. Other objects, however, were likely to show up in one room more than any other. Window shades almost invariably adorned parlors, and small sewing stands were listed in dining rooms. Entries and stair passages seldom contained much beyond a clock, a settee, and possibly a small table. There are, to be sure, also inventories describing households in which some first-floor special accommodations had been made for the final days of the recently deceased. This was certainly the situation of William Stewart in 1844, whose parlor contained nearly every article of furniture normally associated with a parlor and with a dining room, while the second downstairs room simply held a bed and settee.[22]

In practice, a parlor and either a sitting or a dining room occupied the front of the house. Situated behind a balanced facade, entered under a porch, and buffered by a stair passage, these two most elaborate rooms in the house were simultaneously the most

A

Figure 7:27. Domestic service buildings: (A) Monterey, ranged from left to right are an octagonal privy, a smokehouse, and an icehouse; (B) Cochran Grange, combination dairy, storehouse, smokehouse and workshop.

public, due to their disposition at the front of the house, and the least accessible to everyday domestic traffic. Their furnishings emphasized domestic display for Sunday company, and everyday use was held to a minimum. The most heavily used rooms were further back in the house and open to the outside through separate entries. Sitting rooms, nurseries, offices, and kitchens stretched away from the front of the houses in a succession of increasing bustle.

The kitchen, at the very rear of the house, opened directly to the outside and seldom contained more than two tables, a bench or chair, cooking range, and odds and ends ranging from iron kettles to axes and harnesses. By the mid-nineteenth century most cooking was done over built-in masonry and cast-iron ranges, moveable iron stoves that could be backed into a hearth, or open hearths with chimney cranes and trammels (Fig. 7:26). Plans for built-in ranges and hearth-to-stove conversions appeared in local agricultural papers as early as 1808 and were described in terms of making general

B

improvements to the farm (Fig. 7:27).[23] The proponents of the kitchen stove most often couched their arguments in terms of economy of stovewood, the regulating and containing of heat, and economical use of household labor. The notions of domestic economy, functional regulation, and containment as the primary avenues to order are themes that extended well beyond the kitchen to the spatial organization of the entire house and farm. The kitchen, the last remnant of the seventeenth- and eighteenth-century hall, was reorganized and its focus—the hearth—was separated and sealed from the operations which it served. Fire, which once composed the core of domestic attention, had been revalued. It was no longer a force but a utility measured in terms of service.

The first-floor plan of the mid-nineteenth-century house was built around a progression of domestic functions, from parlors to laundry room, and the upstairs arrangement of chambers or bedrooms echoed the same pattern. The chambers at the front of the

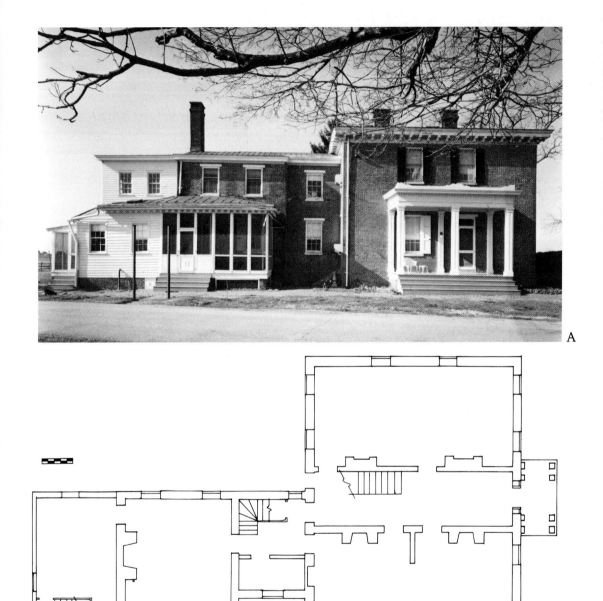

Figure 7:28. Multiple entries: Monterey: (A) sitting room, dining room and kitchen entries, (B) first-floor plan.

house held the most valuable objects. Behind these principal chambers stretched a series of less well-appointed rooms, culminating in servant's quarters or storage over the kitchen. Detached from the main block of the house, but located in the immediate yard, were woodsheds, privys, icehouses, smokehouses, and other household support structures (Fig. 7:28). The agricultural and work buildings of the farm were at the end of a lane behind the dwelling complex.

Metaphors of pure and impure, cold and heat, ritual and work have been advanced to explain the arrangement and utilization of rooms in the house.[24] In American vernacular architecture the phenomenon of household separation and stratification has been recognized for some time as having existed in areas as diverse as late seventeenth-century New England and early nineteenth-century eastern and middle Virginia.[25] The process, almost always associated with significant shifts in building patterns, maintains a self-contradiction based on the inclusion and exclusion of domestic functions under one roof. From the late eighteenth century onward in southern New Castle County, the option for bringing kitchens, quarters, and other operations into the house was exercised increasingly often. At the same time these impure, heated, working spaces were pushed even further back into the rear of the house, leaving the front of the dwelling cold, pristine, and socially ritualized. The construction of multiple entries with different areas of the house, and in some instances separate lanes leading independently to the front, rear, and farmyard, selectively reinforced the pattern of spaces at once unified and divided (Fig. 7:29). The point of departure from similar distinctions made in the colonial period is in a shift from physical and cognitive divisions to purely cognitive separations. The art of planning houses described in the 1857 *Annual Register of Rural Affairs* lay in the manipulation, ordering, and division of space unified under one roof, as opposed to the older concept of expressing a similar order through numerous individual structures.

The changes represented a gradual shift from defining the functions of house and farm as literally separate arrangements to considering them as literally unified but figuratively separate. The rebuilding process amounted finally to a reversal of emphasis. In the decades prior to the 1820s, stress was laid on the actual separation of living and working household functions by the building and maintaining of numerous outbuildings, all of which were perceived as essential to the unified work of the home. But, by the second quarter of the nineteenth century, this emphasis had been inverted. What was made explicit in the rebuilding period was the expression of a unified order. The old physically separated labor, living, and storage spaces were placed in a single building under a single roof. The resulting connection between old ideas and new emphases within traditional architectural design is the crucial thread that bound the rebuilding era to its local past and to its national present.

8. New Farm Buildings

N OT ONLY DID THE REBUILDING PROCESS AFFECT almost every standing dwelling in southern New Castle County, it also had an impact on the design of agricultural buildings. Barns, granaries, corn houses, stables, and related farm structures—often considered by students of vernacular building traditions to be the most conservative architectural forms and the least susceptible to radical change—were literally rebuilt through the middle decades of the 1800s. In the course of this process, farm buildings became the primary vehicles that individual farmers used to communicate the new values of the agricultural reform movement and the character of each particular farm in southern New Castle County. Building types associated with agricultural reform and architectural renewal are granaries or crib barns, bank barns, livestock barns or stables, carriage houses, threshing barns, and cart sheds. Taken together, these buildings emphasize the pervasive nature of agricultural and architectural change in mid-nineteenth-century southern New Castle County.

Toward the end of the first building cycles that shaped southern New Castle County architecture, farmers began to construct farm buildings with specified spaces for designated functions under a single roof. The earliest examples of this notion of carefully allocating work space were tied to the similar idea of incorporating service spaces into the whole dwelling. Earlier barns like Benjamin Wilson's 1802 structure had been designed more for general storage than for specialized usage and might contain some corn in a crib, a cleaning mill, a sleigh, fodder, scythes, and cradles.[1] Although miscellaneous objects continued to fill farm structures throughout the nineteenth century, many farmers began providing precisely defined spaces for farm objects. In the popular codification of this general drive, farmers up and down the eastern seaboard wrote to agricultural journals discussing and illustrating ideas for realizing a new agrarian order. These essays were repeatedly reprinted in journals, almanacs, and book-length agricultural manuals. Everything from plans for pegboards painted with the outlines of hand tools to descriptions of buildings designed for utility and durability regularly appeared in print, but in almost every case these prescriptions, which claimed to be innovative, simply reenforced practices that had already taken hold more than a generation before.[2] Typical of this phenomenon were S. E. Todd's specifications for a barn, claiming to introduce a method for framing principal timbers that he had "never seen laid down in any treatise on architecture" (Fig. 8:1).[3] The innovations Todd takes credit for had been in use with minor variations in the Anglo-American settlements of the mid Atlantic for over a century. The establishment of standard practice and its subsequent codification paralleled the development of southern New Castle County agricultural buildings in the nineteenth century and antedated their publication in contemporary journals by several years (Fig. 8:2).

Of all the agricultural buildings generated in the course of the rebuilding, the timber-frame crib barn, or granary, was the most common (Fig. 8:3). Even today as one drives through lower New Castle County nearly every farm that retains nineteenth-century farm buildings possesses one of these gable-fronted buildings in the farmyard behind the house. The typical crib barn was a one-story-plus-a-loft, braced-frame building with earthen ramps leading from the double doors set in the gable ends of the building. The ground-floor space contained a broad central runway floored with two-inch-thick plank. On either side were equal-sized cribs, generally eight to ten feet wide, running the full length of the building. A stair to the loft was constructed at the end of one crib and finished with battened doors opening on to the runway. The storage space under the steps was often filled with the tenants' feed corn. The interior partition walls were finished with plain wainscot to a height of three to four feet and topped with horizontal lath nailed to the studs and rising to loft height. In several crib barns, the interior walls bear markings such as harvest dates and initials, and one has a miniature leather figure nailed to a door. On the exterior the cribs are sheathed with vertical lath which is nailed to rails tenoned into the principal

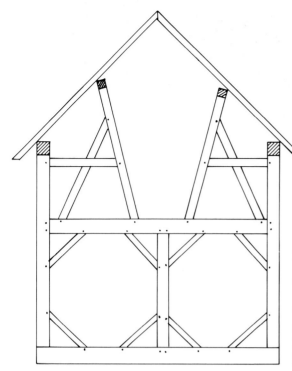

Figure 8:1. "Framing the middle bents of a large barn," based on a drawing in S.E. Todd, *Todd's Country Homes* (1870). Compare Todd's suggested system to the stable framing in Figure 8:2. Drawing: CHAE, William Macintire.

posts. This sheathing covers the exterior from the sills to the eaves. The upper reaches of the crib barns contain a number of plank-walled grain bins, rising to the height of the collar beams (Fig. 8:4). The concept was essentially quite simple: a storage area with a central vehicular passage, with ground-level storage for ears of corn and overhead bins for shelled corn or threshed grain that could be emptied as needed through chutes and hatchways. While the basic design of the crib barn was well established by the 1830s, the structures were subject to improvements throughout the nineteenth century. The earliest dated surviving example of a crib barn is S. H. Black's granary at La Grange (Fig. 8:5), an almost square building with one gable-end entry, rather than a through runway, and a ladder at the other gable end. As the years passed newer crib barns were built for through traffic, and the loft stair was moved to the corner of one of the flanking corncribs or, infrequently, installed as a movable flight of stairs at one end of the runway. The later variations are also found with features such as a third-story hayloft, or appended cart sheds with overhead hay or storage lofts (Fig. 8:6). By 1880, if not before, national publications like *Barn Plans and Outbuildings*

Figure 8:2. Westview stable, Summit vicinity, Pencader Hundred (mid-nineteenth century). Photograph: HABS, David L. Ames.

contained detailed plans, specifications, and elevations of combination corncribs and granaries.[4]

The crib barns in southern New Castle County had local precedent. The Achmester granary, a log structure, contained an elevated threshing floor (precluding wheeled traffic), flanking corncribs, and an overhead loft sealed with board walling so it could hold loose grain (Fig. 4:5). Timber-frame granaries were also built elsewhere on the Delmarva Peninsula.[5] These southern granaries differ from those in New Castle County in that the spaces built on either side of the runway (sometimes open to the roof, but more typically finished with a loft) were often used as cart sheds. Some of these granaries

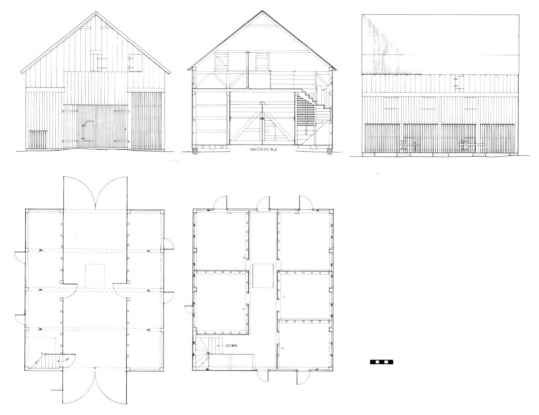

Figure 8:3. Cochran Grange granary (ca. 1830), the design allows for wagon access, mechanical threshing and corn shelling, and grain and corn storage. Drawing: HABS, Charles Bergengren.

originally consisted only of a single unpartitioned block without flanking sheds or cribs. Although such structures are variations, the form of a raised central element with original or appended sheds does appear with a noteworthy frequency throughout the region. What separates these elevated granaries from the crib barns is that the latter had a formal allowance for vehicular traffic (runway), a more precise area to store grain (bins), and an elongated rectangular plan.

Providing wagon ramps and sufficient overhead space for storing loose corn and wheat was a part of the industrialized-agrarian world view that came to characterize the area in the nineteenth century. The New Castle County agricultural society's yearly fairs offered premiums for mechanical farm equipment such as sowing and reaping machines, straw and root cutters, fans, corn shellers, and new inventions. The society also awarded prizes for furniture,

Figure 8:4. Cochran Grange granary, loft with grain bins. Photograph: HABS, David L. Ames.

gunpowder, iron castings, and textiles from the county's northern shops and mills, in addition to fruits, flowers, and vegetables grown throughout the region. At the fairs millers judged the quality of wheat, basing their decisions on how cleanly the grain went through the milling process. Although horses, cattle, oxen, sheep, hogs, and butter were regularly judged and the winners presented with certificates and cash prizes, the biggest prizes were reserved for cereals and for experimental pursuits, such as the best essay on the improved use of manures to increase yields.[6]

In addition to participating in annual fairs, self-proclaimed progressive farmers kept up with technological change and urban markets through regular commerce, correspondence, and visits to nearby milling districts and cities. Philip Reybold, for example, became an honorary member of a Philadelphia-based agricultural society; Richard Mansfield regularly packed up and sent wool shorn from his sheep to be woven into cloth on power looms in the mills along the Red Clay Creek northwest of Wilmington; and Samuel Townsend kept in touch with Philadelphia and New York City wholesale produce establishments.[7]

In light of the agriculturalists' orientation, the compartmentalized storage unit and the adjustments in space to better accommodate the traffic and machinery as it moved through the crib barn were reflections of the same new rural intentions. To allow farmers to better gauge the storage capacity of these barns, mathematical formulas computing volume were regularly published in farming texts or appeared as handwritten addenda on the fly leaves of bound annual volumes of the journals.[8] Not everyone used such computations, however; walls marked with years of bushel counts are common in many crib-barn lofts. Like their predecessors the new compartmentalized granaries stored a variety of grains and miscellaneous objects. In 1866 Alexander Lea's granary had a "Fan and Corn Cradle"; half-bushel and peck measures; hoes, forks, and sundries; 30 bushels corn in the crib; wagon harness; and plow gear. Thomas Clark's granary, inventoried in 1853, had 275 bushels of

Figure 8:5. La Grange granary (ca. 1815). Built by S.H. Black, the granary, although it lacks complete drive-through access, is the earliest example of the new type.

Figure 8:6. Silver Hill granary with attached cartshed, Odessa vicinity, Appoquinimink Hundred (mid-nineteenth century). Photograph: DSA.

white corn, a crowbar, five flour barrels, a corn sheller, a Bamborough fan, 35 grain bags, a half bushel measure, a half dozen split oak baskets, and "one Fly net and Trace."[9] As a locally popular agricultural building, the granary/crib barn represented the continuing economic investment in and dependence on grain and livestock as the district's chief articles of production. The importance of grain was repeatedly stressed: "grain is the great staple of our farmer and in selling the principal article of his production the farmer is interested to have accuracy, certainty, and regular commercial usages observed."[10] Compartmentalized crib barns were not the result of other changes, but were an intimate part of a community in transition and represent the working out and articulation of that community's values in a specific context.

The introduction of the multilevel bank barn into the agricultural landscape of southern New Castle County was another aspect of the on-going changes in nineteenth-century rural work (Fig. 8:7). Although bank barns were a customary form in northern New Castle County and southeastern Pennsylvania, with both English and continental European antecedents, their original range did not extend much further down the peninsula than the fringe of the Piedmont along the fall line. The earliest known English style bank barns in southeastern Pennsylvania date from the fourth quarter of the eighteenth century and had two major levels.[11] Built into the side of a hill or an embankment, the lower level was usually a rubble-stone-walled stabling area opening on to an enclosed barn yard or pound. The second level, which could be of stone, log, or frame construction, contained a central threshing floor flanked by large hay mows. An earthen or dry laid stone ramp on the uphill side of the building led to the threshing floor and to doorways that could be opened to cross-ventilation at both sides.

The characteristic features of the traditional bank barn design—relatively large size, bi-level divisions, and ability to house multiple functions in precisely defined spaces—stimulated a widespread promotion of the form in the second quarter of the nineteenth century. Agricultural publications repeatedly printed plans for variations of it and ascribed their origins to points as far flung as upstate New York and the Midwest. One writer explained:

> With the increase of wealth, and we may add of good sense and enlarged ideas, among the farmers of the country, there is a gradual but very decided improvement in farm architecture. The old custom was to build small barns, to add others on three sides of a yard, perhaps of several yards, and to construct sheds, pigpens, corn houses, and such minor structures as might seem desirable. In the course of a few years the group of roofs, big and little, span and lean-to, in the rear of a large farmer's dwelling, would present the appearance of a small crowded village. Compared with a well-arranged barn, a group of small buildings is inconvenient and extremely expensive to keep in good repair.[12]

A second author provided plans and elevations for a modified bank barn:

> This is the design of a barn partially on the Pennsylvania plan, with under-ground stables, and a stone-walled basement on three sides, with a line of posts standing open on the yard front, and a wall, pierced by doors and windows, retreating 12 feet under the building, giving, in front, a shelter for stock. Two sheds, by way of wings, are run out to any desired length, on each side.[13]

In many ways the bank barn was considered the architectural incorporation of the nineteenth-century agrarian goal prescribed by Black at the first convening of the New Castle agricultural society (1819). One farm journal correspondent ably summarized these values in 1846:

A

Figure 8:7. Bank barns: (A) Thomas Landing, Odessa vicinity, Appoquinimink Hundred (1809), down slope elevation; (B) Cochran farm, Odessa vicinity, St. Georges Hundred (1830–50), ramp elevation.

Perhaps there is no particular feature which more distinctly indicates that perfection than the farm-buildings, certainly there is nothing which more forcibly attracts the stranger's eye on entering within the bounds of that state, where he is at once assured that no niggardly regard to expenditure for useful purposes, influences a Pennsylvania farmer; though his own dwelling be of an unpretending character, the means for housing his crops and sheltering his flocks, are on an ample scale. Poor indeed would he judge that economy to be, which permitted a sheaf to suffer injury for want of an adequate protection.[14]

Several of these large bank barns were erected in southern New Castle County between 1809 and the close of the century, but they never achieved the same widespread popularity found in nearby Pennsylvania, nor did they become as common as the crib barn. The absence of large numbers of bank barns is due in part to the substantial financial expenditure required to undertake their construction—from building an earthen ramp on an otherwise remarkably

B

flat terrain to procuring and processing building materials. The idea of the bank barn in southern New Castle County was imported as part of the thinking and literature spawned through the discourse on better farming practices carried on among the membership of various agricultural societies. These buildings appear only on the farms of the most affluent entrepreneurial farmers and generally only in the most productive and wealthy farming districts in the southern part of the county. Third, although scores of these farm buildings, dating from 1800 to 1900 were built in the Pennsylvania Piedmont region just to the north, their design does not seem to have been carried by any traditional means into the lower half of the county. Farmers of the lower hundreds were undoubtedly acquainted with the multileveled barn and all of its advantages through their trips to Wilmington and Philadelphia, but did not choose to build the bank barn in their own rural neighborhoods; they relied instead on the traditional three-bay English style barn and stables.

Eight bank barns, built between 1809 and 1886, are sufficient to describe the history and variations of this form in southern New

Figure 8:8. Cochran Grange, bank barn (1830–35). Photograph: HABS, David L. Ames.

Castle County.[15] Built in 1835, some ten years before the mansion house, the Cochran Grange barn is a two-level brick structure measuring nearly sixty feet square on the lower level and forty by sixty feet on the main floor (Fig. 8:8). It had mangers for cattle in the main block of the lower level, with a shed roof section providing shelter for unpenned cattle and a fenced enclosure extending out from the sides of the shed. The mangers inside the building were divided by a central aisle entered through round-arched doors at either gable end. Overhead, the main floor was divided into three sections. A central aisle nearly sixteen feet broad ran the width of the building; and two equal-sized mows were on either side. Of particular note is the absence of grain bins or threshing areas in the barns.

The same general plan was used for the Idalia Manor barn, built 1840–50. It contains basement mangers with an overhead aisle and mows, and also lacks provision for grain storage. In fact, spatial arrangement in the Idalia Manor barn reveals no fundamental changes in design from the earliest documented bank barn in southern New Castle County, Thomas Landing barn (1809). The latter is a two-story stone structure with a frame southern elevation (Fig. 8:7). The lower level, entered through a lean-to animal shelter, was divided into three sections, each containing a row of stalls that were framed on cedar struts angled from the ceiling down onto the floor. The main story, entered from an earthen ramp, had a central runway flanked by hay mows. As at Cochran's Grange and Idalia Manor, there was no provision for storage other than hay mows. Grain and corn were processed and stored in a separate granary standing nearby.

The Woodlawn barn represents a considerably later variation on the bank-barn form. Commissioned by J. K. Williams in 1886, the barn was one of five structures erected that year as part of the overhaul of Williams's farm, east of Middletown. All the materials required were imported by rail through the lumber yards of George Hukill in nearby Middletown.[16] When the building project was completed Williams had a new barn, timber-framed cart sheds, a crib barn, and a combination carriage house/chicken coop/piggery (Figs. 8:9 and 8:11). These structures completed the total rebuilding that Williams had begun in the 1850s when he replaced the old house with a new two-and-a-half-story brick house incorporating a rear service ell and bake oven in the cellar, as well as a combination smokehouse/privy in the backyard.

The overall layout of the Woodlawn farm buildings was not dissimilar from those promoted in contemporary agricultural and architectural literature (Fig. 8:10).[17] Like the Cochran Grange barn, the Woodlawn barn had two levels: a lower floor, axially divided, with an aisle centered on the east gable end, and a main floor bisected by a central double runway, flanked by mows. A projecting forebay was finished with board walling for use as a granary (which was rendered superfluous by the simultaneous construction of the crib barn), while providing an overhanging shelter for livestock housed in the floor below. At the west end of the basement level, space was provided for additional mangers and possibly a milking parlor. Two timber-framed, gable-roofed cart sheds (one of which was structurally dependent on the main barn) created a courtyard in front of the barn, which was then enclosed by a simple fence (Fig. 8:11). The whole complex was entered by way of a farm lane leading

A

from the road, past the gable end of the house—a pattern also found at Monterey, Greenlawn, and Cochran Grange (Fig. 8:12). The lane continued past the east cart shed and barn on one side and the carriage house on the other, and past the gable entry of the crib barn; it then jogged to the west and ran to the fields beyond. The barn courtyard thus could be entered from the front, the side, or from the fields via the earthen ramp and timber bridge. Like Cochran Grange, the Woodlawn farm buildings occupied a space secondary to the dwelling, but nonetheless accessible from both the public road and the surrounding fields. In the Woodlawn plan, and other similar arrangements, the house had secondary, gable-end porches and entries that channeled working traffic in and out of the house.

Built in the mid-nineteenth century, the Couper barn, located southwest of New Castle, incorporated both hay and grain storage as well as stabling functions into the main body of the barn (Fig. 8:13). Designed with three levels, the Couper barn provided the maximum

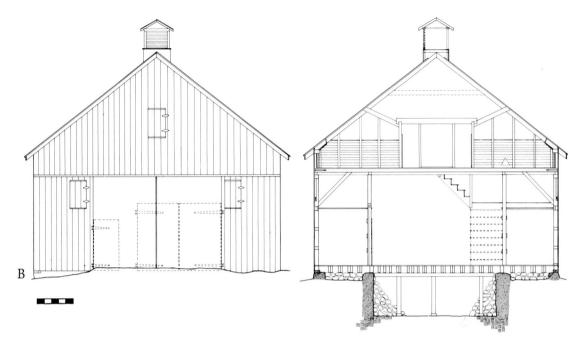

B

Figure 8:9. Woodlawn farm buildings (1885–86): (A) combination carriage barn, chicken house, and piggery; (B) granary elevation and section. Photograph: HABS, David L. Ames. Drawing: HABS, Melinda Fike.

utilization of space. As with other bank barns the ground floor was partitioned into mangers. The access aisles for feeding the stock and mucking out the stalls, however, did not run from gable to gable, but were entered through doors located under the forebay shelter area. The second and third levels were vertically integrated to maximize interior storage possibilities. An earthen ramp extended up to a timber-framed bridge entering the barn at the third level. Using paired king-post trusses, the space was divided into a central runway flanked with slat-sided corn cribs. Where the runway entered the barn, the flanking mows dropped away to the second level. Underneath the elevated runway was a row of plank-sheathed grain bins separated by a narrow aisle. Access to the middle level was through a secondary entry under the bridge house. A work space in the forebay at the other end of the aisle yielded enough space to install and operate a mechanical fan or a corn sheller.

Other bank barns in the area included two with gable-end en-

Figure 8:10. "Design of a barn partially on the Pennsylvania plan," from Lewis F. Allen's *Rural Architecture* (1860). Compare Allen's proposed design to Figures 8:11 and 8:14.

tries and one without a ramp to the second level. The G. Z. Tybout barn, dated 1863, both paralleled and antedated published designs promoting a central block, for hay and grain storage, that faced away from the basement level livestock housing, and that had at least one attached, single-story shed. At the Tybout barn, the shed wing contained box stalls for horses and cattle, and the ground level of the main block was set aside for dairy cows. The main floor held provision for both hay and grain storage and opened to both the lane and road out front, as well as to the fields behind the farm complex. Also built with a gable entry, the Rothwell barn incorporated corn cribs into a covered ramp similar to the Couper barn (Fig. 8:14). The ground level had stables under a forebay. Inside the second level a broad aisle running the length of the structure was flanked by timber trusses that framed the mows on either side (Fig. 8:15). Later additions extended forebays along the two remaining elevations, thus increasing space for hay storage on the main floor and cart and wagon sheds below.

Wheatland barn was erected in the mid 1800s as a two-level

structure with a forebay, but it lacked a ramp to the main floor (Fig. 8:16). A central aisle, open from the ground floor to the roof, provided an avenue for vehicular traffic through the building. The forebay, as in all the other bank barns in the area, served as an animal shelter at the yard level, while providing additional space for hay mows overhead. Built in the image of a bank barn, but without an embankment or man-made ramp, Wheatland barn underscores the tension between these architectural forms as cultural signs and as functional spaces. Since its functions were limited to providing stalls and fodder storage, the building served only as an enlarged stable or cow barn rather than as a multipurpose agricultural structure. The built-in limitations of the Wheatland barn were further emphasized, as at Woodlawn, by the construction of a separate crib barn and other smaller farm buildings.

With their multiple levels and carefully allocated work, storage, and stabling spaces, the Couper, Tybout, and Rothwell barns represent the complete realization of the bank barn's functional potential. This is in sharp contrast to the Cochran Grange, Woodlawn, and Wheatland barns, where space is clearly underutilized. In these instances the grain threshing and storage functions continued to be housed in separate structures set in a farmyard composed of several small buildings clustered around a single larger one—an arrangement whose complex conceptual order and practical use lay somewhere between the old custom of having several small barns and the new ideology of maintaining one well-managed barn. This paradoxical layout reflects two concurrent but fundamentally different cultural perceptions of what a barn should be and is. A similar dilemma was faced by occupants of the first stair-passage-plan dwellings, who discovered that the new arrangement did not easily accommodate old ideas. The established concept of a barn was encapsulated in one 1822 definition: "a sort of house used for storing unthreshed grain, hay, straw, and fodder. But the other use of barns in this country are, to lodge and feed beasts in, to thresh grain. to dress flax, etc."[18] Ambiguity characterizes the very definition. A barn (or several small barns) could be employed for a number of specific purposes; or in a remedial sense, it could be "large enough to serve the farmer for all these purposes."[19] In the rebuilding period of southern New Castle County a barn containing many functions was viewed as the preferred alternative. As an agricultural essayist wrote in 1877, "The first principle to be observed is, so far as possi-

A

ble, to bring everything within the same four walls and under the same roof, and to adjust the size of the structure, not so much to the present requirements, as to the future needs of the farm."[20]

Historically, farmers in eighteenth-century southern New Castle had built and maintained several small buildings for their needs—a pattern followed throughout the lower mid-Atlantic and upper tidewater South. When and where the ideology of agricultural reform encountered established custom, the solutions attempted to reconcile conceptual rift between separation and consolidation. John Cochran, J. K. Williams, and others commissioning large bank barns surrounded them with numerous lesser structures, each possessing certain set functions. Bank barns and crib barns were new in the sense that they were uniformly open to wheeled traffic and provided for the particular separation of functions. They were conservative in the sense that they failed to incorporate all the farm operations within one or two buildings. Basically crop storage re-

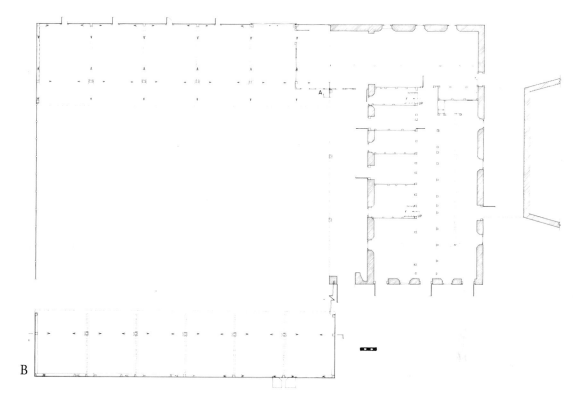

Figure 8:11. Woodlawn bank barn and cartsheds. (A) South elevation; (B) ground-floor plan. Photograph: HABS, David L. Ames. Drawing: HABS, Brian Fletcher.

mained segregated from animal shelter. But those old operations came to be housed in new buildings constructed by progressive, reform-minded, right-thinking farmers who managed large agricultural estates worked by tenants, day laborers, and slaves. The farmers commissioning these barns were consumers of images— images molded to fit a world view they assumed they were changing but one which had taken form a long time before. As a community of builders they could embrace the image but not the substance of the structures they promoted and commissioned to be built: underlying attitudes were not amenable to change that was more than skin deep.

Farmers, who did not build the large bank barns, replaced their old English-style barns with tripartite horse barns that incorporated many of the old uses. On the ground floor these two-story buildings were divided by a central runway with stalls on either side (Fig. 8:17). The second floor was left open for piling loose hay. Because

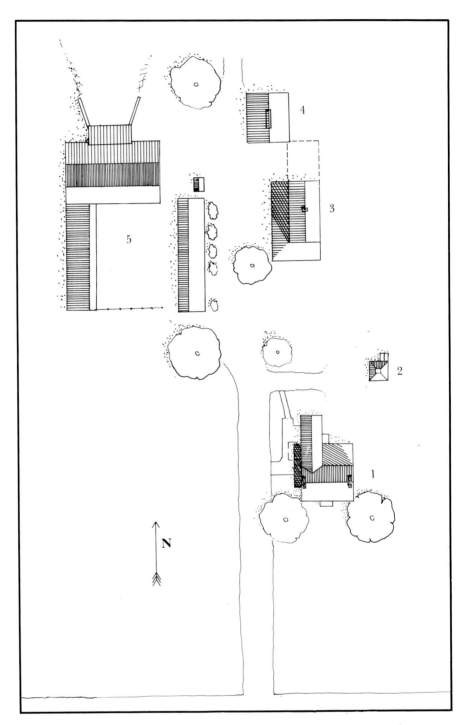

Figure 8:12. Woodlawn, site plan: 1. house; 2. smokehouse; 3. carriage barn/pig-gery; 4. granary; 5. barn and cartsheds. Drawing: CHAE, William Macintire.

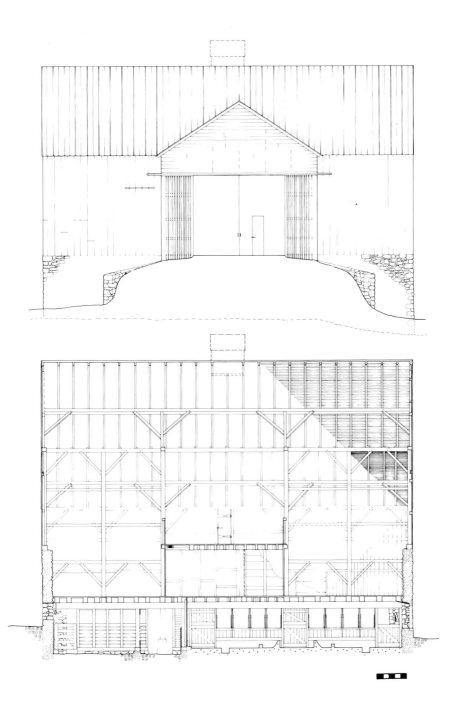

Figure 8:13. Couper bank barn, Tybouts Corner vicinity, New Castle Hundred
(1850–70). Ramp elevation and longitudinal section showing three-level division
of interior space. Drawing: HABS, Charles Bergengren and William Macintire.

Figure 8:14. Rothwell bank barn, Middletown vicinity, Appoquinimink Hundred (mid-nineteenth century). The forebay wraps around three sides of the barn, and the bridge house connecting the barn to the ramp contains corn cribs flanking the aisle.

most farms had the new-style granaries and open cart sheds, these smaller horse barns were not used for threshing or parking farm vehicles. Their primary function was for stabling horses and sheltering dairy cows; consequently, the central runway was often too narrow for anything larger than a wheelbarrow and was used as a corridor to fill feed boxes. Additional entries along the gable ends on secondary elevations provided access for livestock and for farmhands who cleaned out the stalls. Similar in appearance to the traditional barns of the preceding century, the newer barns were different in two important ways. First, they were larger in scale than the average eighteenth century barn—a feature common to all new-style farm buildings and one reiterating their importance to the values of agricultural reform. Second, they were used in a restricted way. Like bank barns they were large enough to house and meet most of the farm's working needs, and yet they were underutilized—their function limited to providing stabling. Both of these features—impressively large exteriors and functionally specific interior spaces—were shared with contemporary dwellings.

Other agricultural buildings erected through the mid 1800s further illustrate the tension between old practices and new at-

Figure 8:15. Rothwell barn. The cantilevered trusses framing in the side aisles were later strengthened with vertical supports.

Figure 8:16. Wheatland barn (1850–70).

titudes. Separate carriage barns with ground-level box stalls and aisles for feeding and cleaning were built with second-story hay lofts. At Greenlawn the carriage barn also contained a small corn-crib, wagon shed, and mounting porch (Fig. 8:18). At Mondamon Farm, hay was stacked in an earthfast, fixed-roof barrack sited away from the stables and barns (Fig. 8:19), a practice also followed at Brick Store Farm in 1850 and 1854, where four barracks, fourteen feet square were situated twenty-five to fifty feet from the barn.[21] Hay barracks were less widely used, but some farmers such as Peter Alrichs, who built one in 1863, continued to rely on them.[22] In the less prosperous areas of the county, particularly in the southwestern part, farmers opted for smaller versions of the agricultural buildings that embodied the new values and grouped them in multiple-structure courts and ranges. On occasion the new buildings were so small that they could not sustain heavy use or accommodate wagons and farm machinery. The Pinder crib barn located in Kenton Hundred, just across the county line, was built with all the requisite ramp and

A

B

Figure 8:17. Horse barns: (A) Woodside (ca. 1860); (B) Westview (mid-nineteenth century), ground-floor horse stalls.

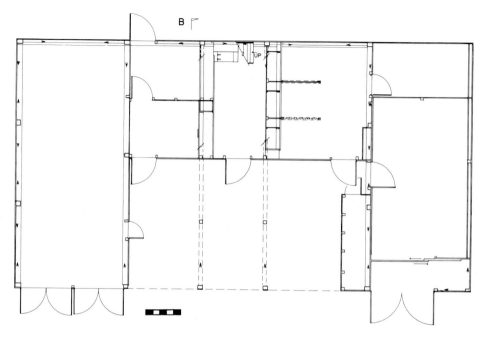

Figure 8:18. Greenlawn carriage barn (ca. 1880), ground-floor plan. Carriage bays at each end of the building flank a central unit composed of a stable area opening onto mounting porch containing a small corn crib. Drawing: HABS, William Macintire.

storage spaces, but its sixteen-by-twenty-foot size rendered it functional only as an old-style elevated granary.

The ideals for reshaping the agrarian landscape are most apparent in the actual construction of the farm buildings. Framing, even for earthfast buildings, became increasingly complex. As ideology attempted to streamline and consolidate the functions of the farm, it prompted increasingly more complicated ways of erecting buildings that reflected that image. Structurally elaborate systems of multiple, diagonally set braces were deployed in a number of buildings. The Achmester crib barn was fitted with double braces running from the principal posts to the tie beams, and at Cochran Grange the threshing barn had double braces supplemented with a second pair set inside the angled space left by the first (Fig. 8:20). The use of king-post trusses, previously limited to short-span timber bridges, was incorporated into the bridge-like ramp at the Couper barn and to support an added forebay on the Rothwell barn. Common rafter roofs in several barns were supported with heavy purlins carried on diagonally set struts that were toed into tie beams and

Figure 8:19. Mondamon barrack, Biddles Corner vicinity, St. Georges Hundred (mid-nineteenth century). Unlike eighteenth-century barracks (see Fig. 4:3), this structure has a fixed and partially sided gable roof and is supported on ten earthfast posts.

braced from the opposite direction with smaller, secondary struts. The mortise-and-tenon joints, where the beams butted principal posts, were not only fixed with wooden pins but reinforced with wrap-around wrought-iron braces, often trenched into the outer face of the posts and fixed to the sides of the beams with iron bolts that were locked into position with nuts and metal keys. Alexander Wilson's Agricultural Works, dating from the 1850s, used iron bolts throughout the structure and, as a testament to Wilson's rainy day blacksmithing skills, included such features as wrought-iron nuts with curled rattail terminals. No single structure better represents the preference for engineering in wood than do the Woodlawn cart sheds (Fig. 8:21). Multiple braces spring in all directions from earthfast principal posts, and the posts stand on flat river cobbles with holes bored through their center to hold heavy iron pins spiked into the underside of the post ends.

Figure 8:20. Cochran Grange threshing barn (1830–35). The elaboration of timber-framing techniques is illustrated by the two pairs of doubled braces joining the posts and tie beams. Photograph: HABS, David L. Ames.

Figure 8:21. Woodlawn cart shed framing (1885–86). Photograph: HABS, David L. Ames.

While some structural elaborations can be explained as displays of competence by rival builders vying for business in a highly competitive market, a large portion of the exercises in constructural complexity were also a projection of the spirit of the times. Just as inventors contended for prizes at annual agricultural fairs and farmers strove to cultivate the finest grain, livestock, and produce, so too did the same farmers—and the carpenters and masons they hired—codify in their new buildings the values summoned up by the agricultural reform. These new buildings were commissioned to house the mandate for revision and consolidation of working spaces. Building technology, as evidenced in fabric, was redefined by local craftsmen and patrons in such a way that it enhanced the perception of how redirected notions of traditional functions were expected to fit into those same forms. Barns, cart sheds, and stables did not contain anything fundamentally different in framing or masonry techniques, but were rebuilt or built anew, using traditional methods in progressive and sometimes novel ways. The solutions, while not structurally required, were necessary signs marking the farm's progress towards becoming an agrarian factory. Established behavior ran against the grain of radical change, but parallel to that was an awareness that pursuit of change was central to the full incorporation of the values promoted and accepted by a rural working society. The elaboration of building technology conveniently presented no threat to an old order and even, through highly visible displays of technique and expense, compensated for the reluctance to accept the new order. Professed changes became the material codifications of a social and agrarian past that remained the firm basis for the architectural organization of work.

9. Ordinary Work

ARCHITECTURE FUNCTIONS ON MANY LEVELS, not the least of
which is as a set of signposts indicating the social and cultural
relationships obtaining in a given time and place. In studying building cycles of southern New Castle County we have observed how
individuals in a community setting used architecture to express
perceptions of society, self, and place. Certain questions, however,
remain. What was the significance of this particular restructuring of
the architectural environment? What sort of building activity took
place following the subsiding of the rebuilding fervor in the 1870s?
What is the place and importance of such building cycles in a larger
American landscape?

Although there seems to have been a unity of action in the
extent of building activity in the mid-nineteenth century, there was
no consensus about whether or not it was beneficial. Those who had
made themselves rich exploiting land, labor, and agriculture praised
the area in glowing terms; those who had lacked opportunity or met
with less success or who were residents new to the lower hundreds
assessed the land and community in more tempered terms. Thus,
George W. Tebo, a real-estate broker, offered properties in "The
Farmers' Klondike" with enthusiasm:

> Are you looking for Gold? Are you desirous of having great riches?
> Would you like to improve your present condition? If so, why journey
> over the glaciers and snow-capped mountains of the North? Why
> become excited by reports of great fortunes picked up in a day and be
> allured to the frozen Klondike by the bubble, "Sudden Riches," the
> pursuit of which, alas! too often ends in an experience like that of the
> belated traveler, who, enticed by the Will-o'the-Wisp, pushes on to
> disappointment, misery and death? Why do this when there is a

Klondike right near home in one of the most delightful spots in the Union, that is a veritable "Eden" for the farmer—not where one occasionally "strikes it rich," but where every man, if he makes a reasonable attempt, is sure of a comfortable living, and by right management, in the course of a few years. he will be able to enjoy a life of comparative ease and luxury.[1]

In contrast stand the observations of newcomer Reverend J. D. Rees, written to his wife in 1891:

I hardly know what to think about Appoquinimink. It will not impress you favorably at first but I think that we will like it when we get acquainted. . . .[2]

Tebo proclaimed the realization of the ideal of a farmer's estate, a world view advocated eighty years earlier by S. H. Black at the first meeting of the New Castle County agricultural society. Rees voiced uncertainty and a subdued optimism about the countryside that was to be his family's new home.

In a meticulously kept daybook, the Nowland family, residing at the former Richard Mansfield's Achmester, recorded expenditures for farm and home at the turn of the century.[3] From 1898 to 1902, the intricacies of their lives were jotted down and given an appropriate cash value. Tenant Isaac Townsend worked off the rent on his house in June and July 1898 by thinning corn, whitewashing two houses, cutting wheat and hay, threshing, and "ordinary work." As he worked, Townsend required additional advances of cash and grain, and at the end of each month owed landlord Nowland anywhere from 85¢ to $4 in rent. Daily expenses for the Nowland household in 1899 included the purchase of fruits, meats, vegetables, staples, and also sundries such as the housekeeper's wages, ice cream, gasoline, church donations, and car fare in the city—all paid for with cash or personal check. Compared to Mansfield's accounts kept in the 1820s, the Nowlands' books represented the continuation of the eighteenth- and nineteenth-century image of the farm as a community within the community. Each season the same laborers came to work in the fields, in the barns, and around the house. Between the entries listed under their laborer's names, the farmer entered his own expenditures, profits, and losses.

What was perfected during the rebuilding period in the middle decades of the 1800s was the architectural ordering of a rural class structure around the concept of an estate which, over time, became a more factory-like agricultural enterprise. The significance of the rebuilding of southern New Castle County is that it articulated in architectural terms a set of social and economic interrelationships. The gradual shift in house form, for example, from open to closed (through the incorporation of primary entries into stair passages) was only one aspect of the overall rethinking of household order. Just as important was the aesthetic equalization of the front rooms (through the types of paneling and ornamentation they received). While front rooms in some houses continued to be decoratively differentiated, the majority began to look very much alike. The old distinction between inner room and outer room in the first building cycles had been replaced with a separation between the front and back. As front rooms assumed equality and formality, rear or gable service wings achieved greater prominence as the spaces where the family actually lived. By the 1850s, the distance from front to back however, was being increased through the addition of intermediary rooms. Kitchens were shoved back as far as possible from the most ornate rooms at the front of the house, all the while remaining under the same roof. Servants' rooms located over the kitchen, for example, often could only be entered from the kitchen below and not from other second floor rooms.

Thus the remodeled and new dwellings of the nineteenth century document, first, the architectural accomplishment of a different domestic order, and, second, the inversion of expressed relationships within the household. The domestic order emerging in the rebuilding process echoed the adage of a place for everything, and everything in its place. Miquon's plan for a pegboard with designated spots for each and every tool was also the sort of image used for organizing the house. Specific rooms were set aside for formal entertaining, sitting, dining, reading, doing business, sleeping, storage, cooking, as well as for keeping children, invalids, and servants. Grouped near the back of the house were other structures including privies, smokehouses, woodsheds, dairies, carriage barns, and stables—some separate, some combined. And beyond the sphere of domestic activity were the new agricultural buildings—barns, stables, corncribs, and granaries. What farmers, builders, townsmen, and others had come to believe was that domestic and agricultural economy was based on the proper organization and allocation of space.

The new arrangement of rooms in the house and farm buildings in the agricultural complex were locally identified as part of a larger progress: "husbandry, the stock, the buildings and appearance of farms had improved, and the price of land had advanced."[4] Improvement, in this case, implied two things: first, increase in an agricultural economy and the material betterment of all things contributing to that economy; second, the stabilization of social and economic relationships. Southern New Castle County farmers called themselves agriculturalists and labeled their farms "estates" early in the nineteenth century. Those nominative gestures were expressed materially in the design and construction of the new dwellings and outbuildings of the mid century.

Defining the mid-nineteenth-century ideal of order was an emphasis that inverted the eighteenth-century sense of spatial/functional separations. Prior to the rebuilding period the unity of home and work was accepted, while the separation of functions, such as house and kitchen, grain storage and cattle shelter, were made literal through the construction of numerous small buildings carefully placed near the house. In the rebuilding, the separation of functions became axiomatic, just as the household and agriculture spaces were unified as single structures. By the close of the period of intense renewal, all but the dirtiest of household activities had been drawn together under one roof, just as the bank barn was intended to unify the functions of the farm. In practice, although the desire for unity was widely professed, many of the old separations remained within the construction of farm buildings and in the household.

The reversal of stressed values in architectural thought is the point on which rebuilding efforts turned. The pursuit of an estate or the streamlining of domestic and agrarian work patterns were not the causes of changes in architecture but were a part of the same revaluing process. Those who controlled the land and built upon it in the nineteenth century possessed a self-image that was profoundly different from that held by their eighteenth-century predecessors. If there was a revolution in the structure of society that found expression in architecture, the cause lay in the relationships between man and land, between individual and community, and in the sense of past and present. Before 1820, development of southern New Castle County went through a series of overlapping building cycles that marked the progression from impermanence to durabiliy and on to social closure and functional unity. The nineteenth-century rebuilding of southern New Castle County transfigured the architectural order in a relatively short period of time. The root of the transfiguration was the control of the land itself. Those who could afford and maintain the luxury of social distance pursued the ideal of a rigidly class-structured community. In the course of architectural renewal, buildings were changed in ways that complemented the attitudinal changes. By century's end both embodied a certain aggressiveness and lack of flexibility that made rural society revolve in ever constricting spheres of interaction. Behind the monumental and tightly balanced facades of houses like Greenlawn and Monterey resided families who came to view their very lives as monuments to the new order they had contracted to be built.

The degree of change, its reenforcement and meaning are further emphasized by the dual character of building activity that occurred after 1870. First, southern New Castle County entered into a period of slowed architectural activity that lasted into the 1940s. Functional unity and conceptual separation of spaces remained the basis for architectural design. Thus, as late as the 1930s, one-room deep, two-story, center-passage plans with service ells were raised throughout the area, as were houses inspired by the popular writings of architect-authors like Gervase Wheeler or the contributors to *Godey's Ladies Book* and *Scientific American*. By the 1920s bungalows were built in towns like Delaware City and Middletown. Although quite different in appearance from the large houses of the nineteenth-century, bungalows continued the movement toward domestic consolidation. The more formal rooms occupied the front of the house, with kitchen, bath, and downstairs bedrooms pushed to the rear; at the same time all supportive functions were contained in a single cube that lacked service wings or ells. More important, bungalows represented a middle-class architecture generally affordable by most individuals with moderate financial means.[5]

Second, the few major building projects that were undertaken in the rural areas of the county in the years after mid century represent the continuation of earlier nineteenth-century concerns. For example, the McCoy House, an arts-and-crafts-influenced mansion designed by architects Voysey and Webb, was commissioned in Red Lion Hundred in 1892, and, in the early twentieth century, the Vogel family had an eight-story water tower built behind their house in Blackbird Hundred. Both buildings followed earlier local precedent in their manipulation of building material and scale as well as in their utilitarian and socially symbolic functions.

Most building activity in the southern hundreds dwindled to the point where new projects were confined to merely maintaining and slightly increasing the housing stock in the still-growing towns or individual replacements for existing buildings. Following the intense activity of the period from 1830 to 1870, southern New Castle County had entered into a period of refinement that continued to uphold architectural and social values worked out and articulated in the previous generations.

Parallel to the slowing of architectural activity was an emerging fascination with local history and biography. Although general histories of Delaware had been compiled in the early decades of the nineteenth century and the Historical Society of Delaware founded in 1864 with the purpose of "the elucidation of history particularly such portions as may refer to this State," it was not until the 1880s that the first in a series of statewide histories with local emphasis began to appear.[6] The first, Scharf's *History of Delaware*, began with a general topical history of Delaware, followed by individual chapters on each of the counties and hundreds.[7] Of particular importance is the fact that Scharf's history was written on subscription, which enabled patrons to include themselves in the text. The resulting two-volume work provided a vehicle for the self-congratulatory history of individuals who had been particularly active in agricultural reform, the rebuilding process, and local political, social, and economic affairs. Once architectural renewal had been accomplished, those who had commissioned improved and new buildings turned their attention to recording a past in which they emerged as the dominant forces for modernism in their communities. Thus, they bought themselves and their ancestors a place in history.

William Wilson of "the Levels" in Appoquinimink Hundred, for example, is described as having devoted himself to agriculture, and made it the business of his life." Scharf continued:

> With wise sagacity and untiring energy he devoted himself to the work of renovating the land and enlarging his domain. He was so successful that years before his death he was the possessor of about thirty-five hundred acres of the choicest land in the Peninsula.[8]

Anthony Madison Higgins of Red Lion Hundred was portrayed as an "agriculturalist" who,

> a prominent citizen of Delaware in his day, was born November 22, 1809, on the place and near the spot where he died [July 1887]. This place is known as Fairview. His father, Anthony Higgins, and grand-

father, Laurence Higgins, had cultivated the same farm, and it is now owned and tilled by John C. Higgins, his oldest son.

Mr. Higgins was not one of the class of men who are content with inferior methods when better may be employed. He believed in going forward to the attainment of the best possible results. Hence, it is not surprising that he made the farm which he tilled advance from an inferior condition to the very front rank of handsome and productive rural estates.[9]

Jacob Benjamin Cazier of southern Pencader Hundred had farmed with equal success and superior achievement:

> After the death of his father, in 1859, he retired from the practical work of farming and removed to "Mt. Vernon Place," his beautiful home. In this farm, Mr. Cazier had taken great interest, and, with pardonable self-satisfaction, has made it one of the most productive and valuable estates in the county.
>
> In 1878 Mr. Cazier took away all of the old family residence except a portion of the outside walls, and rebuilt in a modern style, after plans of his own, making for himself one of the most commodious, richly-finished and elegant mansions in the State [Fig. 9:2].[10]

Andrew Eliason of St. Georges Hundred began his career "a penniless orphan at the early age of sixteen."

> He has been, all his life, engaged in farming, to the practical details of which he has given the closest attention. Every step of his life shows evidence of sound judgement and strong common sense. Commencing life as a driver of teams n the [Chesapeake and Delaware] canal, he has advanced steadily forward, and, by the exercise of the sterling virtues of industry and frugality, had become the owner of four unencumbered farms, embracing nearly nine hundred acres, in St. George's Hundred and Pencader Hundreds.
>
> The old dwelling, purchased with his farm in 1838, and to which he took his young family, was exchanged in 1856 for the commodious mansion in which he now makes his home [Fig. 9:3].[11]

Cazier, Eliason, Higgins, and Wilson were not the only ones to commemorate their passage on the land though the commissioning of both history and architecture. James M. Vandergrift of St. Georges Hundred included in his biography mention of his move in 1860 to Elm Grange where, "He rebuilt the house and completed a beautiful and substantial residence for his family."[12] Thomas Dilworth similarly noted he had improved his land near Port Penn, as did Joshua Clayton at his Choptank-on-the-Hill.

The promise of building biography into history at the close of the nineteenth century lay in the desire and ability of individuals to fix themselves in time. The estates they built in one action and commemorated in a second were monuments of one sort, but even as markers of a kind of change understood within the community these buildings could not fully articulate the degree of change. Dwellings, barns, churches, and town plans remodeled and replaced in the mid-nineteenth century were a product of a pervasive change in the way in which rural society was structured. Those who had wrought those changes did not see the architecture of the rebuilding period as the embodiment of a deeper social change. For them the architecture they authorized was the measure of their own stature. Scharf's biographical sketches, and later on those of Bevan and Conrad, evoke images of devotion and frugality in work, faithfulness and reliance in the home, willingness to serve the causes of agriculture, business, and politics.[13] The men who had commissioned these portraits advanced their own careers as proof of the efficacy of these values. In the mid-nineteenth century they incorporated those same values into their dwellings and farms. The buildings they commissioned evoked the anticipation and attainment of success. When the architectural activity dwindled they turned to constructing history to lend voice to the world they had made.

Just as the rebuilding recorded in southern New Castle County is a phenomenon common to other landscapes at other times, the writing of local histories extolling similar virtues was duplicated in other areas. In some places histories are basically antiquarian texts. On the Eastern Shore of Virginia, Jennings Cropper Wise produced a narrative recounting the seventeenth- and eighteenth-century settlements of Northampton and Accomack Counties. In New England and the mid-Atlantic states local authors penned anecdotal village and county histories.[14] Scharf was a proprietor of a history-writing company producing texts throughout the mid-Atlantic area.[15] The commissioning of local history, like the drive toward rebuilding, was part of an increasing national consciousness. Since, history followed architecture, we can see first the architectural manifestation of social and economic control, and second the textual celebration of those actions. Houses stored and displayed the fruits of profit. Written history provided a narrative about the remembered origin and progress of landholders across the architectural landscape.

Figure 9:1. Streetscape, Townsend, showing late nineteenth-century houses.

From the first substantial occupation of southern New Castle County, through layers of building that yielded a regionally identifiable architecture, through a period of rebuilding in which the architectural landscape was restructured, to the continuation and refinement of architectural values after the 1880s and the writing of

Figure 9:2. Mount Vernon Place, Summit vicinity, Pencader Hundred (1870–1880). Photograph: DSA.

history—the cycles experienced by southern New Castle County epitomize the history of architectural landscapes generally in the eastern United States. Layers of building and rebuilding may have occurred with particular reference to economic, social, and architectural forces at work in specific contexts, but the overall pattern of activity cuts across geographical and temporal lines. Unifying seemingly disparate architectural landscapes are those functions of buildings that go beyond the providing of basic shelter. The house, barn, farm, church, and village are external signs of social organization and symbolize the intricate internal ways in which people materially order their lives. The strength of any architectural sign wears thin with extensive use or with a shift in the perceptions through which the community see themselves or are seen by others.[16] Seemingly simple changes—the widespread acceptance of stair-passage-plan houses, bringing service activities under a common roof, or the building of granaries to accommodate wheeled traffic—reveal profound realignments in the values held by those who commissioned, lived in, and worked within those settings. Complex systems of carpentry, novel applications of stylish finish, the elaboration and enlargement of culturally established architectural spaces represent the refinement of more basic changes.

Basic changes in Delaware included the emergence of a landed middle class and the erosion of customary relationships within the community. Domestic architecture expressed various qualities of social outlook and organization; buildings symbolized social status, economic attainment, and agricultural progress. The architecture of the mid-nineteenth century also expressed the disintegration of local culture in the face of aggressive use of national styles drawn from pattern books and stock decorative elements purchased from urban factories. The shift away from community-based relationships went beyond architectural preferences and agricultural practice. Literacy, for example, was required for keeping account books, writing contracts, and participating through correspondence

Figure 9:3. Andrew Eliason House, Summit vicinity, St. Georges Hundred (1850–60).

and papers in a national forum on farming, household design, and manners. Separately, each of those three expressions threatened established patterns of community interaction; together they contributed to the destruction of an older community founded on customary relationships. The resulting social and economic revolution produced a new conservatism that was expressed in everything from barns to ledgers. The motto, a place for everything, and everything in its place, encompassed corn in the crib, furnishings in the house, and the relationships between social classes.

The first dwellings to incorporate unheated stair-passages and service wings had continued traditions of room-to-room decorative emphasis. The paneled hearth walls of dining rooms (formerly the hall or common room) tokened one form of use and domestic interaction, while the interior finish applied to the parlor bespoke another. Even today, where first-floor interiors date from 1800 to 1830 a visitor can recognize which room is which. Not until the mid-1800s did it become standard practice to treat the front rooms with nearly identical trim and thereby signify that the entire front of the house was fundamentally different from the back and its individual rooms roughly interchangeable.

In a like manner, the mid-nineteenth-century development of unusually intricate framing systems for agricultural buildings did not result from the introduction of new types of barns and farm structures into the area. Although some barns, like the Cochran Grange complex, did employ displays of complicated timber framing techniques as early as the 1830s, the general appearance of double braces, wrought-iron clamps on principal posts and ties, and similar elements did not occur until the mid-nineteenth century. Elaborate displays of framing techniques were used only where they could be readily seen by outsiders or visitors. The intricate bracing systems developed for barns, granaries, and cart sheds were not used in houses or outbuildings that had ceilings and walls which would cover these features. Furthermore, intricate technological devices appeared at a time when a large number of skilled builders still lived in the district. This factor, coupled with the element of visibility, suggests that the sophisticated techniques used in buildings like the Cochran Grange threshing barn and the Woodlawn cart sheds were displays made by the builder and not the client. In effect, they were a form of self-promotion, advertising superior skill and ability in an increasingly constricted and highly competitive marketplace. After the rebuilding fervor had quieted, combination corncrib/granaries with runways for wagons, large dairy barns, and stables continued to be raised, but the reliance on complicated carpentry techniques gradually waned.

For house, barn, farm, and village the most significant changes were in matters of form. Where space was reshaped, social relationships and cultural attitudes were given direction. New choices in architectural ornament and its application, and innovations in the technology of building served to gloss the meaning and impact of spatial arrangements.

Architectural statements passing through time are subject to physical alterations of all sorts and become above-ground archaeological sites. By analytically stripping away layers of occupancy we can discover the house or barn as it existed in a given historic moment. Through the close analysis of individual sites, which we can identify by owner and place within a community, we can extrapolate collective reasoning and the bases of common communication. The dynamic stored up in our architectural heritage is as complex as it is fluid, and in our perceptions of action in time and context we perceive patterns of history. The history charted by vernacular building, however, is a history from the inside out. Frequently, the history wrapped up in this non-verbal, traditional process is at odds with later, written histories that chronicle key lives and institutional events which are deemed important from the vantage point of outside looking in.[17]

In some histories of southern New Castle County the cause of nineteenth-century architectural change has been assigned to the introduction of peach and fruit cultivation for market.[18] However, the heyday for these perishable crops spanned the decade from 1870 to 1880—well after the majority of building activity was underway or had been completed. Other narratives identify the cause as the opening of the Chesapeake and Delaware Canal or the extension of the railroad southward down the spine of the Delmarva Peninsula. Transportation certainly provided the means for the improved movement of goods in and out of the area. But access to the market was not the impetus leading to architectural change, although it may have increased the farmer's ability to take better advantage of regional markets and thus accrue the capital necessary to finance building projects. The cause for change lies in the fact that those who pursued the rebuilding and consolidated its values had embraced new ideas about the way in which home, farm, and village were socially structured. Where a sense of social class, stratified by the ability to hold land and acquire money, emerged as an organizing principal of community, those individuals with the power conferred by material possessions raised monuments to their own lives and progressive achievements in architecture and then memorialized themselves in subscription histories. The motivation and ability to realize social stratification based on material wealth was part of a national process felt at different times in different places. Over the broad region of the eastern United States architectural change heralding a new order was uneven, but in the end the result was equivalent.

The nineteenth-century architectural renewals of southern New Castle County slowed and came to a close in the 1880s. Farm values, as reflected in the United States agricultural census returns, had dramatically and steadily climbed between 1850 and 1870. In 1880, however, farm assessments plunged 30 to 60 percent throughout the area. The root of the collapse in value lay not in problems of production, pestilence, or soil quality, but in the relocation of most American grain production and commercial flour milling to the Midwest. Following the Civil War, an improved transportation system with better established land and water trade routes and the creation of farm equipment especially suited to vast expanses of flat, fertile, treeless, and rockless land allowed the Midwest to assume the role of the pre-eminent American grain belt—a distinction that had belonged to the middle-Atlantic region in the eighteenth and early nineteenth centuries.

Southern New Castle County was not the only area to experience a decline in its agricultural economy. The pattern of altered or vanished markets afflicted rural communities from Maryland to Maine, and each area sought its own panacea by marketing more perishable goods, ranging from fresh eggs to orchard produce.[19] In the wake of diminished farm incomes, the preoccupation with domestic and agricultural building projects likewise decreased. While a few individuals continued to commission occasional buildings, most of their neighbors had become preoccupied with other more pressing economic concerns.

Common architectural landscapes describe society in time and in motion. Each house or barn as it stands in time exists in one sense as a site-specific synthesis of a complex series of formal, construction, decorative, social, cultural, and contextually bound options. The reality of material choice also provides an index to a larger range of possibilities limiting, inspiring, diverting, and shaping future statements. Each building in every moment of its history from inception to destruction becomes an emblem of continuity and change. As an environment the architectural landscape is the distillation of memory and the perception of cultural order and social knowledge.

The architectural history of particular places breathes life into the body of theoretical speculation, lending abstract notions of society and material life the reality of time and place. The cycles of building and rebuilding characteristic of southern New Castle County are not unique to one place or a given time but are part of the greater American landscape. It is our task to find pattern in cultural behavior across regional and temporal boundaries and, at the same time, to discover the degree to which individual changes are peculiar to time and place or are part of a larger continuum. We are, as one New Castle County farmer wrote in 1820, ". . . industriously pursuing the traceless paths of investigation and discovery in order that the reflections of a winter's day may be made to produce, if nothing better offers, something to augment our stock of theoretical speculations."[20]

Glossary

Architrave. The trim, often molded, surrounding openings such as doors and windows.

Ashlar. Stone masonry of regularly shaped and finished blocks laid in even courses.

Baseboard. A plank used to decoratively finish the juncture of an interior wall and the floor. Baseboards also provide a tight and even interior seal between wall and floor.

Bay. A portion of a structure marked off by sections of framing or dimensional units. A bay also denotes the openings along the first-floor line in the fenestration of a structure.

Bead. A rounded molding run with a plane along the edge of a timber or board.

Belt course. A projecting, sometimes decorative, band of exterior masonry visually delineating an internal division between stories or acting as flashing for a pent or porch roof.

Bent. A lateral section of framing defining one side of a bay.

Block. A heavy piece of unworked timber (such as a section of tree trunk) averaging two to three feet in height and employed as a foundation supporting the underframe of a building.

Brace. In timber framing, a diagonally set timber stiffening the frame and preventing twisting or distortion.

Brick bonds. The pattern employed in laying brick in courses. Examples found in southern New Castle County commonly include:
Flemish bond—alternating headers and stretchers in a single course laid in such a manner that a header in one course typically lines up over a stretcher in the below;
English bond—alternating courses of headers and stretchers;
Common bond—where each course of headers alternates with multiple (usually three, five, or seven) courses of stretchers;
Stretcher bond—all stretcher courses.

Chair rail. A strip of molding running around the walls of a room at about three feet above the floor.

Chamfer. A bevel-edge molding cut along the exposed surface of framing members. A chamfer may terminate in a straight stop, sloped ending, or decorative terminal.

Chinking. The material used to fill the space between horizontal members in a log or a plank wall.

Collar. A roof-framing member serving as a tie between opposing pairs of rafter blades. The earliest examples are fixed to the rafters with half-dovetailed lap joints and pinned in place, while in late nineteenth-century structures they are nailed in place to the sides of the rafters.

Common rafter. One of a series of equal-sized rafters, usually on two-foot centers, carrying the roof covering.

Cornice. A molding of wood, plaster, or other material at the base of the roof and top of the lateral surface of an exterior wall or at the juncture of an interior wall and ceiling.

Course. A horizontal row of bricks in a wall.

Ell. A wing or addition built at right angles to one side of the structure, creating an L-shaped plan.

False plate. A timber or plank set into or across the upper ends of joists, extending beyond the face of the structure and providing a seat for the rafter feet. Also known as a raising plate.

Girt. In framed buildings, a horizontal member in a bent supporting ceilings or floors. The topmost girts in southern New Castle County houses are often the end joists.

Graining. The application of paint to achieve a visually textured effect resembling wood grain.

Header. The butt end of brick.

Joist. A timber spanning the width of a building and supporting the floors and, at the attic level, the base of the roof framing.

Lath. Strip of riven or sawn wood to which shingles or plaster are applied.

Lean-to. A shed addition, usually no more than one room deep and one story in elevation.

Marbleizing. The application of paint in such a manner so as to suggest masonry materials, most typically marble.

Mortise and tenon. A framing joint in which a tongue of one timber is inserted into a pocket cut in the other and locked into place with a wooden pin or nails.

Nailer. A block or length of timber set into a masonry surface such as a chimney pile or brick wall and to which mantels, paneling, or other trim can be nailed.

Nogging. Fill, usually of soft brick, inserted into the framed walls of a building.

Overmantel. A section of paneling or plaster work circumscribed by a molding and located above the mantel surrounding the fireplace opening.

Passage. The modern equivalent of

this term would be hall or corridor. Usually an unheated space containing stairs, connecting other rooms, and providing access between floors or to the outside.

Pent. In Delaware Valley architecture, a shallow shed-like roof, framed on extended joists between floors or at the base of the gable.

Piers. Masonry footings placed at intervals to support a frame or log structure above the ground.

Pile. 1) Referring to the depth of a building, usually in terms of structural bays defining rooms. A single-pile dwelling for example, is one room deep; 2) the mass of a chimney.

Plate. The horizontal timber carried across the tops of the framing posts or at the top of a masonry wall that provides the base for the attic and roof framing.

Post. 1) A vertical, load-bearing member used in braced-frame construction; 2) a vertical timber set in the ground as a support for the base of a structure.

Post-and-plank. A combination of log and frame walling where horizontal logs are joined to corner posts.

Principals. In braced-frame construction, major load-bearing members usually arranged as opposing pairs.

Purlin. A lateral timber running across the face of a roof parallel to the ridge. Purlins in the lower Delaware Valley are usually found in principal rafter roofs and bear the weight of the common rafters.

Rail. A section of timber framing running at right angles between two posts and providing a nailing surface for vertical board siding.

Relieving arch. A round arch in the cellar carrying the weight of the chimney pile. It is often mistakenly assumed that these arches are closed up fireplaces.

Round. An eighteenth-century term designating a log in a wall. For example, a log building might be described as nine rounds high.

Sill. In timber framing, the base member carrying the first-floor joists and seating posts and studs.

Stretcher. The side face of a brick.

Stud. A vertical member running between sill and plate or sill and girt. In braced-frame construction, these are not necessarily load-bearing members, but serve as nailing surfaces for lath and siding.

Tie beam. A framing timber binding two opposing framing members or units together. For example, a collar beam acting as a tension member between two opposing rafters.

Water table. In masonry structures, the offset on the external walls where the foundation walls thin out into the upper walls. On brick structures, the water table may be simply offset or finished with beveled or molded bricks.

Notes

CHAPTER I

1. Delaware State Archives, New Castle County Orphans Court (1778), F-1-20. Hereafter: DSA, orphans.
2. Gray (1958), 75–131.
3. Scharf (1888), Eckman (1955), Hoffecker (1977), Munroe (1979).
4. Kalm (1966), 273–74, 727–28; Hempstead (1901), 525.
5. For studies on the industrial development of northern Delaware, see Wallace (1980), Ferguson (1980), Hoffecker (1974). The agricultural profiles of Delaware cited here are the product of the Rural History and Community Studies Project, American Studies Program, University of Delaware (1981–83). The Rural History project was designed and implemented by David F. Allmendinger, Jr., and H. John Michel, Jr.
6. Matthews and Lavole (1970).
7. Tilton (1789), 156–80, 217–20.
8. Ibid., 157.
9. Spurrier (1793); see especially pp. 11–21 for Spurrier's views on the spirit and design of agriculture.
10. Eckman (1955). 519–29.
11. An example of these perspectives on Delaware architecture can be found in Eberlein and Hubbard (1962), 3–12. Bennett (1932) exhibits "period" details for use as source material for architects.
12. Intensive architectural survey work has been continuous in New Castle County since 1977 and has been made possible through matching grants provided by the Delaware Division of Historical and Cultural Affairs, Bureau of Archaeology and Historic Preservation.
13. The county atlases consulted for New Castle County include Rea and Price (1849), Beers and Lake (1860), Beers (1868). Hopkins (1881), Baist (1893).
14. All the field data from these surveys are deposited with the Bureau of Archaeology and Historic Preservation within the Delaware Division of Historical and Cultural Affairs.
15. Laslett (1971), Hoskins (1965), Bloch (1966), MacFarlane (1977), Tate and Ammerman (1979), Michel (1981).
16. Handsman (1983), Stone (1971), Sturtevant (1966), Carson (1978).
17. Structuralists' perspectives on history are contained in Robey (1972), Lane (1970), Levi-Strauss (1963), Kurzweil (1980).
18. Thomas (1878), 129.

CHAPTER 2

1. Glassie (1968–69), 32–39.
2. For discussions of typologies based on form, fabric, fashion and context, see: Herman and Orr (1975), 307–27; Marshall (1981); Brunskill (1971), 30–32.
3. Henry Glassie's work on the identification and analysis of building forms continues to set the standard for most current American scholarship. Glassie (1968–69); Glassie, (1975a); Upton (1982); Chappell (1980).
4. Carson (1974); Stiverson (1977), 56–84; Earle (1975), 136–38.
5. DSA, orphans (1805), I-1-291.
6. Delaware State Archives, New Castle County Inventories (hereafter DSA and name of inventory), Christopher Vandergrift inventory (1818).
7. DSA, Thomas Adams inventory (1790); Twiss-Garrity (1983), 17–18.
8. DSA, John Hales inventory (1723).
9. DSA, orphans (1775), E-1-47.
10. Carson (1974).
11. DSA, David Ross inventory (1818).
12. DSA, orphans (1792), G-1-339.
13. DSA, John Jacquet inventory (1692). The appraisers of Jacquet's estate listed the frame of a house thirty-five by twenty feet and two-and-a-half stories in elevation. The dimensions, which at the least are those of a hall-parlor plan, describe what would have been an unusually large house for the period.
14. The terms "Penn plan" and "Quaker plan" refer to three-room and double-pile, two-room house types. The confusion surrounding the definitions of these types is considerable. See: Johnston and Waterman (1941), 173–74; Herman (1978). The relationship of these plans to urban counterparts in southeastern Pennsylvania is the subject of current research by Alice Kent Schooler.
15. DSA, Ingeber Lefevre inventory (1807).
16. Carson et al. (1981), 141–44.
17. Glassie (1975a), 88–89; Deetz (1977), 39–40; Morrison (1952), 300–317; Kimball (1966), 56–63; Waterman (1945), 3–17.
18. Forman (1934), 149.
19. Two examples are the Allee House, Kent County, Delaware, and Mount Pleasant, Northampton County, Virginia. The latter is illustrated in Whitelaw (1968), 337–38.
20. DSA, David Stewart inventory (1829).
21. Sweeney (1959) contains a full account of the Corbit House, including reference to surrounding contemporary structures.
22. DSA, orphans (1801), I-1-157.
23. DSA, John Golden inventory (1790).
24. DSA, orphans (1801), I-1-157; (1794), H-1-123.
25. Ibid., 161.
26. Webb (1984), 3–163.
27. Nash (1979); Isaac (1982), 285–93 and 320–22.
28. Warner (1968), 3–4.

CHAPTER 3

1. Latrobe (1805), section of Delaware Street. For information on hierarchies of finish, see Chappell (1984). Other examples of the social significance of doorways are presented in Sweeney (1984), 242–43 and 248–49.

2. Sickler (1949); Love (1955), 182–208.

3. Gowans (1964), 10–14.

4. Sickler (1949), 57–58. The Gregg House is located near Kennett Square, Chester County, Pennsylvania.

5. Carson et al. (1981), 169–70; Melchor, Lohr, and Melchor (1982). The furniture presented by Lohr and the Melchors bears out Carson and his co-author's thesis that early colonial Chesapeake Bay builders found it "better to put profits back into production and spend disposable income on material comforts that could be enjoyed immediately."

CHAPTER 4

1. Redfield (1973), Beeman (1977), Fenton (1973).

2. DSA, orphans (1775), E-1-47.

3. Bourcier (1984).

4. DSA, orphans (1774), D-1-482; (1773), D-1-421.

5. DSA, orphans (1792), G-1-379; (1794), H-1-123.

6. DSA, Joshua Clayton inventory (1798).

7. Thomas Evans accounts (1793).

8. John Dickinson papers (1799). The references cited here are from the collected and edited papers compiled by the Delaware Bureau of Museums for the John Dickinson Mansion Project, Kent County.

9. DSA, orphans (1793), H-1-85.

10. DSA, David Ross inventory (1818).

11. DSA, orphans (1792), G-1-381; (1808), I-1-637.

12. Glassie (1975b), 9–19; St. George (1982b), 7–23.

13. DSA, orphans (1795), H-1-187.

14. Jicha (1984), Shoemaker (1959),

Dornbusch and Heyl (1958), Ball (1974).

15. William Clarke, Portrait of Captain William Frazer 1798, accession no. 30.38.01, Historical Society of Delaware.

16. DSA, Isaac Cleaver inventory (1832).

17. DSA, orphans (1776), E-1-64.

18. DSA, David Ross inventory (1818); DSA, John Alrichs inventory (1829).

19. DSA, orphans (1779), F-1-240.

20. Tilton (1789), 217.

21. DSA, orphans (1795), H-1-187.

22. Ibid. (1779), F-1-8.

23. Ibid. (1810), I-1-665.

24. DSA, David Ross inventory (1818); DSA, John Alrich inventory (1829); DSA, John Cleaver inventory (1820).

25. DSA, Edward Congo inventory (1811).

26. DSA, Jacob Fariss inventory (1818).

27. DSA, orphans (1801), I-1-162; DSA, John Janvier inventory (1801).

28. Richard Mansfield accounts (1825–44).

29. U.S. Secretary of the Treasury (1833). For a detailed and readily comprehensible overview of milling, see Reynolds (1970).

30. DSA, orphans (1779), F-1-81.

31. U.S. Secretary of the Treasury (1833), 774–75.

32. DSA, orphans (1805), I-1-446; (1799), H-1-737.

33. U.S. Secretary of the Treasury (1833), 744–57.

34. DSA, orphans (1801), I-1-105.

35. U.S. Secretary of the Treasury (1833), 827.

36. Ibid., 756–57.

37. Hazen (1837), 67–69.

38. DSA, orphans (1801), I-1-105.

39. DSA, orphans (1773), D-1-84; (1793), H-1-164.

40. Clarke (1981).

41. Heite (1978).

42. Stewart papers (1810); Port Penn papers (1794).

CHAPTER 5

1. Carson et al. (1981).

2. Ibid., 141.

3. Archaeological excavations conducted by Cara Wise at the site in the summer of 1979 identified post holes, a board-lined cellar, and remnants of a clay-lined, post-and-wattle chimney.

4. DSA, orphans (1775), D-1-532.

5. Ibid., E-1-47.

6. McKee (1976), 82–84; Brunskill and Clifton-Taylor (1977), 15–16; Noël Hume (1974), 32–36; Cooper (1814), 386–404.

7. Loth (1974), 82–120.

8. Upton (1976), 22–43; Upton (1981), 51–75; Buchanan (1976), 54–73.

9. DSA, New Castle County tax assessments, 1803–04 and 1816–17. These record groups were the subject of a statistical project undertaken by David Allmendinger, Jr., and Laura Tuthill in 1978–79.

10. Herman (1982), 183.

11. DSA, orphans (1795), H-1-180; (1792) G-1-320 (1775) D-1-534.

12. Patterson (1931), 122–24.

13. Ridout (1978). This mode of construction has been identified in sawn-plank and hewn-log buildings from North Carolina through Pennsylvania. I am grateful to Orlando Ridout V and Paul Touart for their field observations in Maryland and North Carolina.

14. Glassie (1968b), 343–47, 350.

15. Jordan (1985); Mercer (1976), 18–31; Case (1976).

16. Glassie (1968b), 347–50; Jordan (1984).

17. Upton (1981), 36–84; Cummings (1979); Whiffen (1960).

18. Glassie (1974).

19. Glassie (1975a), 122–33; Glassie (1974), 212–17; Upton (1976), 22–43.

20. Upton (1979), 176–77.

21. Upton (1981), 65–67.

22. For regional variations in purlin roofs see Upton (1981), 42, 49–50, 67–68, 76, 80–81.

23. Upton (1976), 22–43.

24. There are a number of excellent regional studies on the vernacular architecture of the British Isles, including Mercer, (1975), Smith (1975), Fenton and Walker (1981), Gailey (1984), Machin (1978), Barley (1961), and Wood-Jones (1963).

25. Kniffen (1965), 549–77; Glassie (1968); Cummings (1979), 202–9.

CHAPTER 6

1. DSA, New Castle County tax assessments, 1816–17, St. Georges Hundred. The statistical evidence cited here was developed by Laura Tuthill and David Allmendinger, Jr., in 1978–79.

2. The evidence for the basis of these explanations was developed by H. John Michel, Jr., and David Allmendinger, Jr., in the course of the Rural History Project conducted by the American Studies Program at the University of Delaware, 1982–83. The sources for the data were the 1850 and 1870 United States Census manuscript schedules for Delaware.

3. Michel (1984), 15.

4. Ibid., 19 and 22.

5. U.S. Secretary of the Treasury (1833), 744–57. The day-to-day transactions of the tanning busi-

ness are recorded in the Corbit
family accounts 1795–1826.

6. Michel (1984), 42.

7. Black (1820), 9–11 ff.

8. Ibid., 9.

9. Ibid.

10. Ibid., 10.

11. Suydam (1847), 4.

12. Bushman (1982), 27–49. David Allmendinger, Jr., and Laura Tuthill
examined United States Census,
manuscript schedules, Schedules
of Population for the years 1800–
20 and found a significant out-
migration from the countryside in
that twenty-year period.

13. Pritts (1845), 202–6.

14. "A Good Suggestion" (1836–37),
14.

15. Niagra (1836), 37.

16. Bond (1983); Biggs accounts (1854).

17. Biggs accounts (1855).

18. Upton (1982), 98; Barthes (1968),
56–57.

19. Holly (1863), 57–58.

20. Eberlein and Hubbard (1962), 142–
43.

21. For the relationship between orchard crops and transportation see
Pyle (1879), 194–99.

22. Ibid., 194.

23. Ibid., 198.

24. Deetz (1977), 92–117; Glassie
(1975), 185–93.

25. Hoskins (1965), 131–48; Harris
(1978), 50–52; Barley (1961), 57–
179; Machin (1977a); Machin
(1977b); Hutton (1977); Alcock
(1983).

26. Glassie (1975a), 182–88; Deetz
(1977), 115–17; Upton (1982); Bonta (1979), 131–224.

27. Hoskins (1965), 137.

28. Smith (1969); Lawrence (1983), 22;
Ginzburg (1982), xiv–xx; Barnett
(1953), 291–312.

29. Upton (1979), 173–75.

30. Whitelaw (1968), 156–57; Chiaramonte (1970), 19–46; Cummings
(1979), 193–221.

31. In architectural histories, cities
have been cited as the centers for
innovative design—especially in
terms of the work of individual
architects. Kirker (1969), Alexander (1974), Mumford (1955).

32. Loth (1974), 109.

33. The information on builders and
tradesmen in southern New Castle
County through the latter half of
the nineteenth century was compiled from United States Census,
manuscript schedules, Schedule of
Population by Rebecca S. Siders.

34. Richard Mansfield accounts (1829):
June through August.

35. Note found in a house on High
Street, Odessa. Reference courtesy
of Marcia Jarrell.

36. Note found in a house in Appoquinimink Hundred. Reference
courtesy of Valerie Cesna.

37. U.S. Census Schedule of Manufactures (1870).

38. Samuel Townsend accounts (1864).

39. U.S. Census Schedule of Manufactures (1850, 1860, 1870, 1880).

40. Cochran (1855).

41. Thompson (1982), 6–7.

42. Bennett Downs accounts (1815–
17).

CHAPTER 7

1. Sweeney (1959), 41–44.

2. Several individuals have examined
the Christopher Vandergrift House
and contributed to unraveling its
complicated physical history. I
would like to thank Dean Nelson,
W. Brown Morton III, Charles

Bergengren, and Doug Reed for
their insights.

3. The publication and distribution of nineteenth-century builders' guides and pattern books were extensive. Among the many titles known to have circulated in the lower Delaware Valley are Cleveland, Backus and Backus (1856), Vaux (1869), Wheeler (1855), Woodward (1867), and Allen (1860).

4. Glassie (1982), 327–424 and 589–608.

5. Woodward (1867), 98–101.

6. I am grateful to Stuart Rafert for sharing his research on Fairview. The quote is from the narrative of the 1982 National Register of Historic Places nomination prepared by the office of the New Castle County historic preservation planner.

7. William Brady described the patterns of building hierarchies and field rotation at Greenlawn, as he remembered them, in a series of conversations during the summer of 1982.

8. This quote comes from a letter written by William Wilson to Alexander Wilson of Pencader Hundred (Wilson Correspondence, 1874).

9. DSA, orphans (1829), N-1-206.

10. Cobbett (1803), 134–39, 185–86, pls. XIV and XV.

11. Mansfield accounts (1827–44), entries for June through August, 1829. A final settlement date September 1, 1829, reads, "Settled with Robert MacFarlan for carpenters work, he and Willis having worked for me 102 day[s] together a[t] $1 for day."

12. I am indebted to Henry Vaughan for the use of Mansfield and Nowland family records and for permis-

sion to reproduce the view of Achmester in Figure 8:19.

13. DSA, Richard Mansfield inventory (1846).

14. DSA, David Stewart inventory (1829).

15. DSA, David Ross inventory (1818).

16. Matthews and Lavole (1970). Statistical studies by H. John Michel, Jr., of manuscript agricultural census returns for 1850 demonstrate a direct correspondence between soil types and aspects of agricultural production such as investment in farm machinery, cultivation of certain grains, and the rearing of cattle and sheep.

17. Thomas (1857), 314–23.

18. Ibid., 314–16.

19. DSA, Thomas Janvier inventory (1856).

20. DSA, David Craven inventory (1862).

21. DSA, William Cleaver inventory (1859).

22. DSA, William Stewart inventory (1844).

23. Dickey (1808), 290–95.

24. Glassie (1982), 405–14; St. George (1982a), 161 and 169–72.

25. Glassie (1975a), 66–113; St. George (1982), 170–73; Upton (1982), 104–7.

CHAPTER 8

1. DSA, Benjamin Wilson inventory (1802).

2. A sample of nineteenth-century agricultural papers circulating all along the eastern seaboard includes *The American Farmer, Genessee Farmer, The Farmer's Cabinet, The Southern Planter,* and *The Agriculturalist.*

3. Todd (1870), 239.

4. Halsted (1884), 183–86.

5. Forman (1975), 165 and 269.

6. Agricultural Society of New Castle County (1836–72), entry for September 17, 1845.

7. Samuel Townsend accounts (1857–1873); Richard Mansfield accounts (1825–44); Philadelphia Society for the Promotion of Agriculture (1939), 218.

8. An instance of such a formula penciled into a bound annual volume of *The Farmer's Cabinet* runs ". . . to ascertain the quantity of corn in a crib or house multiply the length, breadth & depth together then the whole product by 4, cut off the right hand figure of the last product and you have the bushels of shelled corn." (Collection of the author.)

9. DSA, Alexander Lea inventory (1866).

10. Agricultural Society of New Castle County (1836–72), entry for January 13, 1855.

11. There is little detailed information on the regional development of English-style bank barns in the lower Delaware River Valley. The best Delaware field study is Jicha (1984). See also Brunskill (1974), 76–86.

12. Halsted (1884), 13.

13. Allen (1860), 290.

14. *The American Agriculturalist* (1847), 24–26.

15. Several of the barns discussed in the text were recorded through large format photography and measured drawings in 1982. The recording project was made possible through a grant from the University of Delaware Research Foundation.

16. The receipt for the purchase and delivery of building materials for farmbuildings to be commissioned by Williams is in possession of the William Cross family, who are the current farm owners.

17. Allen (1860), 290–98; Waring (1877), 69–73.

18. Deane (1822), 16.

19. Ibid., 16.

20. Waring (1877), 50.

21. Kent County Mutual Assurance, policies for George Cummins dated August 9, 1850 and January 2, 1854.

22. DSA, Peter Alrichs inventory (1866).

CHAPTER 9

1. Tebo (1900), 1.

2. Butler (1980), 2.

3. Nowland family accounts (1898–1902).

4. Scharf (1888), 434.

5. Wright (1980), 106–49; Wright (1981), 240–61.

6. Simmons (1964), 7–8.

7. Scharf (1888). Scharf's history is presented in two volumes, with the first containing a general history of the state and its institutions and the second divided into county and hundred histories.

8. Ibid., 1018.

9. Ibid., 961–62.

10. Ibid., 949–50.

11. Ibid., 984.

12. Ibid., 988.

13. Bevan (1929); Conrad (1908).

14. Wise (1967); Shourds (1876); Temple (1875).

15. Scharf (1879), Scharf (1882), Scharf (1884), Scharf and Westcott (1884), Scharf (1886), Scharf (1888).

16. Bonta (1979), 200–2.

17. Carson (1978), Glassie (1972).

18. Scharf (1888), 440–41.

19. Shannon (1945), 245–67.

20. Mendenhall (1820), 75.

Bibliography

"An Act to Incorporate a Society, under the Name and Style of the Agricultural Society of the County of New Castle." *American Farmer* 2, no. 1 (March 31, 1820), 1–3.

Adams, Thomas. *Outline of Town and City Planning: A Review of Past Efforts and Modern Aims.* New York: Russell Sage Foundation, 1935.

Alcock, N. W. "The Great Rebuilding and Its Later Stages." *Vernacular Architecture* 14 (1983), 45–48.

Alexander, Christopher. *Notes on the Synthesis of Form.* Cambridge: Harvard Univ. Press, 1964.

Alexander, Robert L. *The Architecture of Maximillian Godefroy.* Baltimore: Johns Hopkins Univ. Press, 1974.

Allen, Lewis F. *Rural Architecture, Being a Complete Description of Farm Houses, Cottages and Out Buildings.* New York: C. M. Saxton, Banner and Co., 1860.

Armstrong, Robert Plant. *The Affecting Presence: An Essay in Humanistic Anthropology.* Urbana: Univ. of Illinois Press, 1971.

Bachelard, Gaston. *The Poetics of Space.* Boston: Beacon Press, 1958/1969.

Baist, G. William. *Atlas of New Castle County, Delaware.* Philadelphia: G. William Baist, 1893.

Ball, Bernice. *Barns of Chester County, Pennsylvania.* West Chester, Pa.: Chester County Day Committee of the Women's Auxilliary, Chester County Hospital, 1974.

Barley, M. W. *The English Farmhouse and Cottage.* London: Routledge and Kegan Paul, 1961.

Barnett, H. G. *Innovation: The Basis of Cultural Change.* New York: McGraw-Hill, 1953.

Barthes, Roland. *Elements of Semiology.* New York: Hill and Wang, 1968.

Beeman, Richard R. "The New Social History and the Search for 'Community' in Colonial America." *American Quarterly* 39, no. 4 (Fall 1977), 422–43.

Beers, D. G. *Atlas of the State of Delaware.* Philadelphia: Pomeroy and Beers, 1868.

Beers, S. N., and D. J. Lake. *Map of the Vicinity of Philadelphia.* Philadelphia: John E. Gillette and C. K. Stone, 1860.

Bennett, George Fletcher. *Early Architecture of Delaware.* Wilmington, Del.: Historical Press, 1932.

Bevan, Wilson Lloyd, ed. *History of Delaware, Past and Present.* New York: Lewis Historical Publishing Co., 1929.

Biggs, Benjamin. Day Book, 1847–57. Special Collections, Morris Library, Univ. of Delaware, Newark, Del.

Binford, Lewis. *An Archeological Perspective.* New York: Seminar Press, 1972.

Bishir, Catherine. "Jacob W. Holt: An American Builder." *Winterthur Portfolio* 16, no. 1 (Spring 1981), 1–31.

Black, Samuel Henry. Extract Book 1810 [Farm Accounts]. Special Collections, Morris Library, Univ. of Delaware, Newark, Del.

———. "An Essay, On the Intrinsic Value of Arable Land; With some General Remarks on the Science of Agriculture." *American Farmer* 2 (1820), 9–11, 17–18, 25–27, 33–35, 41–43, 49–51.

Bloch, Marc. *French Rural History: An Essay on its Basic Characteristics.* English translation. Berkeley: Univ. of California Press, 1966.

Bond, Hallie E. "The Modernization of Delaware Agriculture: A Case Study of its Impact on Labor." Unpublished paper, 1983.

Bonta, Juan Pablo. *Architecture and Its Interpretation: A Study of Expressive Systems in Architecture.* New York: Rizzoli International Publications, 1979.

Bourcier, Paul G. " 'In Excellent Order': The Gentleman Farmer Views His Fences, 1790–1860." *Agricultural History* 58, no. 4 (1984), 546–64.

Brady, Ethel W. *Sketch of the Brady-Macintire Families.* Typescript, ca. 1950. William Brady Collection, Middletown, Del.

Braudel, Fernand. *The Wheels of Commerce.* New York: Harper and Row, 1979.

Brunskill, R. W. *Illustrated Handbook of Vernacular Architecture.* New York: Universe Books, 1971.

———. *Vernacular Architecture of the Lake Counties: A Field Handbook.* London: Faber and Faber, 1974.

Brunskill, Ronald, and Alec Clifton-Taylor. *Brickwork.* New York: Van Nostrand Reinhold, 1977.

Buchanan, Paul E. "The Eighteenth-Century Frame Houses of Tidewater Virginia." In *Building Early America: Contributions Toward the History of a Great Industry,* edited by Charles E. Peterson, 54–73. Radnor, Pa.: Chilton Book Co., 1976.

Bushman, Claudia. "The Wilson Family in Delaware and Indiana." *Delaware History* 20, no. 1 (Spring–Summer 1982), 27–49.

Butler, William. *The Legacy of the Landscape: A Study of Tenant Farming in Appoquinimink Hundred.* Bristol, R.I.: by the author, 1980.

Carson, Cary. "Doing History with Material Culture." In *Material Culture and the Study of American Life,* edited by Ian M. G. Quimby, 41–64. New York: W. W. Norton, 1978.

———. "The 'Virginia House' in Maryland." *Maryland Historical Magazine* 69, no. 2 (Summer 1974), 185–96.

Carson, Cary, Norman F. Barka, William M. Kelso, Garry Wheeler Stone, and Dell Upton. "Impermanent Architecture in the Southern American Colonies." *Winterthur Portfolio* 16, no. 2/3 (Summer/Autumn 1981), 135–96.

Case, Lynn M. *A Swedish Log Cabin: Three Centuries of History on Dar-*

by Creek. Philadelphia: by the author, 1976.

Chappell, Edward A. "Acculturation in the Shenandoah Valley: Rhenish Houses of the Massanutten Settlement." *Proceedings of the American Philosophical Society*, 124, no. 1 (Feb. 1980), 55–89.

——. "Looking at Buildings." *Fresh Advices: A Research Supplement* (Nov. 1984), i–vi.

Chiaramonte, Louis J. *Craftsman-Client Contracts: Interpersonal Relations in a Newfoundland Fishing Community*. St. Johns: Institute of Social and Economic Research, Memorial University of Newfoundland, 1970.

Clarke, Ruth Anne. "An Architectural Study of the 'Brick Stone' Built 1767 in Appoquinimink Hundred, Delaware." Unpublished paper, 1981.

Clemens, Paul G. *The Atlantic Economy and Colonial Maryland's Eastern Shore: From Tobacco to Grain*. Ithaca: Cornell Univ. Press, 1980.

Cleveland, Henry W., William Backus, and Samuel D. Backus. *Village and Farm Cottages: The Requirements of American Village Homes Considered and Suggested; With Designs for Such Houses of Moderate Cost*. New York: D. Appleton and Co., 1856.

Cobbett, William. *An Epitome of Mr. Forsyth's Treatise on the Culture and Management of Fruit Trees*. Philadelphia: T. L. Plowman, 1803.

Cochran, John P. "Notice to Builders and Contractors." *The Delaware Gazette* 64, no. 10 (Feb. 2, 1855), 1.

Cohn, Jan. *The Palace or the Poor House: The American House as a Cultural Symbol*. East Lansing: Michigan State Univ. Press, 1979.

Conrad. Henry Clay. *History of the State of Delaware, by Henry C. Conrad, From the Earliest Settlements to the Year 1907*. Wilmington: by the author, 1908.

Constitution and Minutes of the Agricultural Society of New Castle County, 1836–72. Historical Society of Delaware manuscript collections. Wilmington, Del.

Cooper, Thomas. "On the Art and Method of Brick Making." *The Emporium of Arts and Sciences* 4, no. 3 (March 1814), 386–404.

Corbit, Daniel. Ledger, 1821–26. Corbit-Sharp House, Winterthur Museum, Odessa, Del.

Corbit, Pennell. Ledger, 1795–1826. Corbit-Sharp House, Winterthur Museum, Odessa, Del.

Corbit, William. Accounts, 1798–1814. Corbit-Sharp House, Winterthur Museum, Odessa, Del.

——. Day Book, 1795–1823. Corbit-Sharp House, Winterthur Museum, Odessa, Del.

Cummings, Abbott Lowell. *The Framed Houses of Massachusetts Bay, 1625–1725*. Cambridge: Belknap/Harvard Univ. Press, 1979.

——, ed. *Architecture in Colonial Massachusetts*. Boston: The Colonial Society of Massachusetts, 1979.

Deane, Samuel. *The New-England Farmer, or Georgical Dictionary*. Boston: Wells and Lilly, 1822.

Deetz, James. *Invitation to Archaeology*. Garden City, N.Y.: Natural History Press for the American Musuem of Natural History, 1967.

——. *In Small Things Forgotten: The Archaeology of Early American Life*. Garden City, N.Y.: Anchor Press/Doubleday, 1977.

Delaware Bureau of Archaeology and Historic Preservation. Cultural Resource Survey. Dover: Delaware Division of Historical and Cultural Affairs.

Delaware State Archives. New Castle County Orphans Court, 1680–1850. Dover: Hall of Records, Delaware Division of Historical and Cultural Affairs.

———. New Castle County Probate Inventories, 1680–1925. Dover: Hall of Records, Delaware Division of Historical and Cultural Affairs.

———. New Castle County Tax Assessments, 1803–4. Dover: Hall of Records, Delaware Division of Historical and Cultural Affairs.

———. New Castle County Tax Assessments, 1816–1817. Dover: Hall of Records, Delaware Division of Historical and Cultural Affairs.

Demos, John. *A Little Commonwealth: Family Life in Plymouth Colony.* New York: Oxford Univ. Press, 1970.

Dickey, Samuel. "Description of a Kitchen Stove." *Memoirs of the Philadelphia Society for Promoting Agriculture* 1 (1808), 290–95.

Dornbusch, Charles H., and John K. Heyl. *Pennsylvania German Barns.* Pennsylvania German Folklore Society 21. Allentown, Pa.: Schlecter's, 1958.

Downes, Bennett. Account Book, 1793–1821. Delaware State Archives, Delaware Division of Historical and Cultural Affairs, Hall of Records, Dover, Del.

Downing, A. J. *The Architecture of Country Houses, Including Designs for Cottages, and Farm-Houses, and Villas, with Remarks on Interiors, Furniture, and the Best Modes of Warming and Ventilating.* New York: Dover Publications, 1969. Reprint of 1850 edition.

Earle, Carville. *The Evolution of a Tidewater Settlement System: All Hallows Parish, Maryland, 1650–1783.* Chicago: Univ. of Chicago, Department of Geography, 1975.

Eberlein, Harold Donaldson, and Cortlandt V. D. Hubbard. *Historic Houses and Buildings of Delaware.* Dover, Del.: Public Archives Commission, 1962.

Eckman, Jeanette, Ed. *Delaware: A Guide to the First State.* New York: Hastings House, 1955. Revised edition.

Evans, Thomas. Account Book, 1792–99. Special Collections, Morris Library, Univ. of Delaware, Newark, Del.

Fenton, Alexander. "The Scope of Regional Ethnography." *Folklife* 2 (1973), 5–14.

Fenton, Alexander and Bruce Walker. *The Rural Architecture of Scotland.* Edinburgh: John Donald Publications, 1981.

Ferguson, Engene S. *Oliver Evans: Inventive Genius of the American Industrial Revolution.* Greenville, Del.: Hagley Museum, 1980.

Ferguson, Leland, ed. *Historical Archaeology and the Importance of Material Things.* Special Publication Series, no. 2. Society for Historic Archaeology (1977).

Fitchen, John. *The New World Dutch Barn: A Study of its Characteristics, Its Structural System, and Its Probable Erectional Procedures.* Syracuse, N.Y.: Syracuse Univ. Press, 1968.

Forman, Henry Chandlee. *Early Manor and Plantation Houses of Maryland.* Easton, Md.: by the author, 1934.

———. *The Virginia Eastern Shore and Its British Origins: History, Gardens, and Antiquities.* Easton,

Md.: Eastern Shore Publishers' Associates, 1975.

Gailey, Alan. *Rural Houses of the North of Ireland.* Edinburgh: John Donald Publishers, 1984.

Giedion, Siegfried. *Mechanization Takes Command: A Contribution to Anonymous History.* New York: W. W. Norton, 1969. Reprint of 1948 edition.

Ginzburg, Carlo. *The Cheese and the Worms: The Cosmos of a Sixteenth-Century Miller.* New York: Penguin Books, 1982.

Glassie, Henry. *Pattern in the Material Folk Culture of the Eastern United States.* Philadelphia: Univ. of Pennsylvania Press, 1968a.

_____. "Types of the Southern Mountain Cabin." In *The Study of American Folklore,* edited by Jan Harold Brunvand, 338–70. New York: W. W. Norton, 1968b.

_____. "A Central Chimney Continental Log House." *Pennsylvania Folklife* 18, no. 2 (Winter 1968–69), 32–39.

_____. "Eighteenth-Century Cultural Process in Delaware Valley Folk Building." In *Winterthur Portfolio* 7 ed. by Ian M. G. Quimby, 29–57. Charlottesville: Univ. Press of Virginia, 1972.

_____. "Structure and Function, Folklore and the Artifact." *Semiotica* 7, no. 4 (1973), 313–51.

_____. "The Variation of Concepts Within Tradition: Barn Building in Otsego County, New York." In *Geoscience and Man,* Vol. 5: *Man and Cultural Heritage,* edited by H. J. Walker and W. G. Haag, 177–235. Baton Rouge: Louisiana State Univ. School of Geoscience, 1974.

_____. *Folk Housing in Middle Virginia: A Structural Analysis of Historic Artifacts.* Knoxville: Univ. of Tennessee Press, 1975a.

_____. "Barns Across Southern England: A Note on Trans-Atlantic Comparison and Architectural Meanings." *Pioneer America* 7, no. 1 (Jan. 1975b), 9–19.

_____. "Meaningful Things and Appropriate Myths: The Artifact's Place in American Studies." *Prospects* 3 (1977), 1–49.

_____. *Passing the Time in Ballymenone: Culture and History of an Ulster Community.* Philadelphia: Univ. of Pennsylvania Press. 1982.

Goffman, Erving. *The Presentation of Self in Everyday Life.* Garden City, N.Y.: Doubleday/Anchor Books, 1959.

"A Good Suggestion." *The Farmer's Cabinet* 1, no. 1 (1836–37), 14.

Gowans, Alan. *Architecture in New Jersey: A Record of American Civilization.* New Jersey Historical Series, Vol. G. Princeton: D. Van Nostrand, 1964.

Gray, Ralph D. "Delaware and Its Canal: The Early History of the Chesapeake and Delaware Canal, 1769–1829." M. A. Thesis, Univ. of Delaware, 1958.

Greiff, Constance M. *Lost America: From the Atlantic to the Mississippi.* Princeton: The Pyne Press, 1971.

Hall, Edward T. *The Hidden Dimension.* Garden City, N.Y.: Anchor/Doubleday, 1969.

Hall, Robert DeZouche, ed. *A Bibliography on Vernacular Architecture.* Newton Abbot: David & Charles, 1972.

Halsted, Byron D. *Barn Plans and Outbuildings.* New York: Orange, Judd Company, 1884.

Harris, Richard. *Discovering Timber-Framed Buildings.* Buckinghamshire, Shire Publications, 1978.

Harrison, Barry and Barbara Hutton. *Vernacular Houses in North Yorkshire and Cleveland.* Edinburgh: John Donald Publishers. 1984.

Hazen, Edward. *The Panorama or Professions and Trades; or Every Man's Book.* Philadelphia: Uriah Hunt, 1837.

Heite, Louise B. "Appoquinimink, A Seventeenth-Century Delaware Town." Unpublished paper, 1978.

Hempstead, Joshua. *Diary of Joshua Hempstead of New London, Connecticut, Covering A Period of Forty-Seven Years, From September 1711, To November, 1758.* New London, Conn.: New London County Historical Society, 1901.

Herman, Bernard L. "Continuity and Change in Traditional Architecture: The Continental Plan Farmhouse in Middle North Carolina." In *Carolina Dwelling. Towards Preservation of Place: In Celebration of the Vernacular Landscape,* edited by Doug Swaim, 160–71. Raleigh: Student Publication of the School of Design, North Carolina State Univ., 1978.

———. "Delaware Vernacular: Folk Housing in Three Counties." In *Perspectives in Vernacular Architecture,* edited by Camille Wells, 183–93. Annapolis: Vernacular Architecture Forum, 1982.

———. "Multiple Materials/Multiple Meanings: The Fortunes of Thomas Mendenhall." *Winterthur Portfolio* 19, no. 1 (Spring 1984), 67–86.

Herman, Bernard L., and David G. Orr. "Pear Valley *et al.*: An Excursion into the Analysis of Southern Vernacular Architecture." *Southern Folklore Quarterly* 39, no. 4 (Dec. 1975), 307–27.

"Historical Archaeology and Capitalism, Subscriptions and Separations: The Production of Individualism." *North American Archaeologist* 4, no. 1 (1983), 63–79.

Hoffecker, Carol E. *Brandywine Village: The Story of a Milling Community.* Wilmington, Del.: Old Brandywine Village, 1974.

———. *Delaware: A Bicentennial History.* New York: W. W. Norton, 1977.

Holly, Henry Hudson. *Holly's Country Seats: Containing Lithographic Designs for Cottages, Villas, Mansions, etc., with Their Accompanying Outbuildings: Also, Country Churches, City Buildings, Railway Stations, Etc.* New York: D. Appleton and Co., 1863.

Hopkins, G. M. *Map of New Castle County, Delaware.* Philadelphia: G. M. Hopkins and Co., 1881.

Hoskins, W. G. *Provincial England: Essays in Social and Economic History.* London: Macmillan, 1965.

Hubka, Thomas C. *Big House, Little House, Back House, Barn: The Connected Farm Buildings of New England.* Hanover, N.H.: Univ. Press of New England, 1984.

Hukill, George. Receipt for building materials to J. K. Williams from George Hukill, Middletown, Del., Oct. 8, 1886. William Cross Collection, Odessa, Del.

Hutton, Barbara. "Rebuilding in Yorkshire: The Evidence of Inscribed Dates." *Vernacular Architecture* 8 (1977), 819–24.

Isaac, Rhys. *The Transformation of Virginia, 1740–1790.* Chapel Hill: Univ. of North Carolina Press, 1982.

Jensen, Joan. "Churns and Butter Making in the Mid-Atlantic Farm Economy, 1750–1850." *Working Papers From the Regional Economic History Research Center* 5, nos. 2 and 3

(1982), 60–100.

Jicha, Hubert F. "Bank Barns in Mill Creek Hundred, Delaware." Honors Thesis, Univ. of Delaware, 1984.

Johnston, Frances Benjamin, and Thomas Tileston Waterman. *The Early Architecture of North Carolina.* Chapel Hill: Univ. of North Carolina Press, 1941 and 1947.

Jordan, Terry G. *American Log Buildings: An Old World Heritage.* Chapel Hill: Univ. of North Carolina Press, 1985.

Kalm, Peter. *The America of 1750: Peter Kalm's Travels in North America, The English Version of 1770.* Edited by Adolph B. Benson. New York: Dover Publications, 1966. Reprint of 1937 edition.

Kimball, Fiske. *Domestic Architecture of the American Colonies and the Early Republic.* New York: Dover Publications, 1966. Reprint of 1922 edition.

Kirker, Harold. *The Architecture of Charles Bullfinch.* Cambridge: Harvard Univ. Press, 1969.

Kniffen, Fred. "Folk Housing: Key to Diffusion." *Annals of the Association of American Geographers* 55, no. 4 (Dec. 1965), 549–77.

Kuhn, Thomas S. *The Structure of Scientific Revolutions.* International Encyclopedia of Unified Science, vol. 2, no. 2. Chicago: Univ. of Chicago Press, 1962. Revised, 1970.

Kurzweil, Edith. *The Age of Structuralism: Levi-Strauss to Focault.* New York: Columbia Univ. Press, 1980.

Lane, Michael. *Introduction to Structuralism.* New York: Basic Books, 1970.

Laslett, Peter. *The World We Have Lost: England Before the Industrial Age.* New York: Scribner's, 1965. Second edition, 1971.

Latrobe, Benjamin Henry. Plan of the Town of New Castle State of Delaware 1805. Delaware State Archives, Delaware Division of Historical and Cultural Affairs, Hall of Records, Dover, Del.

Lawrence, Roderick J. "The Interpretation of Vernacular Architecture." *Vernacular Architecture* 14 (1983), 19–28.

Lemon, James T. *The Best Poor Mans' Country: A Geographical Study of Early Southeastern Pennsylvania.* New York: W. W. Norton, 1972.

Levi-Strauss, Claude. *Structural Anthropology.* New York: Basic Books, 1963.

Loth, Calder. "Notes on the Evolution of Virginia Brickwork from the Seventeenth Century to the late Nineteenth Century." *Bulletin of the Association for Preservation Technology* 6, no. 2 (1974), 82–120.

Lounsbury, Carl. "Vernacular Construction in the Survey." In *Historic America: Buildings, Structures, and Sites,* edited by C. Ford Peatross, 182–95. Washington, D.C.: Library of Congress, 1983.

Love, Paul. "Patterned Brickwork in Southern New Jersey." *Proceedings of the New Jersey Historical Society* 73, no. 3 (July 1955), 182–208.

Macaulay, David. *Motel of the Mysteries.* Boston: Houghton Mifflin, 1979.

McDaniel, George W. *Hearth and Home: Preserving a People's Culture.* Philadelphia: Temple Univ. Press, 1982.

MacFarlane, Alan. *Reconstructing Historical Communities.* Cambridge, Eng.: Cambridge Univ. Press, 1977.
———. *The Origins of English Individualism: The Family, Property and Social Transition.* New York: Cambridge Univ. Press, 1979.

Machin, R. "The Great Rebuilding: A Reassessment." *Past and Present* 77 (Nov. 1977a), 33–56.

———. "The Mechanism of the Pre-Industrial Building Cycle." *Vernacular Architecture* 8 (1977b), 815–19.

———. *The Houses of Yetminster.* Bristol, Eng.: University of Bristol, Department of Extra-mural Studies, 1978.

McKee, Harley J. "Brick and Stone: Handicraft to Machine." In *Building Early America: Contributions Toward the History of a Great Industry,* edited by Charles Peterson, 74–95. Radnor, Pa.: Chilton Book Co., 1976.

McMurry, Sally Ann. "American Farm Families and Their Houses: Vernacular Design and Social Change in the Rural North, 1830–1900." Ph.D. Diss., Cornell University, 1984.

———. "Progressive Farm Families and Their Houses, 1830–55: A Study in Independent Design." *Agricultural History* 58, no. 3 (1984), 330–46.

Mannion, John J. *Irish Settlements in Eastern Canada: A Study of Cultural Transfer and Adaptation.* Toronto: Univ. of Toronto Press, 1974.

Mansfield, Richard. Farm Accounts, 1825–44. Delaware State Archives, Delaware Division of Historical and Cultural Affairs, Hall of Records, Dover, Del.

Marshall, Howard Wight. *American Folk Architecture: A Selected Bibliography.* Publications of the American Folklife Center, no. 8. Washington, D.C.: Library of Congress, 1981a.

———. *Folk Architecture in Little Dixie: A Regional Culture in Missouri.* Columbia: Univ. of Missouri Press, 1981b.

Martin, Charles E. *Hollybush: Folk Building and Social Change in an Appalachian Community.* Knoxville: Univ. of Tennessee Press, 1984.

Matthews, Earle D., and Oscar L. Lavole. *Soil Survey of New Castle County, Delaware.* Washington, D.C.: U.S. Government Printing Office, 1970.

Melchor, James R., Gordon Lohr, and Marilyn S. Melchor. *Eastern Shore, Virginia, Raised Panel Furniture, 1730–1830.* Norfolk, Va.: The Chrysler Museum, 1982.

Mendenhall, Thomas. "On the Cultivation of Potatoes." *American Farmer* 2, no. 10 (June 2, 1820), 75.

Mercer, Eric. *English Vernacular Houses: A Study of Traditional Farmhouses and Cottages.* London: Her Majesty's Stationery Office, 1975.

Mercer, Henry C. *The Origin of Log Houses in the United States.* Doylestown, Pa: Bucks County Historical Society, 1976. Reprint of 1924 essay.

Michel, H. John, Jr. "'In a Manner and Fashion Suitable to Their Degree:' A Preliminary Investigation of the Material Culture of Early Rural Pennsylvania." *Working Papers from the Regional Economic History Center* 5, no. 1 (1981).

———. "A Typology of Delaware Farms, 1850." Paper delivered at the Organization of American Historians Annual Meeting, Los Angeles, April 1984.

———. *The Regional Organization of Delaware Agriculture, 1849.* Philadelphia: by the author, 1985.

Michelmore, D. J. H. *A Current Bibli-*

ography of Vernacular Architecture. Vol. 1. 1970–1976. Little Stonegate, York: Vernacular Architecture Group, 1979.

Morris, William. On Art and Socialism. London: Chiltern Library, 1947.

Morrison, Hugh. Early American Architecture from the First Colonial Settlements to the National Period. New York: Oxford Univ. Press, 1952.

Mumford, Lewis. Sticks and Stones: A Study of American Architecture and Civilization. New York: Dover Publications, 1955. Reprint of 1924 edition.

Munroe, John A. History of Delaware. Newark: Univ. of Delaware Press, 1979.

Nash, Gary B. The Urban Crucible: Social Change, Political Consciousness, and the Origins of the American Revolution. Cambridge: Harvard Univ. Press, 1979.

Niagra. "Last Leaf of the Farmer's Leger." The Farmer's Cabinet 1, no. 3 (1836–37) 37–38.

Noël Hume, Ivor. Digging for Carters Grove. Colonial Williamsburg Archaeological Series, no. 8. Williamsburg: Colonial Williamsburg Foundation, 1974.

Nowland Family Accounts, 1898–1902. Henry Vaughan Collection, Philadelphia.

Otterbein, Keith F. Changing House Types in Long Bay Cays. New Haven: Human Relations Area Files, 1975.

Patterson, H. W. Small Boat Building. New York: Macmillan, 1931.

"A Pennsylvania Barn." The American Agriculturalist 6, no. 1 (Jan. 1841), 24–26.

Peterson, Charles E. Building Early America: Contributions Toward the

History of a Great Industry. Radnor, Pa.: Chilton Book Co., 1976.

Philadelphia Society for Promoting Agriculture. Sketch of the History of the Philadelphia Society for Promoting Agriculture. Philadelphia: Philadelphia Society for Promoting Agriculture, 1939.

Platt, Colin. The English Mediaeval Town. London: Paladin Books, 1979.

Port Penn Papers. Historical Society of Delaware, Wilmington, Del.

Pritts, J., comp. The Farmer's Book and Family Instructor. Chambersburg, Pa.: by subscription, 1845.

Pye, David. The Nature and Art of Workmanship. New York: Van Nostrand Reinhold, 1968.

Pyle, Howard. "A Peninsular Canaan: III—Delaware." Harper's New Monthly Magazine 59, no. 350 (July 1879), 193–208.

Rea, Samuel, and Jacob Price. Map of New Castle County, Delaware. Philadelphia: Smith and Wistar, 1849.

Redfield, Robert. The Little Community/Peasant Society and Culture. Chicago: Univ. of Chicago Press, 1960.

Reps, John W. Tidewater Towers: City Planning in Colonial Virginia and Maryland. Charlottesville: The Univ. Press of Virginia for the Colonial Williamsburg Foundation, 1972.

Reynolds, John. Windmills and Watermills. London: Hugh Evelyn, 1970.

Ridout, Orlando V. "Post-and-Plank Construction in Tidewater Maryland." Paper presented to the Maryland Historical Trust Historic Preservation Conference, Annapolis, Md., Nov., 1978.

Riesenweber, Julie. Order in Domestic Space: House Plans and Room Use in the Vernacular Dwellings of Salem County, New Jersey, 1700–1774. M.A. Thesis, Univ. of Delaware, 1984.

Robey, David, Ed. *Structuralism: An Introduction.* Wolfson College Lectures, 1972. Oxford: Clarendon Press, 1973.

Ruskin, John. *The Seven Lamps of Architecture.* New York: Noonday Press, 1974. Reprint of 1849 edition.

———. *The Stones of Venice.* New York: Peter Fenelon Collier and Son, 1900 edition.

Scharf, Thomas. *History of Maryland From the Earliest Period to the Present Day.* Hatboro, Pa.: Tradition Press, 1967. Reprint of 1879 edition.

———. *History of Western Maryland.* Baltimore: Regional Publishing Company, 1968. Reprint of 1882 edition.

———. *History of West Chester County, New York, Including Morrisania, Kings Bridge, and West Farms, Which Have Been Annexed to New York City.* Philadelphia: Preston, 1886.

———. *History of Delaware, 1609–1888.* Philadelphia: L. J. Richards and Co., 1888.

Scharf, John Thomas and Thompson Westcott. *History of Philadelphia, 1609–1884.* Philadelphia: L. H. Everts and Co., 1884.

Schuyler, Robert L., ed. *Historical Archaeology: A Guide to Substantive and Theoretical Contributions.* Farmingdale, N.Y.: Baywood Publishing Co., 1978.

Shannon, Fred A. *The Farmer's Last Frontier: Agriculture, 1860–1897.* New York: Holt, Rinehart and Winston, 1945.

Shoemaker, Alfred L., ed. *The Pennsyl-vania Barn.* Kutztown, Pa.: Pennsylvania Folklife Society, 1959.

Shourds, Thomas. *History and Genealogy of Fenwick's Colony [New Jersey].* Bridgetown, N.J.: George F. Nixon, 1876.

Sickler, Joseph S. *The Old Houses of Salem County.* Salem, N.J.: Sunbeam Publishing Company, 1949.

Simmons, Richard L. "The Historical Society of Delaware, 1864–1964," *Delaware History* 10, no. 1 (April 1964), 3–34.

Smith, J. T. "The Concept of Diffusion in its Application to Vernacular Building." In *Studies in Folk Life: Essays in Honour of Iowerth C. Peate,* edited by Geraint Jenkins, 60–78. London: Routledge and Kegan Paul, 1969.

Smith, Peter, *Houses of the Welsh Countryside: A Study in Historical Geography.* London: Her Majesty's Stationery Office, 1975.

Spurrier, John. *The Practical Farmer: Being A New and Compendious System of Husbandry, Adapted to the Different Soils and Climates of America.* Wilmington, Del.: Brynberg and Andrews, 1793.

St. George, Robert Blair. *The Wrought Covenant: Source Material for the Study of Craftsmen and Community in Southeastern New England, 1620–1700.* Brockton, Mass.: Brockton Art Center–Fuller Memorial, 1979.

———. "'Set Thine House in Order': The Domestication of the Yeomanry in Seventeenth-Century New England." In *New England Begins: The Seventeenth Century,* vol. 2: 159–201. Boston: Museum of Fine Arts, 1982a.

———. "The Stanley-Lake Barn in Topsfield, Massachusetts: Some Comments on Agricultural Buildings in Early New England." In *Perspectives in Vernacular Architecture,* edited by Camille Wells, 7–23. Annapolis, Md.: Vernacular Architecture Forum, 1982b.

Stewarts of Port Penn Papers. Small Manuscripts Collection. Delaware State Archives, Delaware Division of Historical and Cultural Affairs, Hall of Records, Dover, Del.

Stilgoe, John R. *Common Landscape of America, 1580 to 1845.* New Haven, Conn.: Yale Univ. Press, 1982.

Stiverson, Gregory A. *Poverty in a Land of Plenty: Tenancy in Eighteenth-Century Maryland.* Baltimore: Johns Hopkins Univ. Press, 1977.

Stone, Lawrence. "Prosopography." *Daedalus: Historical Studies Today* 100, no. 1 (Winter 1971), 46–79.

Sturtevant, William C. "Anthropology, History, and Ethnohistory." *Ethnohistory* 13, nos 1–2 (Winter–Spring 1966), 1–51.

Suydam, Elder C. *The Farmer's Manure System; or, General Directory for the Preparation and Use of Manure.* Lambertsville, N.J.: Lange and Hughes, 1847.

Swaim, Doug, ed. *Carolina Dwelling. Towards Preservation of Place: In Celebration of the North Carolina Vernacular Landscape.* Raleigh: The Student Publication of the School of Design, North Carolina State Univ., 1978.

Sweeney, John A. *Grandeur on the Appoquinimink: The House of William Corbit at Odessa, Delaware.* Newark, Del.: Univ. of Delaware Press, 1959.

Sweeney, Kevin M. "Mansion People: Kinship, Class, and Architecture in Western Massachusetts in the Mid Eighteenth Century." *Winterthur Portfolio* 19, no. 4 (Winter 1984), 231–56.

Tate. Thad W., and David L. Ammerman, editors. *The Chesapeake in the Seventeenth Century: Essays on Anglo-American Society and Politics.* New York: W. W. Norton, 1979.

Tebo, George W. *The Farmers' Klondike: A Descriptive Catalogue and List of Farms for Sale.* Dover, Del.: Sentinel Printing Co., 1900.

Temple, J. H., and George Sheldon. *History of the Town of Northfield, Massachusetts, for 150 Years. With an Account of the Prior Occupation of the Territory by the Squarheags: and With Family Genealogies.* Albany, N.Y.: Joel Munsell, 1875.

Thomas, J. J. *The Illustrated Annual Register of Rural Affairs and Cultivator Almanac, for the Year 1857.* Albany, N.Y.: Luther Tucker and Son, 1857.

————. *Illustrated Annual Register of Rural Affairs for 1864-5-6.* Albany, N.Y.: Tucker and Son, 1878.

Thompson, Pricilla M. *Hedgelawn.* Wilmington, Del.: The History Store, 1982.

[Tilton, James]. "Answers to Queries on the Present State of Husbandry and Agriculture in the Delaware State." *The Columbian Magazine* 3 (1789), 156–60, 217–20.

Todd, S. E. *Todd's Country Homes and How to Save Money.* Hartford, Conn.: Hartford Publishing Company, 1870.

Townsend, Samuel. Farm Accounts, 1857–75. Ruth Tindall Collection, Middletown, Del.

Trent, Robert F. *Hearts and Crowns: Folk Chairs of the Connecticut Coast, 1720–1840.* New Haven, Conn.: New Haven Colony Historical Society, 1977.

Tuan, Yi-Fu. *Landscapes of Fear.* Minneapolis: Univ. of Minnesota Press, 1979.

———. *Segmented Worlds and Self: Group Life and Individual Consciousness.* Minneapolis: Univ. of Minnesota Press, 1982.

Tuthill, Laura. "1804 and 1816 Tax Assessment Study." Unpublished paper, 1979.

Twiss-Garrity, Beth Ann. "Getting the Comfortable Fit: House Forms and Furnishings in Rural Delaware, 1780–1820." M.A. Thesis, Univ. of Delaware, 1983.

United States Census. Schedule of Agriculture, State of Delaware. Manuscript Returns, 1850, 1860, 1870, 1880. Delaware State Archives, Division of Historical and Cultural Affairs, Hall of Records, Dover, Del.

United States Census. Schedule of Manufactures, State of Delaware, Manuscript Returns, 1850, 1860, 1870, 1880. Delaware State Archives, Division of Historical and Cultural Affairs, Hall of Records, Dover, Del.

United States Census. Schedule of Population, State of Delaware, Manuscript Returns, 1800, 1810, 1820, 1830, 1840, 1850, 1860, 1870, 1880. Washington, D.C.: National Archives.

United States Secretary of the Treasury. *Documents Relative to the Manufactures in the United States Collected and Transmitted to the House of Representatives.* 2 vols. Washington, D.C.: Duff Green, 1833.

Upton, Dell. "Board Roofing in Tidewater Virginia." *Bulletin of the Association for Preservation Technology* 8, no. 4 (1976), 22–43.

———. "Current Bibliography." *Vernacular Architecture Newsletter.*

Published quarterly by the Vernacular Architecture Forum. Annapolis, Md.

———. "Toward A Performance Theory of Vernacular Architecture: Early Tidewater Virginia as A Case Study." *Folklore Forum* 12, nos. 2–3 (1979), 173–96.

———. "Traditional Timber Framing." In *Material Culture of the Wooden Age,* edited by Brooke Hindle, 35–93. Tarrytown, N.Y.: Sleepy Hollow Press, 1981.

———. "Vernacular Domestic Architecture in Eighteenth-Century Virginia." *Winterthur Portfolio* 17, nos. 2–3 (Summer–Autumn 1982), 95–120.

Vaux, Calvert, *Villas and Cottages: A Series of Designs Prepared for Execution in the United States.* New York: Harper and Brothers, 1869.

Wallace, Anthony F. C. *Rockdale: The Growth of an American Village in the Early Industrial Revolution.* New York: Alfred A. Knopf. 1978.

Waring, George E., Jr. *Waring's Book of the Farm; Being a Revised Edition of the Handy-Book of Husbandry.* Philadelphia: Porter & Coates, 1877.

Warner, Sam Bass, Jr. *The Private City: Philadelphia in Three Periods of its Growth.* Philadelphia: Univ. of Pennsylvania Press, 1968.

Waterman, Thomas Tileston. *The Mansions of Virginia, 1706–1776.* Chapel Hill: Univ. of North Carolina Press, 1945.

Waters, Deborah Dependahl. *Plain and Ornamental: Delaware Furniture, 1740–1890.* Wilmington: Historical Society of Delaware, 1984.

Webb, Stephen Saunders. *1676: The End of American Independence.* New York: Alfred A. Knopf, 1984.

Wells, Camille. *Perspectives in Ver-*

nacular Architecture. Annapolis, Md.: Vernacular Architecture Forum, 1982.

Welsch, Roger L. "Beating A Live Horse: Yet Another Note on Definitions and Defining." In Perspectives on American Folk Art, edited by Ian M. G. Quimby and Scott T. Swank, 218–33. New York: W. W. Norton, 1980.

Wheeler, Gervase. Homes for the People, in Suburbs and Country; The Villa, the Mansion, and the Cottage, Adapted to American Climate and Wants. New York: Charles Scribner, 1855.

Whiffen, Marcus. The Eighteenth-Century Houses of Williamsburg: A Study of Architecture and Building in the Colonial Capital of Virginia. Williamsburg, Va.: Colonial Williamsburg, 1960.

White, Charles E., Jr. The Bungalow Book. New York: Macmillan Co., 1929.

Whitelaw, Ralph T. Virginia's Eastern Shore: A History of Northampton and Accomack Counties. Gloucester, Mass.: Peter Smith, 1968. Reprint of 1951 edition.

Willard, X. A. Willard's Practical Butter Book. New York: Rural Publishing Co., 1875.

Wilson, Alexander. Business Accounts, 1850–1900. Sarah Wilson Slack Collection, Newark, Del.

———. Business Correspondence 1850–1900. Special Collections, Morris Library, Univ. of Delaware, Newark, Del.

Wise, Jennings Cropper. Ye Kingdome of Accawmake on the Eastern Shore of Virginia, in the Seventeenth Century. Baltimore: Regional Publishing Company, 1967. Reprint of 1911 edition.

Wood-Jones, Raymond B. Traditional Domestic Architecture in the Banbury Region. Manchester: Manchester University Press, 1963.

Woodward, George E. Woodward's Cottages and Farmhouses. New York: George E. Woodward & Co., 1867.

Wright, Gwendolyn. Moralism and the Model Home: Domestic Architecture and Cultural Conflict in Chicago, 1873–1913. Chicago: Univ. of Chicago Press, 1980.

———. Building the Dream: A Social History of Housing in America. New York: Pantheon Books, 1981.

Index

Locust Grove, 186
log construction, 62, 64, 83, 84–85, 88–89, 91–94, 99, 109, 134, ill. 91, 93, 135; ethnicity in, 5, 94; related to finish, 47–48
lumber yards, 132, 211

McCoy House, 233
McDonough House. *See* Trap
McFarlan, John, 139
McFarlan, Robert, 139
McMurphy, Alexander, house, 39
machinery, 115, 203, 205, 213
Mailley granary, ill. 164
Mansfield, Richard, 73, 121, 139, 171–72, 204. *See* Achmester
Mansion Farm, 48
mantels. *See* fireplace paneling
Maples, 175
Marldale, 175, 179
Mayfield, 162, ill. 167
meathouses. *See* smokehouses
Melvin, John, 143
Michel, Jack, 114, 116
Middlesex, 162, ill. 160
Middletown, 80–81, 82, 125, 146
Miller, Lewis, 142
milling, 74–76, 242
mills; buildings associated with, 74; grist and flour, 74–76, 146, ill. 75; merchant, 74; old process, 74; saw, 74
Mondamon Farm barrack, 222, ill. 225
Monterey, 171, 175, 212, 233, ill. 181, 196; outbuildings, 194
mortar, 86
Mount Hope kitchen, ill. 192
Mount Jones, 26, 47, ill. 25, 47, 57, 59
Mount Vernon Place, 235, ill. 238
Muddy Branch, 171, 173–77, ill. 177; interior finish, 174–75, ill. 178
Murphy, John, 63

naming; process of, 122–23
Nash, Gary, 40
Naudain house, 104, ill. 28

Newry, 106, 110, ill. 107
Nile's Weekly Register, 171
nogging, 95–96
Nowland family, 230
Noxon House, 32–33, 52, 56, 98, 104
Noxontown, 80
Noxontown Mill, 74–75, 94, 98–99, ill. 74

oakum, 89
Odessa, 23, 80–81, 82, 125, 146
Okolona, 176, ill. 182
Old Drawyers Church, 45, 81, ill. 46
orchards, 8, 65, 124–27, 242
order, 118–19, 127–29, 181–82, 200, 230–33, 236–43
orphans court, 1, 62, 67, 83, 84–85, 88
outbuildings; types built after 1820, 197, 231–32; types built prior to 1820, 61–63; village, 81
oxen, 114–15

paneling, 49, 52–56, ill. 52, 54–55. *See* interior finishes
peach houses, 126
peaches. *See* orchards
Penn, William, 5, 23, 84
pent roof, 46–47, 86–87
Philadelphia, 22
pillows, 70, 99
Pinder crib barn, 222, 224
plan for a pegboard, 119, 231, ill. 120
plates, 87–88, 92, 101, 103–4, ill. 102; false or raising, 88, 92, 101–3, ill. 89, 102
population changes; nineteenth-century, 112–13
Port Penn, 23, 80–81, 82, 125, ill. 80
Preston, Jonas, 78
purlins, 104–6
Pyle, Howard, 126

Quaker meetinghouses, 81
Quaker plan, 22, 24
Quakers, 48

Architecture and Rural Life in Central Delaware,

was designed by Dariel Mayer; composed by
The Composing Room of Michigan, Inc., Grand Rapids,
Michigan; printed by Thomson-Shore, Inc., Dexter, Michigan;
and bound by John H. Dekker & Sons, Grand Rapids, Michigan.
The book was set in 11/14 Trump Mediaeval with Trump
Mediaeval display and printed on 70-lb. Warren's Patina.